PASSAGE ACROSS THE MERSEY

Passage Across the Mersey

Robert Bhatia

HarperCollins*Publishers*

HarperCollins*Publishers*
The News Building,
1 London Bridge Street,
London SE1 9GF

www.harpercollins.co.uk

Published by HarperCollinsPublishers 2017
1

With grateful thanks to the following for permission to reproduce extracts:
Liverpool Daisy, copyright © Helen Forrester, originally published by Robert Hale (now The Crowood Press)
Invisible Immigrants: The English in Canada Since 1945, copyright © Marilyn Barber and Murray Watson, published by the University of Manitoba Press
Quips, Quotes and Quanta: An Anecdotal History of Physics, copyright © Anton Z. Capri, published by World Scientific Publishing Co.

Photographs reproduced courtesy of the estate of Jamunadevi Bhatia

Photo of Helen and Robert 1959 copyright © Edmonton Journal

A catalogue record for this book
is available from the British Library

ISBN: 978-0-00-816886-5

Set in Sabon LT Std by Palimpsest Book Production Limited,
Falkirk, Stirlingshire

Printed and bound in Great Britain by
Clays Ltd, St Ives plc

I would like to thank Gill Paul for bringing her outstanding editing skills to bear on the sometimes challenging raw material I had and for her patience, diligence and empathy.

To my parents, whose love was a shining light

Prologue

A bright April sun has warmed the covered porch of our bungalow in Edmonton, Canada. My mother is dressed in a fine sari, off-white with a pattern along the edges. She looks happy, as if nothing can spoil this moment. She is beautiful, a half-smile on her lips, and her soft brown hair is neatly arranged in a roll on the top of her head.

Aged three and a half, I am sitting looking up at her with an expression of obstinacy and triumph. The photographer from the *Edmonton Journal* only wanted a picture of Mum, to accompany their article about a local housewife having a novel published in Great Britain. But I insisted on being part of it. I knew it was an important moment and I didn't want to be left out.

'All right, dear,' she agreed a bit resignedly, smoothing my hair neatly to one side before letting me join her in front of the camera.

It was April 1959 and the novel was *Alien There Is None* (later republished as *Thursday's Child*). Mum and I had both been very excited a few weeks earlier when a large package, as big as a suitcase and tied securely with rope, arrived. Inside were dozens of hardback copies of her first book, with an illustration of an Indian village woman and an ox cart on the cover. It had been written before I was born.

My mother was a wonderful storyteller and often told me tales about her childhood, her life in India, her jobs, and about living in Liverpool during the Second World War. It seemed natural to me that she could write stories down and have them published in a book.

Of course, I had no idea how difficult it was to write a book, never mind get it published, and I never had a moment's concern that this activity would take her away from my afternoon playtime. My mother had two overriding priorities: one was to devote as much time as possible to caring for me, playing with me and feeling her way through raising a child in a society far from her homeland; the other was to care for, and support, my father, a brilliant theoretical physicist at the University of Alberta.

There was so much I didn't understand back then. It would certainly never have occurred to me how lonely and isolated Mum was in that foreign country. Snow lay deeply on the ground most of the time between late October and early April and, more importantly to her, the community seemed colder too. She was used to strangers passing the time of day in the streets of Liverpool, and neighbours having a chat and a laugh with each other when they met in the shops. People in Edmonton seemed more reserved, their sense of humour was different, and she found it hard to make social connections. It would only be much later when I understood that being an outsider was a key theme in my mother's life. Back then, all I knew was that she was the most wonderful mum anyone could ever wish for.

That cold spring began a unique privilege for me. For the next half-century, I observed and shared in the frustrations and triumphs as Mum became Helen Forrester, an accomplished and successful author. A couple of decades after hijacking her press photograph at the age of three, I became a trusted reader and confidant. She would frequently talk about her ideas and what her characters were doing, or might do in the future. Later I would receive a draft manuscript for my opinion, a role I always found a tremendous honour.

My mother wrote four volumes of memoirs, first published in the 1970s and 80s, but those books cover only about fifteen years of her life. I am delighted to have this chance to tell a more complete story and to answer some of her readers' questions about what happened before and after. As far as possible, I have used her own words from previously unpublished letters and speeches, adding my memories of her recollections and of events to which I was privy.

Part I covers the years from her birth until the end of the Second World War, and shows her looking back as an adult to try to understand the damaged family she was part of and the mistakes her parents made – mistakes that could easily have had fatal consequences for her and her siblings.

Part II tells of the love story between Mum and my dad, Avadh Bhatia, an Indian academic. My parents met in Liverpool in March 1949 but my father had to return to India in December after completing the work for his PhD in theoretical physics. From January to April 1950 they exchanged letters almost daily, letters in which they planned the life that lay before them and tried to resolve the many difficulties that threatened to spoil their chance of happiness.

For four and a half months, Mum's future hung in the balance before she set sail, with great courage, to join my father in an exotic foreign land. On the first day of her voyage she wrote to him:

> Yesterday I was frightfully sad about leaving England and my family but today I have turned my face towards you and am happy because I do love you so – I remember your dear face and every flicker of expression on it and it is ever before me. I do want to make you happy very much.

It was the start of a huge adventure, and a lifelong love story. She kept all the correspondence between them during the difficult months of their courtship and edited extracts now form the very heart of this book.

My mother's bestselling volumes of memoir ended in 1945, four years before she met my father. She wrote a couple of novels loosely based on her experiences in India but no overall autobiography. However, she kept impeccable records, and it has been a joy for me to piece together the rest of her story in Part III of this book, describing her decades away from her homeland and her journey to literary success.

I hope readers will enjoy these extra insights into the author of *Twopence to Cross the Mersey*, *A Cuppa Tea and an Aspirin*, *Liverpool Daisy*, and many other wonderful books. I have used the name Helen Forrester to refer to my mother throughout this book, because that is how she is best known to her readers.

My mum led a remarkable life that included terrible hardship, breathtaking romance, perseverance and extraordinarily hard work. It was an unusual life in many respects, and one she lived to the full.

PART I

Chapter One

In my more comfortable early life, my six siblings and I did not communicate much with our parents. Theirs was a truly awful First World War marriage.

My mother was born on 6 June 1919 in Hoylake, then part of Cheshire, where her paternal grandmother, Elizabeth Huband, lived. It was to this home she so passionately wanted to return twelve years later when she yearned for 'twopence to cross the Mersey', a wish that would provide the title for her first volume of memoirs in 1974.

Mum's father, Paul Huband, came from a cultured family with a pedigree traceable back to before the Battle of Hastings in 1066. My great-grandfather had been a successful wine merchant and property owner as well as a director of a railway company that later became Great Western Railway. Sadly, he passed away in 1900, when Paul was just six years old. Helen spoke of the abrupt turn this caused to the family's fortunes in a speech she gave in later life.

> My grandfather built a very pleasant house 'out in the country' in Tynwald Hill, off Green Lane [about

> five kilometres east of the centre of Liverpool]. I saw it at the beginning of the [Second World] war, when it had become home to a mass of poverty-stricken Chinese. When, at the age of 46, my grandfather died, my grandmother was persuaded by his executor thoroughly dishonest executor that she was now quite poor. She was a typical Victorian woman, who had never even bought a train ticket for herself, never mind done any business. She therefore sold her home and most of its contents – perhaps I should say more correctly, allowed it to be sold by the executor. She then retired to a tiny, but very pretty little house in Hoylake together with a widowed daughter [Stella] and her granddaughter, Marjorie, and another single daughter [Phyllis]. Despite the threat of poverty, they lived very well and the money left by Grandpa must have been quite considerable, since one of my cousins, who finally inherited it, still lives very comfortably on it – and when one remembers the amount of inflation which must have occurred since Grandpa died in 1900 – this is no mean feat.
>
> My grandmother submerged herself in black satin, with black-veiled bonnets and hats, which she wore for the next fifty years, Queen Victoria having made it the fashion. As a Victorian lady who had always been looked after, she was assured by her grown-up daughters and her lawyer that she could not possibly cope with bringing up her little son. So he was sent to a preparatory boarding school, where he also spent some of the holidays because of distance.

My grandfather might well have been sent to boarding school anyway, as so many other boys of his era and class were. I am not sure whether his older brothers, Percy and

Frank, went to boarding school, too, but it seems likely. My mother believed this enforced exile from the age of just six years contributed to my grandfather's later difficulty in coping with his own children. She wrote to her brother, Tony, in 2000:

> It always amazed me how much Father survived in his life. He had a rotten childhood. You probably know that his father died when he was six, and he was sent to a Preparatory Boarding School in Wales, until he was old enough to be sent to Denstone – I don't know whether you have seen Denstone, but I did when I was about eight years old – a horrible gloomy freezing cold place, stone floored, with huge dormitories for the boys. No electric light.

Denstone College in Staffordshire is now a co-educational boarding school, and the facilities have been brought up to date since then. My grandfather was a boarder there until the age of eighteen and received an excellent education, particularly excelling in mathematics. He emerged in 1912 to get work as a clerk in a bank. It was a respectable job for an upper-middle-class boy, and one that held good prospects. He might have been promoted to branch manager and possibly in time to a role in head office, but two years later circumstances intervened when Britain suddenly found herself at war with Germany.

The naval arms race between the two nations had been rumbling on for years. Few had paid much attention to the assassination of Austro-Hungarian Archduke Franz Ferdinand in Bosnia on 28 June 1914, but the repercussions would snowball over the next few weeks. By 28 July, Austria-Hungary had declared war on Serbia, then Germany declared war on Russia on 1 August, marched into Luxembourg on the 2nd and declared war on France on the 3rd. Still trying to hold out, British Prime Minister Herbert Asquith asked the German Kaiser for a reassurance that Belgium would remain neutral. At 11 p.m. on 4 August, when that assurance had not been received, Britain was officially at war with Germany – something few would have predicted at the start of the summer.

My grandfather joined the 17th Service Battalion of the Liverpool Regiment, a volunteer force raised from men in the North-West, and in November 1915 his company was sent out to the trenches of the Somme. He was like many stiff-upper-lipped men of his generation who put up with the sea of mud, the deafening explosions of shells, and the sight of friends and comrades dying of horrific wounds, and just got on with it.

The 17th Service Battalion took part in the 1916 Battle of the Transloy Ridges, when heavy rain turned the ground into a swamp; the Battle of Arras in April and May 1917, when they pushed the Germans back but were unable to achieve a breakthrough; and some 1918 battles at the Somme as they resisted the German spring offensive. Altogether 13,795 men of the Liverpool Regiment died during the war, an average of 615 per battalion of 1,000 men, and the 17th had so few left by June 1918 they were 'reduced to cadre' – i.e. there was just a basic core left, which was used to train new recruits. My grandfather later told Helen that only three men remained from his old batallion, and that he would never forget all the comrades he had lost.

In the midst of the war, in 1917, Lance-Corporal Huband was home on leave and recuperating from a sports accident when he happened to go into a library in Llandudno in North Wales and got chatting to a young woman with 'fashionable short black curls and large, pale blue eyes' who was working there. Her name was Lavinia Prosser-Baker, and she was a great beauty. Paul was soon smitten and asked for her hand in marriage. She agreed, and they were married on 22 February 1918 in St Hildeburgh's Church in Hoylake.

Very little is known about my grandmother's origins. There is no definitive record of her parents despite extensive genealogical research undertaken by Helen's sister, Avril. In later life, she and Helen exchanged several letters on the subject of their mother's background. Helen remembered: 'Mother did tell me, when I was quite young, that her father was a physician who was swept overboard on his way to the States to establish a practice and a home there. Somehow, I did not believe her.'

They did know that Lavinia was raised in a convent, where her welfare was overseen by a guardian. She and Helen's father had that in common: both had been raised in institutions from a young age. Avril's research suggested that Lavinia may have been illegitimate. Helen responded to this:

> Because of the awful load of being illegitimate – people were so cruel in the nineteenth and early twentieth century about it – she is likely to have concocted a story which would defend her against such unkindness. If such were the case, I wish she had confided in us, because it would have explained so much about her. Her awful tantrums (even when I was very little), having so many children, perhaps, to create the family she had never had – though without the foggiest notion, for years, of how to manage them! The awful frustration of being so gifted – and she was – and yet not being able, in the general chaos of her life, to train to use those gifts.

Helen's cousin Marjorie also maintained that Lavinia was illegitimate and believed that was why Paul's sisters, Phyllis and Stella, did not approve of her. There was also some indication that Lavinia had a half-sister who visited the Hubands with her husband when Helen was about nine years old. Her parents entertained her but, in their snobbish way, refused to speak to him because he was just a cobbler.

In the convent, Lavinia 'learned all the social graces of a woman with money – all the smatterings of this and that felt necessary for a graceful woman of those days. She learned to sing well and to embroider beautifully – but not plain sewing – like patching. She learned nothing whatever about cooking, children, running a home, and was never exposed to family life at all. She had, like most convent girls, a wild interest in men.'

Lavinia spent school holidays in the convent, looked after by the nuns, as she had no home to go to. At the age of fifteen, she left the convent school and went to live with her guardian. He owned several private libraries and trained her to be a librarian. When he married unexpectedly three years later, she couldn't get along with the new wife. Instead, she ran away and found herself a job in a private library in North Wales, which is where she met my grandfather.

Lavinia later told Helen she had been engaged before meeting Paul. Her first fiancé was the youngest son of a widow, who had inherited a cotton mill from her late husband. She lost her other sons in the war, but this one stayed at home to run the mill. Lavinia told Helen, 'He was very handsome. I loved him very much.' But tragedy struck. 'One day, he was walking through the mill, when the floor above him collapsed under the weight of the machinery – and he was crushed to death.'

Was she still on the rebound when she agreed to marry

Paul Huband? Or did she feel he was a kindred spirit with a similarly lonely background to hers?

'A wartime marriage was just about the worst thing that she could have done, especially to a man who had no real home life,' Helen wrote to Avril. Their father had not sustained any serious physical wounds but was obviously haunted by memories of all he had experienced at the Western Front and could not settle down to domestic life. Instead, as the First World War drew to a close in 1918, he re-enlisted as a regular soldier to sail out to Russia and fight another war, leaving Lavinia behind in Hoylake, expecting his child.

When writing in *Twopence to Cross the Mersey,* about her troubled relationship with her mother, Helen dated it back to this: 'the only sin I had committed was to be born to my mother at a time when she would otherwise have divorced my father. She could never forgive me for it.' Certainly it's understandable if my grandmother was furious that her new husband left her alone and pregnant the year after their marriage to fight a war he need not have fought, a war that did not affect British national interests directly. She must have been terrified for her own welfare and that of her unborn child.

After the Bolsheviks took power in Russia in October 1917 and subsequently signed a peace treaty with Germany, the Allies became concerned about the possible spread of Communism. For this and other strategic reasons, starting in 1918, Britain, Canada, the United States and a few other countries sent troops to fight alongside the White Russians, a loose confederation of anti-Communist forces resisting Bolshevik rule. Why Paul Huband joined them is a matter of speculation but it was likely that the difficulty of re-integrating into civilian life, along with a strong sense of obligation, was a factor.

During the winter of 1918–19 my grandfather travelled right into the very heart of the country, from Archangel in the frozen north down to a little town called Pless, around 320 kilometres from Moscow. He wrote a diary in the early months of his time there.

> We commenced the experience of a lifetime. A trek through Russia . . . The road consisted of a track cut through a forest as big as England. No surface to the road. It was frozen like iron and it was marvellous we had so few sprained ankles. At times we passed through desolate marsh, it was like the end of the World, no news and absolutely dependent on our own rations . . . Our grub was bully beef and biscuits. Never shall I forget the vivid imagination one had of fine meals and a comfortable room, as we struggled along.

In March 1919 he succumbed to shock brought on by exposure in the harsh temperatures, which averaged around -15°C, and spent two days in hospital thawing out before rejoining his small patrol. He recalled 'sharp encounters with the enemy, in pathless forests, where my greatest fear always was that I would get lost'. A shed that had been turned into an improvised hospital was set alight during a raid and several of his wounded friends died inside: 'It was a hopeless inferno in seconds,' he later told Helen. And then there was an ambush, in which he became separated from his comrades. It must have been unbelievably terrifying. My mother later wrote to Avril about it:

> I read again Father's description of a small troop of them being sent out into a sort of no man's land, of icy ridges and no population, of their being cut off from any news whatever of what was happening to

> the rest of the British force. No wonder that he was hopelessly lost, when he was the sole survivor of a small patrol. Presumably, it was Bolsheviki who did the ambush and the killing, and it was ironical that it was a Bolshevik who found him and took him home.

That Bolshevik was a man named Stupan. He took my grandfather back to his farm, where he used him as a labourer in an arrangement that may have started out as a prisoner/gaoler situation but soon became more about companionship. Within months the two men were close friends and Helen later wrote, 'I sometimes think that Stupan, the Bolshevik, was the only real friend my father made after his school days. He still had his photo with him when he went into hospital and died.'

Conditions were harsh, though, and when Paul was eventually found by a British patrol and given a medical examination, it was found that his hands were so badly affected by frostbite that surgeons considered amputating them on the ship home. Fortunately for him, they decided they could be saved, although for the rest of his life they would lose circulation and cause him a lot of pain in cold weather.

While my grandfather was holed up in the wilds of central Russia, Lavinia was working as the first lady cashier in the National Provincial Bank in London Road, Liverpool, presumably to be near to her new husband's family home in Hoylake. And then in June 1919, her baby was born. Helen wrote about her arrival in the world to a friend in Ireland; I presume she heard the story from one of her aunts.

> In 1919, my mother had booked herself into a nursing home [a private hospital in Hoylake called Brynmor]. My father was missing, presumed killed, in Russia, though he did come home eventually, a broken neurasthenic after being a prisoner of the Bolsheviki.
>
> When my mother presented herself at the nursing home, her pains having started, it was packed with desperately wounded men awaiting places in military hospitals for long-term treatment.
>
> Since I could not be left on the sidewalk to be born, they let mother in. A soldier who could walk gave up his bed and there I was born, with him assisting a hastily called in midwife. It was he who brought food to my mother, washed my first diapers and generally looked after the pair of us for ten days lying-in. He himself slept on the floor.
>
> My mother, being a very spoiled beauty, seems to have accepted this help as of right. She never thought of keeping in touch with such a humble, kind man. If it had been me, I would have taken a lifelong interest in him and his family.

On Helen's baptismal certificate, Paul Huband's occupation is given as private in the King's Liverpool Regiment and as bank clerk, the job he had done before going into the army. The baby's name is listed as June Elizabeth Louise Huband.

My mother wrote to her sister Avril about how her names were selected: 'June was a natural choice for me. They were going to call me Joan (Auntie Phyllis's second name) but she [Auntie Phyllis] said that June would be similar but prettier. So they added Elizabeth after Granny Huband and Louise after Uncle Percy's wife, who was one of my godmothers.'

Her father missed her christening because he was still in

Russia and believed lost by his relatives back home. He stayed on Stupan's farm until a British Army squad was sent in many months later to round up stragglers. So far from civilisation, he would have had no way of getting back to England on his own.

No one is entirely clear when my grandfather returned to Hoylake to meet his little daughter. Helen said he told her that 'if he had been there, I would have been called Milinki, which, I think, means little girl in Russian.' The name he had in mind was likely 'Milinkaia', which translates roughly as 'cute', or Malenkaia, which means 'little'. He did not think that June was a nice name to give a girl, in view of the notoriety of June, Lady Inverclyde, the mistress of the Prince of Wales. (I imagine it was a bit like calling a child Madonna nowadays!) When I was little, of course, I did not understand the inferences of it all!'

It is clear that Paul had been psychologically damaged by the war. Helen described him as 'neurasthenic', a somewhat vague disorder commonly diagnosed at the time. Today we would likely say that he suffered from post-traumatic stress disorder. He woke screaming in the middle of the night and 'was in such a mental state that he badly needed a calm, gentle, loving wife to help him heal. Instead, Father said that coming home to my mother was like getting into bed with a perfect stranger: not a very good beginning to any marriage. They managed another two babies, Alan and Fiona, within two years, and they fought like cats.'

The First World War ruined many lives, and it seems clear that my grandmother and grandfather's were among them.

Chapter Two

> *It is impossible for me to ever love my parents; the best I can do is to remember that neither of them had much home life or training in family life, and just found children a damned nuisance.*

Soon after Paul returned from Russia, the Huband family moved to Ludlow in Shropshire, where he got a job in a bank. At first they stayed in an apartment in what is now the Feathers Hotel in the centre of town. My mother later wrote:

> Accommodation was very difficult to find, immediately after the First World War, and we expected to spend some years in our apartment. However, one night its Elizabethan fireplace fell out. Termites had been very busy in the beams. So we had to find somewhere else. My father served in the army with the Earl [of Plymouth] at the beginning of the war, and he very kindly rented us one of a row of brand-new cottages he had built for his staff returning after the war.

The earl's cottage was in the village of Bromfield, three kilometres north-west of Ludlow. There my grandparents kept several servants, although I imagine that in order to do so they were living well beyond the means of a bank clerk. A nanny called Edith was hired to look after the children while their parents enjoyed a hectic social life.

'The times were quite wild,' Helen wrote. 'They were known as the Roaring Twenties. The hippies of the 1960s and 1970s had nothing on their parents of the 1920s.' She mused to one of her editors about writing a novel about this time but unfortunately chose not to. 'I had at one point thought about going back to my beginnings and writing a child's view of a rather wild period, encompassing the days of the flappers, the General Strike, the excitement of owning a motor car, the Hunt Balls, County Balls, etc., that my parents used to go to. Probably it has been done already. There was a great poignancy in that period.'

Her parents threw lavish parties at the house and had a large set of friends, mostly 'men who had served in the war and their wives'. In *Twopence*, Helen remembered the women as 'doll-like creatures . . . in short, beige georgette dresses, their Marcel-waved hair covered by deep cloche hats'. Afternoon tea or cocktails were served by a parlour-maid wearing a black-and-white uniform. Helen was allowed to attend daytime parties, dressed up in a smart frock, where she would sit nibbling cake and watching the guests.

> They were intelligent and well educated, business and professional men, and I learned a lot from their conversations about law courts and stock exchanges and medicine and foreign countries, and, of course, about the First World War.
>
> My father was a strong conservative and politics were a favourite subject of conversation and argu-

> ment. One thing that sticks with me, especially in these cynical days, was the absolute love of these men for their country. There was no place like England, no one like the English. Scots and Welsh were brethren with different histories. Anything that touched England touched them personally. Anything that hurt English interests was a personal loss to them.

The war cast its shadow, with many of the men still affected by their wounds. Helen remembered one man who let her 'reach up and touch the silver plate the doctors had implanted to replace the top of his skull'; another had 'an artificial leg which creaked when he walked'. They were 'bereaved, disillusioned, wounded in a war of frightful, unnecessary suffering'.

In a letter to my dad, Avadh, in 1950, Helen described the visits of two local aristocrats.

> I can remember as a small girl of four or five years sitting in my bath in front of a roaring fire in a largish cottage we had in the country, playing with wooden ducks brought me by a couple of gentlemen who used to ride over on horseback. They were the Earl of Plymouth and Viscount Boyne. Both of them lived in young palaces, but they loved to come to our cottage, sit in the steam and warmth and drink hot tea with rum in it. They used to stay and talk literature and country law with my mother and father and then back they would go home. I often laugh and say that I must be one of the few ladies in the land who had a couple of Earls to bath her at one time! But the real point of the story is that wealthy people often enjoy simple comforts for a time because they are different from the normal routine.

Paul and Lavinia were generous hosts, who were able to contribute to the intelligent conversation and present a public front as a glamorous young couple of means, but as soon as the last guest left, they were at each other's throats. My mother wrote about their vicious arguments in a letter to her brother Alan when they were both grown up and living their own family lives. 'I used to lie in bed, simply terrified, as they screamed at each other. I clung to Edith [the nanny], and kept out of the way of Mother as much as possible.'

She remembered that the rows were 'often over stupid, small things', and speculated on the many tensions in their relationship.

> Their marriage did not really have much chance: neither knew the first thing about family life or managing money, because they were both consigned to boarding schools by the age of six. Though they knew each other for some time before their wartime marriage, the coming of the war and the separation caused by it, complicated the relationship.
>
> I think that they certainly started out by being in love, and, despite anything I think they held together because their experience from infancy was similar, yet different from that of the circles in which they lived.
>
> Father was not by nature aggressive, but he drank a lot, like ex-soldiers did in those days, and could become irritated by the children and aggressive in regard to them. Mother went into the attack like a trained defence dog. I suspect that, with no parents to help at all, she had had to defend herself all through her young life. I dreaded her. Nowadays, I feel sorry for a very talented woman with good brains, who never had much chance.

At the schools he attended my grandfather had been beaten for every small misbehaviour so it is not surprising that he considered it normal to hit his children. Helen recalled:

> Reading was such a quiet pursuit that it rarely got me into trouble! My eldest brother was not so lucky – he was much more energetic – he had a marvellous ability to fall out of trees and have to be stitched up, break things, spill things, shout in the garden, forget to say, 'please' or 'thank you', etc., ad infinitum. I used to feel quite smug, until parental wrath caught up with me, too, for some dreadful misdemeanour, like smirking over my brother's fall from grace – or simply looking sulky – or being in a room in which children were not allowed. The pair of us were slapped, slippered and occasionally, caned. Our nanny, who protected us as much as she could, scolded us as a 'pair of little varmints'. She saw no hope for us.

Despite the chastisement (which was doled out by both parents), Helen had a soft spot for her father. She wrote: 'He was quite a gentle person in his way and would tell us funny stories about his time in Russia. His college had taught him Shakespeare's plays so well that he could recite some of them from beginning to end. But imagine his trying to cope with the real world – after a World War.'

An army doctor suggested to Helen's father that if he could tell someone about his horrific experiences, it might improve his nerves. He was sure his wife would not understand so the doctor suggested he tell his children instead. At first he was shocked at the idea of telling them about the brutal cruelty of real war and of the horrors of the civil war in Russia but the doctor persuaded him by pointing out that fairy tales are very often gruesome.

'Gradually, small channels of communication were opened up between Father, Alan and me,' Helen wrote. 'We soon learned that if, after Tea, we could get him going on Russia, we could be sure of not being sent to bed before at least nine o'clock.'

As well as describing his war experiences he taught them other lessons as well: 'My father had a friend who owned a string of race horses, and we used to go to the Ludlow races to watch them. And Father introduced me to betting. I did not like losing the sixpences he gave me, but I learned to love the horses – and some of them knew me.'

She might have enjoyed spending snatches of time with her father but it was not fun to be around her mother. Lavinia was too volatile. She had a terrifying temper and could fly off the handle on the flimsiest pretexts. Servants came and went as they got fed up with receiving the sharp edge of her tongue, or were sacked for some imagined misdeed. 'I remember her screaming like a maniac at me and at the servants,' Helen wrote.

> I was afraid of [her] and up to the age of six, always sought refuge with my nanny. I am sure that up to the age of seven, had I met my mother in the street, I would not have recognized her. By the time I was six, I knew my father all right, because he formed the habit of taking me for a walk occasionally. It was the most split up kind of household that I have ever come across.

*

The name of Edith, the nanny, came up frequently in my mother's stories of her early childhood. She was obviously a very special woman who provided much-needed stability for the children: 'I clung to her,' Helen recalled. 'She was a grey-eyed, plump country woman used to caring for half a dozen small siblings, and naturally at ease with children.' From Edith, young Helen learned a love of nature that would stay with her all her life.

> Edith would pick a primrose, count the petals – so that I learned to count – show me the stamens and the pollen and explain how insects carried the pollen from one flower to another. To this day, I find interest in watching insects.
>
> She would point out birds in flight – and say that spring or winter was coming – and explain migration.
>
> She could recognize a person from half a mile away. 'I know by the tilt of her head – or the way she walks,' she would say. So I learned that the body talks as well as the tongue.

The children sometimes caught rabbits in the field next to the Bromfield house (likely with a makeshift snare or net) intending to turn them into pets, but found they either died or escaped in no time at all. In a letter to Alan, Helen reminisced about those rabbits and also recalled a rather terrifying incident involving Edith: 'I remember that same field one harvest, all golden, and I walked out into it – the stalks were as high as me – and it caught fire from a spark from the railway train passing at the bottom of the garden. I remember Edith rushing into the crop to haul me out – and, do you know, I have always been terrified of fire ever since.'

Helen loved roaming the countryside on the earl's estate and watching the people she came across. She recalled poachers lying on the banks of streams tickling the trout under an overhang until they were relaxed enough to be caught by hand. A band of gypsies camped nearby and she knew the ones who worked in the stables at the racecourse from when she went there with her father. She also knew the local farmers and their dairymaids, shepherds, cowherds and ploughmen, and enjoyed seeing them at seasonal events such as May Day, horse shows, market days and harvest festivals.

In the 1990s, my mother and I visited Bromfield together, and as we toured the area she spoke warmly of her early memories of growing up in the countryside, somehow managing to separate these happy recollections from all the pain of life behind closed doors in the Huband household. We found the racecourse and St Mary's Parish Church but try as we might we couldn't find the cottages. In the dark and the rain, we both felt that Ludlow itself seemed rather melancholy after that. Mum described the trip to a friend.

> It is possible that the rain made the town more depressing than it really is. It did not seem to have any life in it. My kilt was so soaked that it felt a dead weight, and Robert was not much better.
>
> Like many English villages, Bromfield, so lovingly described by Ellis Peters in her Father [sic] Cadfael novels, is barely surviving. Even the church was being held up by scaffolding. The house in which I had lived had been bulldozed to make way for what looked like a small factory. I felt quite sad.

However, she remembered her child's-eye view of the village with great vividness.

> We knew everything that went on in Bromfield, from all the heavy innuendo of adult conversation. Hatches, matches and dispatches were all part of our little world, together with delicious scandals, which we did not quite understand, amongst a bunch of genuine Welsh

border peasants – not a dull character amongst them.

With the aid of a lot of old lace curtains plus long-abandoned bowler hats, ladies' hats, walking sticks, ancient handbags, and other discarded clothing, the whole pantomime of life was re-enacted in our play in the back garden.

Our long-suffering cats, wrapped in shawls, became dead babies, tenderly laid in a shoe box by weeping mothers – they always seemed to escape before being actually buried in a flowerbed. Though, once we did give a dead pet rabbit a full funeral, together with practically all the flowers from the front garden. I will pass over the row which resulted from a bare front garden!

With one of my father's old collars turned back to front and a walking stick, my eldest brother became the image of our rather pompous Vicar.

For myself, I can remember wrapping myself in trailing lace curtains, as I imitated my mother going to a Ball in full regalia.

With a large dock leaf for a mirror and a stone for a lipstick, I peered into the dock leaf and applied the pebble, while I said, 'Goodnight, darlings!' and NEVER glanced back at my brother and sister who were pretending to go to bed.

This was all very well but it did not make up for the lack of loving parents. As Helen remarked: 'Children learn from what they observe and they know very well when no one cares about them.'

*

With her parents engaged in their mad social whirl and with Edith busy caring for the two younger children, Helen was thought to be in the way. For several months at a time she was sent to stay with her father's mother in Hoylake, and these periods would become incredibly important to her. In 1992, she gave a speech in which she sang her grandmother's praises and explained just how important an influence she had been.

> My parents did not believe that it was really necessary to educate their girls; girls got married. What else did they need? But, I had a grandmother, who had been educated by her grandmother, born in the eighteenth century. I usually spent about six months of each year with her, until I was ten.
>
> She taught me patience, fortitude, endurance, persistence, a stiff, narrow kind of honesty, at the same time as she taught me to knit, first on a pair of butcher's wooden skewers, and, later on a threepenny pair of bone knitting needles. Finally, she bought me a set of four real steel pins. Promotion at last! She also taught me to sew and to mend, which was just as well, when I, later, had nine sets of socks, stockings and other garments to mend, patch or darn.
>
> But, most important of all, she taught me to read out of the King James Version of the Bible, a huge tome with big letters, bound in leather and having a lock to close it when not in use. If you are used to hearing the familiar forms – thee, thou, thy, etc., it is not a difficult book – and it has wonderful stories in it.
>
> So very early I was exposed to one of the most beautiful examples of the English language that there is. She would not, however, let me read the Songs of Solomon and she did not seem very keen on Hosea. These books were closed off to me by a clothes peg at the top and another at the bottom of the pages –

and to this day I use clothes pegs to hold my chapters and other papers together.

Since Grandma started me off at the age of three, I did not understand a lot of what I read – and Grandma had to do a lot of helping out. She once explained that Mary Magdalene was a *Fallen Woman* – which did not help me much. She also taught me to print. I never did learn cursive writing – I had to do what I could by experimenting with joining up the printed letters that I knew.

Helen was a natural reader and soon began exploring her grandmother's personal library.

Grandma had complete sets of the works of Dickens and Sir Walter Scott and the Brontë sisters, plus a number of books by a man called Lever, whose heroines always had swanlike necks and alabaster arms. I read the lot. Recently, I was browsing over *Nicholas Nickleby*, and I wondered how on earth I got through it.

In another bookcase, my two aunts had a huge collection of Edwardian novels, which they allowed me to read. I have long since forgotten their names, but I do remember that they all seemed to have heroines, determined to be free and live alone, for various reasons. They all seemed to end up in country cottages covered with climbing roses. The books, like most books in those days, were illustrated, and all the heroines wore straw boaters from which fetching strands of golden hair emerged around their necks. They often had freckles and snub noses. All the books ended with a tender kiss from a tall, dark, very rich man. No wonder I married a dark man!

Both my parents read a lot too. They bought books

> and they did not seem to mind if I took them out of the bookcases to read. So I read many of the authors of the 1920s, including a number of books by various army generals, on the First World War, and a lot of eighteenth-century French history, which was, all my father's life, his particular interest.

Helen's grandmother was the first person to encourage her to write. 'When I was little, my grandmother taught me how to write pleasant letters of thanks for gifts or for invitations to parties. When I was not staying with Grandma, I wrote a letter to her every week, telling her what had happened in my life during that week.' These letters must have provided an early form of training in how to describe her life in an entertaining way, a talent that would stand her in good stead in later life. In 1985, she wrote to thank a teacher whose class had written letters to her, saying, 'I think letter writing is one of the best ways of learning to write, and at the same time it gives pleasure to the persons who received the letters!'

At her grandmother's tea parties, Helen learned to hand round cake, talk about the weather, listen while the old ladies described their various 'indispositions', and gasp at the latest escapades of their sons or nephews – girls did not seem to have escapades officially. She was also allowed to play with some hand-picked local children – something that was strictly forbidden in Bromfield: 'One of the Earl's labourers lived next door to us with his family. But we were not allowed even to peer through the hedge at them – they were working class and therefore beneath us!'

Auntie Phyllis sometimes took my mother down to the seashore to dig holes in the sand and learn a little about marine life. They went to inspect the local fishing fleet's catch of the day and always bought fish directly from the fishermen.

Sundays in Hoylake meant spending the morning in church, with a silver threepenny piece in hand for the collection. Helen recalled:

> I thought it was wonderful theatre. My mother sang in amateur opera; and to give Nanny a break she sometimes took me to rehearsals; since nobody told me otherwise, I imagined for a long time, that the church service was a theatre show made for God.
>
> At an early age, Grandma taught me to say my prayers. 'Gentle Jesus, meek and mild, look upon a little child,' and also to sing, 'There's a Friend for little children above the bright blue sky.' She also taught me the 23rd Psalm, 'The Lord is my Shepherd; I shall not want.' She implanted in me a firm belief that above the clouds walked a Friend for little children called Jesus.
>
> The idea of this friend was crucial to me and stayed with me all through the terrifying years I would later face; it kept me alive, that he would one day take me out of the misery I was enduring.

The time Helen spent at her grandmother's house provided a refuge from the trauma of home life: listening to her parents' endless arguments, being beaten by her father and tongue-lashed by her mother. She must have dreaded the day when each visit came to an end and it was time to leave that little house in Hoylake and head back to the unpredictable chaos of home.

Chapter Three

Because I did not get to school much – in fact, very little at all – and did not therefore have a circle of friends, I thought all boys and girls had the same kind of family life as we did: unmitigated quarrelling. I am told by psychiatrists that children just accept what they see daily as normal but ours was a pretty odd family, and Alan and I would, nowadays, be considered definitely abused.

In 1924, the Hubands had another baby – Brian – followed in 1927 by Tony, bringing the number of children to five by the time Helen reached her eighth birthday. Avril was born when Helen was nine, then her brother Edward when she was eleven. It 'was absolute insanity', Helen wrote in later life, 'at a time when none of their friends to my knowledge had any children at all; and birth control was quite widely practised by the middle classes.'

Her parents' limited resources had to be stretched even further to feed each new arrival and their marriage deteriorated to new depths under the strain of raising all those young children. Helen believed that her parents were often unfaithful to each other and at one point she tried to make light of it: 'I am not sure what the DNA of we children would show!' If any of the children were not my grandfather's, it might help to explain the atmosphere of tension and the frequent battles in that volatile household.

Some time after Helen's sixth birthday, her parents enrolled her in a girls' school in the local market town, Ludlow. No one had explained to her that all children have to go to school and she had very little experience of socializing with other children, so it came as a huge shock.

> School descended upon me totally unexpectedly one morning when Nanny dressed me in a white cotton blouse, a black serge gymslip, a black blazer – and black woollen stockings and laced-up shoes. Have you ever worn coarse black woollen stockings? They itch unmercifully; and I had never worn laced-up shoes before. Since they had been bought without fitting me, they hurt. Nanny said soothingly that I had to have them for school, so that I could learn to read and write.
>
> Since I had been able to do both for a number of years, I thought she was just being awkward, and I rebelled promptly.
>
> It was a very tearstained little girl, with a bottom which must have been very red – though veiled, of course, by thick fleecy-lined bloomers – who was delivered to the school by an irate father.
>
> The teachers were not trained teachers; they were simply middle-class women who had set up a school; and the main idea was to turn out refined young women with a modicum of French and music and of the classics, but, most important, with the correct English accent, which would indicate their place in the class

> structure. In such schools, manners were very important, also.
>
> After the first half hour of colouring a picture, I became bored. I loudly asked where I could find something to read. That was the second spanking of the day – for impudence, this time.
>
> Father picked me up in the afternoon, one of the few times I was glad to see him. I remember my tearful, total bewilderment among these strange women who shouted at me and shoved me about. It seemed as if my world had gone mad. I had no idea what a teacher was. No idea what I had done to be banished to this awful place.
>
> My father was not pleased at the report hastily poured into his ears by the teacher who handed me over. She said something which I did not understand, but it sounded bad so I remembered it. She said, 'We'll break her in time.'

Helen endured about two weeks of fairly constant battles with the teachers at that school and a couple of canings from her father at home, before succumbing to a bad case of measles. She became so ill that her eyesight was significantly affected. She could still read with her nose pressed right up against the page, so for a couple of years none of the family noticed.

While she was recovering from measles her brother Alan caught the disease. In those days, no child could attend school if another member of the family had a contagious disease and the isolation period was three weeks after the last spot had disappeared. Helen's little sister Fiona came out in spots on the day Alan was declared clear of spots, so the return to school was delayed even longer. Helen and Alan spent their months' long convalescence in the back garden, 'making mud pies and burying a dead rabbit several times over with full funeral rites, as far as we knew them'. Nanny had to watch Fiona very carefully, because she was a delicate child with precarious health, but she pulled through her bout of measles unscathed.

Helen did not return to her school after Fiona recovered because it was time for her to visit her grandmother. While there, she was educated in different ways.

> Auntie Phil [Phyllis] ran a little prep school in the dining room, and I sat in on it – and technically was at school! But I spent most of my time reading my way through the enormous number of adult books in the house. I don't seem to have been any trouble with either Granny or the Aunts, because I don't ever remember even being scolded, never mind hit. Grandma once tried sending me to the local girls' school, but I went home in mid-term, thus wasting the fees, so she did not try again.

Her grandmother began to teach Helen French, and she also taught her musical notation and embroidery, so she was getting an education at that time, albeit in a piecemeal fashion. Auntie Phil also taught Helen to draw with perspective and light and shade.

Not all of the lessons were intentional, however. In 1997, she told an audience aboard the *Queen Elizabeth II*:

> Grandma never realized that little Big Ears sitting under her velvet-draped tea table, playing with an old Victorian toy tea set, was listening to her discussions with her daughters: and also to her discussions with her solicitor, who was also her financial adviser – in those days, solicitors made home visits. No

> wonder I know a fair amount of family law of the period!
>
> My father would have had a fit, if he had known how much his six-year-old daughter knew about him and about his brothers. And about lawyers. Those conversations have sparked many good ideas.

These were by far the happiest times of my mother's childhood. She was almost the sole focus of her grandmother and her aunts' attention, since her siblings rarely came on these visits, for reasons that were never explained. Perhaps they were considered too young to be sent on the train unaccompanied. At any rate, she was fussed over by those three ladies and became very fond of them.

When Helen got back to Bromfield after her 1925 visit, she found that her parents were packing up to move to Ross-on-Wye, where her father had a new job. It was the first in a succession of moves the family would make as their financial difficulties increased. At that age Helen did not know the reasons for the move but she found it difficult yet again being the new girl in school, and before long she was clashing with the teachers.

> Children are rarely kind to newcomers who are late in starting the school year. All the friendly cliques have already been formed. And, anyway, I was always in trouble for failing to answer questions correctly and, once, I was sent to Headmistress, because I had stood up and told the History teacher that she had not got her facts right. I had to stay after school and write, I must learn not to be impudent, five hundred times. In a haphazard way, I had read a fair amount of history, which fascinated me. I had also accepted as history *The Iliad*, *The Odyssey* and a book of Scandinavian sagas,

> not to speak of several children's books on Egyptian Gods and myths.

Just as she had memorized her classmates' names and begun to make friends, it seemed the family were moving on to the next town and it was time for yet another change. Helen yearned for the kind of life she saw other girls leading.

> It began to dawn on me that other girls had regular schools, birthday parties and Christmas parties, family holidays and picnics – and none of these things seemed to happen to me. Once or twice, I had been to other little girls' parties, where I knew no one – and do not to this day know how I was included.
>
> In one school, I managed to learn my arithmetic tables, so essential in the days before pocket calculators. A girl also taught me to skip. And in another school, a girl taught me how to play wall games with a bouncing tennis ball – with all the little rhymes that went with the games.

But just as soon as Helen began to form a budding new friendship, it was time to go back to her grandmother's, or her parents decided to move house again. Tensions also increased at home and Helen grew increasingly wary of her parents.

> As my beautifully spoken parents moved around the house, if they noticed a grammatical error in my brother's or my speech, they would automatically slap us across the head and correct us. I think this must have happened to both of them in boarding school. It is certainly one way of teaching grammar!
>
> While I struggled through a childhood which was

so unpredictable, I learned to keep out of the way of adults. I watched their faces, so that I could react quickly if I thought I was going to be hit. I also learned to keep away from school bullies.

I took refuge in hall cupboards and in wardrobes, sometimes with my brother, while our parents screamed with rage at each other.

*

The domestic staff at home provided a different kind of education, as Helen later recalled. 'I listened to the maids talking and learned a few extraordinary facts of life, which were confirmed to me by the animals in the farm fields around us – no artificial insemination in those days.'

In 1997 she told an audience at the Daphne du Maurier Festival of Arts and Literature:

> I listened to the cook, our nanny and the housemaid talking round the nursery fire in the evenings, about their boyfriends and the new films they had seen in Ludlow. I learned about who was dead or dying or needed money at home, and how much these women contributed to their families.
>
> At one point, when two babies [Tony and Avril] arrived within eleven months, a charlady was recruited from the local workhouse to help with the cleaning. She was a tall thin woman, grey hair scraped back in an old-fashioned bun, dressed in workhouse uniform and a black shawl. We liked each other.
>
> And she whistled as she worked. She whistled her way down the long staircases and down the back and front steps, as she scrubbed and scrubbed. And she would talk to me. She fascinated me – and looking back, I realize what an old dear she was, though at

> the time I mostly feared that she was bound for hell for her musical efforts. She sometimes turns up in my books.
>
> One of the many old men who worked on the Estate on which our village home stood, taught me how to whistle, as he cleaned out ditches round the field adjacent to us.
>
> 'A girl who whistled was bound for hell,' I was shocked to discover. 'A whistling girl or a crowing hen ain't no good for gentlemen,' said Nanny, as she proceeded to slap the habit out of me.

Religion played a part in her home life as well as at her grandmother's, but it was the nanny and not Helen's parents who took the children to church on Sundays.

> There I heard the works of many of the great composers played on good organs. The local choirs sang mighty works, Cantatas, oratorios and anthems, on Festival days. All the churches had fine stained-glass windows for careful examination by bored little girls; some churches had good paintings donated in memory of dead parishioners. The churchyards were filled with elaborately carved gravestones so I became aware that men could carve wonderful things, like angels standing on tiptoe holding up a wreath, or women clad in a kind of Roman toga, on their knees embracing a marble cross decked with marble flowers. There was an inordinate number of plump cherubim and baby angels on children's graves, too. Inside the churches, my grubby fingers explored other monuments with the figures of men and women in armour or stiff ruffs; and I remember being startled when I saw, on the walls, plaques to soldiers killed in action in Daddy's war.

Every November 11th, I was taken to the cenotaph, and watched aghast, as women draped in black wept. I wore a Flanders poppy and Father wore his medals, and looked as if he might cry, too. It worried me very much.

*

Helen's parents were not unusual in 1920s England in being very class-conscious, and although they could not afford an upper-middle-class lifestyle on Paul Huband's earnings, they were determined to demonstrate all the outward trappings. Unbeknownst to Helen, their debts were continuing to multiply throughout the decade.

My brother and I observed another world moving round us, though we were not allowed to connect with it in any way. It was the working-class world, kept separate from us because we were upper middle-class and mixed with County people. At that time, I might not know much else, but I knew exactly how I fitted into the class structure and that I was Church of England.

Rough and noisy children tumbled past our gate on their way to and from the village, presumably going to school. On Sundays they came by dressed for church, and I remember, in the summer, envying the girls their long fair hair crowned with bright yellow straw hats decked with yards of pink ribbon. My hair was cut short. In winter, I wore a boy's cap exactly like my brother, and in summer a round sailor hat with a white top, and a navy ribbon round it with H.M.S. *Rodney* on the front – with matching sailor suits and sailor dresses. It was a long-lasting fashion.

Some of the despised working class came into our

> house or garden quite regularly. They were mostly men, the postman, hedgers and ditchers and thatchers and pond cleaners, well diggers, delivery boys, bricklayers, the gardener, the local blacksmith with a new wrought-iron gate, tramps begging for food, gypsies wanting to sell clothes pegs and tell your fortune. A wonderful collection of characters.
>
> The workmen who came would always talk to a watching little boy and girl, and I think they were the first people I ever talked freely to.

Another thing that separated them from local people was religion: Helen and Alan were not allowed to play with Roman Catholic children. The prohibition by her parents was so strict that it seemed to Helen as if Roman Catholic children must carry an infectious disease.

They moved to Ross-on-Wye and Helen was sent to Ross High School, where she made her first proper friend, a girl called Joan Brawn, who was the daughter of a newly widowed lady who lived nearby. Helen's parents approved of the connection but Joan's mother seemed curiously reluctant to let her daughter visit the Huband household. As Helen explained later, 'Joan told me it was because my parents had a bad reputation. I knew, in Ludlow, from Edith talking to the daily cleaning lady, who came in, that it was the same story. Scandal went round these tiny towns faster than flood water.'

The scandal to which she referred was largely to do with her parents running up debts all over the place, then fleeing from their creditors, which was particularly frowned upon in someone who worked for a bank. 'Things began to fall apart. I heard someone say that my father was in financial difficulties, whatever that might mean,' Helen recalled.

If Helen was right in thinking her parents were unfaithful

to each other, perhaps that was also a factor in tarnishing their good name. And there was one more thing she was aware of, but likely did not grasp the significance of at the time: her father had suffered a heart attack in 1928, when he was just thirty-three years old, which must have made it even harder for him to deal with the pressure he was under.

The family moved once again, probably fleeing all the creditors on their tails, and this time they relocated to Nottingham, so Helen was separated from Joan.

> My parents rented a very big town house – a very nice one. They sublet a lot of it. My brother and I were sent to a school, which seemed very much rougher to me.
>
> In Nottingham, I went to Trent Boulevard School for a few weeks, and there I met Mary Southall, the daughter of the Methodist minister of the chapel further up Bridgford Road than us.
>
> They obviously decided that I needed to be 'saved' from my surroundings, so I spent a lot of time in their house and at their chapel. What they taught me, gently, of integrity, honesty, common decency, has remained with me. I shudder to think what my life might have been in Liverpool, if they had not explained about chastity and 'fallen women'. They are the family to whom I really owe an awful lot.

In 1930 Helen noticed that her parents had stopped entertaining visitors at the house, and one day she realized that her mother's collection of Georgian silver had vanished from the antique sideboard. She asked where it had gone but was told by Lavinia: 'Girls should not poke their noses into the business of grown-ups.' And then their housemaid,

Mary Ann, left and it became clear she wasn't planning to come back. Something odd was going on, but Helen had no idea what.

Lavinia was admitted to hospital to give birth to her seventh child, Edward, and immediately afterwards had to have a hysterectomy. While she was recuperating in hospital, her husband was declared bankrupt. Helen was told about it by a schoolfriend.

She wrote in *Twopence to Cross the Mersey* that it was 'a not uncommon occurrence in the world of 1930, but strange to me. I had heard vaguely that going bankrupt was an American disease which had struck Wall Street in New York, and that Americans committed suicide when this happened to them; mentally, I saw dozens of them hurling themselves off the tops of skyscrapers, and I wondered where Father would find a skyscraper.'

When my grandfather's employers found out about his bankruptcy, it was the final straw and they fired him. He was out of work, with seven children to feed, just as the world teetered on the brink of the Great Depression triggered by the Wall Street Crash. Stock prices tumbled, manufacturing industries failed, and unemployment began to rise. By 1933, 2.5 million would be unemployed in Britain, a staggering twenty-five per cent of the workforce.

When Helen's mother heard the news in her hospital bed that her husband had lost his job, she must have been devastated. None of them had any idea yet of what the effects of bankruptcy would be on the whole family, or that my grandfather, in his naïvety, was about to make a string of disastrous decisions that would threaten the very existence of them all.

Chapter Four

When I came to Liverpool as a young girl, I was simply terrified by it – it was so black with soot – and a lot of its people were misshapen and ugly from the awful circumstances in which they lived and worked – people who face the utmost poverty are rarely pretty, and about the streets were many people who reminded me of the hobgoblins in my story books and, what's more, I couldn't understand a word of the language!

It's difficult to put myself in my grandfather's shoes as he tried to decide what to do in the aftermath of the bankruptcy and the loss of his job. He was well-educated, and surely a sensible man with less false pride would have sought advice before making any hasty decisions. But events moved quickly: the domestic staff walked out, one of them taking my grandmother's clothes in lieu of unpaid wages; creditors were desperately clamouring for repayment; and, with his wife still in hospital, Grandfather relied on Helen to look after her younger siblings during those desperate days. I presume he tried to negotiate with his creditors, but none of them would give him any more leeway after hearing he had lost his job. Besides, it must have been well known that he had run away from previous debts; he was not a good credit risk.

In *Twopence to Cross the Mersey*, my mother explains his next actions.

> Father had no knowledge of the legal rights of a bankrupt to clothing and bedding, so he sent the key of our house to his main creditor, a moneylender, with instructions to sell the house and its contents, and to reimburse himself from the proceeds. From a misguided sense of honour, he left everything we possessed, except the clothing in which he and his family were dressed, taking only a pair of blankets in which to wrap my mother and the new baby, Edward.

With the last ten pounds in his pocket, he bought tickets for the whole family to travel to Liverpool, city of his birth, imagining there must be work in such a big port, with industries that had been thriving at the turn of the century based on the wealth of the Empire. Helen's brother Alan recalled their father telling him, at the time, that 'by stealth' they were going to try to get to Liverpool and that there were a number of old friends who had promised to help. These promises, however, did not materialize.

In the middle of the nineteenth century, the port of Liverpool had been second only to London as a hub through which goods were imported and exported to serve the needs of the nation. The opening of the Manchester Ship Canal in 1894 secured its status by allowing the industrial heartlands easy access to the port facilities. Liverpool's main industries were shipbuilding, glass manufacture, iron foundries and soap making. In the early twentieth century, the city's wealth was displayed for all to see in the grand buildings erected along the waterfront: the Port of Liverpool Building, the Liver Building and the Cunard Building, jointly known as The Three Graces. Much later, Helen would grow to love that waterfront and its magnificent buildings, which now have UNESCO World Heritage status.

But while there were rich pickings for the wealthy, there was a dark side to the story. In 1928, the year before the Wall Street Crash, fourteen per cent of the population of Liverpool were in a state of poverty, barely able to feed themselves and living huddled together in overcrowded slums that were breeding grounds for infectious diseases. Immediately after the Wall Street Crash in October 1929, the American Government clamped down on the import of foreign goods and demanded repayment of outstanding loans. Both of these actions had instant effects on Liverpool's docks, leading to a massive drop in revenues and to hundreds of workers being laid off. Worldwide, prices fell and foreign imports were taxed, causing the value of British exports to halve in just a year. My grandfather obviously had not been reading the newspapers closely, because by the time he arrived in Liverpool with his family in the winter of 1930–31, the unemployment rate there was double the national average. It would continue to rise until, at its worst, almost a third of working-age men were unable to find jobs.

Britain's northern industrial cities, such as Glasgow, Manchester, Sheffield and Liverpool, were badly hit in the Depression, while the South, where light industries – chemicals and electrical goods – dominated, remained relatively unscathed. My grandfather would have done better to have stayed in Nottingham but perhaps he was too ashamed. He was under immense pressure. I understand his uncertainty and despair.

The family arrived in Liverpool on a dismal, wet, grey

day. Helen's mother was still very weak from her operation and could not walk unaided, so she lay in the station waiting room surrounded by her children while my grandfather went out to look for accommodation for them. All he could find was a single room, with 'a suffocating odour of unwashed bodies, old cooking and cats'. After buying some bread, milk and sausages, his cash ran out and they could not afford a bag of coal to heat the place. A Roman Catholic priest helped that first time, but he warned my grandparents that unemployment was rising and that finding a job would not be easy.

Gradually their disastrous situation began to sink in. After hearing her parents tell the priest a well-edited version of their story, Helen, aged ten and a half, understood more of what was happening and felt a sense of foreboding.

> Now, at last, I knew why we were in Liverpool and what the word 'bankruptcy' really meant to our family. I knew with terrible clarity that I would never see my bosom friend, Joan, again, never play with my doll's house, never be the captain of the hockey team or be in the Easter pageant. My little world was swept away.
>
> I looked at Alan, who was standing equally silently by the window. His eyes met mine and we shared the same sense of desolation. Then his golden eyelashes covered his eyes and shone with tears, half-hidden.

My grandfather went to the authorities to claim unemployment benefit but he didn't realize that it was paid at the level given by the last town in which they had registered as residents. In Nottingham in early 1931, this was forty-three shillings a week – less than he would have got had he been a Liverpool resident, and a ridiculously tiny amount on which to feed and house a family of nine.

Permanent accommodation was eventually found at a private house in the south of the city: two top-floor rooms and an attic in very run-down condition. Neither of my grandparents realized that the twenty-seven shillings a week charged by the landlady was way above the going rate – yet another example of their poor financial skills. Alan, Fiona, Brian, Tony and Avril were registered at a local school, which at least had the benefit of being heated during the day, but Helen was kept at home to look after baby Edward, while both of her parents tried to find work. At the age of eleven, she was put in charge of cooking, cleaning, laundry, and trying to make a shilling a day (equivalent to five pence in modern British currency) stretch so she could produce an evening meal for the whole family. A pint of milk for the baby cost twopence, leaving ten old pennies for a loaf of bread, a bag of potatoes, and possibly a penny worth of bacon or margarine. Their staple diet was boiled potatoes, and gnawing hunger pains were a sensation they soon got used to.

Other people were poor in Liverpool in 1930, but Helen stood out as 'not like them':

> In a middle-class school uniform, with a very cultivated speech, with a small baby in my arms, I ventured into a world where other children jeered and laughed at me. I had been taught by my grandmother that property was sacred, so I could not steal as other children did. She also taught me that food that had been dropped on the ground or into garbage cans must never be touched – it would probably poison me and I would die. So, as if I was a high-caste Hindu, I left such things untouched.

Perhaps my grandfather thought, when he moved to Liverpool, that his mother would be forced to help them but he had burnt his boats in that respect many years earlier. She still had her home in Hoylake, a ferry ride across the Mersey, and a decent income, but there had been a falling-out between her and Helen's parents a few years earlier. Now Helen's grandmother was unwilling to help them in their time of need. Paul's brother Frank had died in 1923 and his other brother Percy had himself been declared bankrupt. Of the five siblings, only the girls were to be provided for. Helen wrote to Avril about it in later life.

> Grandfather's monies were held in trust, so that Grandma could live on the interest and the capital distributed amongst his children after she died. All the monies which our father would have inherited went to Auntie Phyllis, most of it as interest on small loans she made him when we were little.
>
> When we lived in Ross, Granny came to see us, and made an agreement with Daddy – which she had already made with Uncle Percy (Uncle Frank was by then dead) – that her home and its contents should be left to Aunties Phyllis and Stella. She was anxious that they not be uprooted and made homeless by a legal challenge to her own will. Of course, Father agreed, because he had, at that time, a good job and real prospects.
>
> Daddy had borrowed from his sister, Phyllis, regularly and signed agreements that she should be repaid after Granny's death out of his share of their father's reversionary interest. What he had not reckoned on was that the courts ruled that Auntie Phyllis was entitled, by the agreements he had signed, to collect INTEREST on 20-year-old loans! So our family ended up without a cent. In fact, Father still owed money to his sister.

From time to time, when they were in Liverpool, a small package would be delivered with a Hoylake postmark.

> It always contained a pair of very soft, finely knitted children's combinations; there was never any note. I wondered sometimes what Grandma thought about during the long afternoons when she must have sat, as was her custom, in her sunny, lace-curtained sitting room, cat on knee, and knitted. Did she grieve? Or was she sustained by righteous indignation? Had she any inkling at all about what was happening to us, that we looked like children who had suffered in an Indian famine?

One of the most difficult things for anyone to understand about Helen's story is how her grandmother could have abandoned the family. In 1997, Helen spoke to a class of children at Wyedean School in Gloucestershire. Afterwards, the pupils did a variety of exercises, including composing imaginary letters from Helen to her grandmother asking for assistance. Helen wrote to the English teacher with the following explanation of why her grandmother did not help the struggling family.

> My grandmother was bitter that two of her sons made a mess of their lives – but she expected them to get on and clear up the mess. Hardship was punishment for their stupidity. The Bible says that God 'visits the sins of the fathers upon the children', and that was part of the attitude.
>
> In those days, real suffering was much more common than we realize, and people were accustomed to the idea of it. For example, even basic medical care was not always available or affordable.

After the First World War, there was a lot of what was called 'genteel poverty'. Many well-educated people who had lost their money as a result of the war lived in extreme poverty, which they hid from their neighbours as much as possible.

You were told that 'the Lord made the burden and He knows how much you can bear' so you got on with your miserable life and bore it. You did not give up easily. These people maintained their good manners and their pride in family but they were very poor. I think that is how my grandmother viewed my parents. I don't think she would have been particularly sympathetic to a whining letter from me.

She would simply think that, well, lots of nice people are poor; she would not, never having seen it (remember there were no televisions with pictures of starving people to enlighten her), believe that anyone could actually starve in Britain. She would tend to say that they should get up off their butts and work.

My grandmother was, indeed, a very nice woman, for her time; yet she held ideas which are alien to us nowadays.

My great-grandmother was eighty-three years old in 1931, and had two daughters and Helen's cousin at least partially dependent on her – and the aunts, too, had very little sympathy for Helen's family. Help was not going to be forthcoming from that quarter. They were on their own.

It wasn't long before the effects of the Hubands' poor diet were evident: the weight dropped off the children, leaving them skinny-limbed and prone to catching all the bugs doing the rounds, then struggling to fight them off again; my grandmother's teeth fell out, marring her once-beautiful looks, and my grandfather fell into a state of hopelessness and depression. When Helen became seriously ill with an ear infection and was referred to a hospital specialist, he was aghast at the sight of her protruding ribs and the buttocks that were so bony it hurt her to sit on a chair. 'Even in this city,' he said sternly, 'it is some time since I saw such a shocking case of malnutrition.'

Helen said in later life that she believed that doctor saved her hearing and, quite possibly, her life when he 'tore into my mother about the need to see that I was fed. From that moment, my life took a tiny turn for the better.' In a lecture in 1992, she added: 'It was only when, after the war, I saw the pictures of the inmates of Auschwitz that I fully understood how close to death we had been.'

Many years later, Alan wrote to my mother that social services had visited while she was out one day and that the children were lucky not to have been taken into care. It seems likely that Helen's malnutrition had been reported to the authorities, and possibly Brian's had been noted when he was in hospital with quinsy (a serious throat infection). In some ways my grandparents can be excused for their lack of financial common sense, but when I read in my mother's memoirs that her parents still borrowed money to subsidize their smoking habits, their callousness seems incomprehensible.

My mother was lucky not to suffer any long-term ill effects from the starvation she experienced for several years from the age of eleven. It helped that she had been well fed up to that age, by Edith the nanny and other domestic staff at their previous houses, and also when staying with her grandmother. Once she was earning her own money, from the age of fifteen onwards, gradually she began to return to a healthy weight.

In adult life my mother always appreciated good plain

food and was genuinely concerned for anyone who didn't seem to eat enough. It is no wonder that Edmonton's food bank was one of her favourite charities or that she felt quite comfortable talking with homeless men drifting in and out of the river valley near her home.

Helen felt deeply the unfairness that her siblings were allowed to go to school while she, by dint of being the eldest, was not. 'I became housekeeper, nanny, general factotum, to six uncaring siblings and two incapable and bad-tempered parents. I discovered that the one at home must always do without, because she did not have to go to school or work.' This fundamental injustice was one of the most important lessons I took from my mother's story and, as a result, I have always been very sensitive about treating my own children scrupulously fairly.

Helen had a thirst for knowledge and a love of reading that had been stimulated by her grandmother and now there were no outlets for either in the daily drudgery of her life. She was befriended by an elderly Lebanese gentleman she met in a local park, a man who spoke many languages and had worked as an interpreter. His wife and three sons were dead and now he was awaiting his own death, but still he enjoyed books and sitting outdoors in the sunshine. Helen began to sit with him regularly during the summer of 1931 and haltingly confided in him about her family's difficulties. He counselled that her present difficulties were only temporary and advised that she should read as much as possible: 'One day, you will have the opportunity to make use of the knowledge that you will accumulate,' he said, adding that scholarship might not earn you much money but that it enriched your mind.

Of course, my mother loved books and in particular she

loved libraries, describing them as 'beacons of light in a dark world'. For an anniversary celebration of the Edmonton Public Library, she recalled, 'In his destitution, my father also felt the loss of books. With two precious pennies he enrolled himself in the local Carnegie public library, full of volumes often so tattered that pages were missing. He could also read the newspapers there.

'Dressed in garments which barely covered me, and with my filthy baby brother on my hip, I borrowed his card and faced irate librarians who wanted to send me to the children's department. I insisted in my high-bred English accent that I had to get books for my father. They let me in. They became my friends.'

There were other uplifting moments when Helen could forget her situation for a while.

> Every week the Salvation Army Band came to our street corner, all dressed up in their uniforms, cymbals clashing, drums rattling, trumpets blowing. They would play all kinds of lively hymn tunes, while we stood and listened, and sometimes joined in the singing. Another musical effort was that of the hurdy-gurdy man. He had a monkey with him, who used to carry a hat round the audience to collect pennies from us. Then there were sad Welsh miners, standing in the gutters and singing superbly their Welsh songs for pennies.

But before long something would remind her of the family's desperate circumstances. It must have been a bitter blow when she spotted her old friend Joan in the streets of Liverpool one wintry day, on an outing with her mother, and neither would acknowledge her. It was just over a year since they had last seen each other but in that time everything had changed. Suddenly Helen saw herself through their eyes.

> Coming towards me, amid the well-dressed shoppers, was an apparition. A very thin thing draped in an indescribably dirty woollen garment which flapped hopelessly, hair which hung in rat's tails over a wraith-like face, thin legs partially encased in black stockings torn at the knees and gaping at the thighs, flapping, broken canvas covering the feet.
>
> I slowed down nervously, and then stared with dawning horror.
>
> I was looking at myself in a dress shop window.

I have read it many times now but my mother's inspired description of herself still fills me with sadness.

In the spring of 1932, after months of fruitless trudging to the labour exchange, Helen's father obtained a poorly paid job as a clerk for the city, helped by a policeman who noticed his Denstone school tie; by coincidence, he had also attended Denstone. The school's benevolent fund gave my grandfather the money to buy some decent clothes to wear to an interview, as well as a haircut, and the policeman provided a reference that secured him the job. Meanwhile, my grandmother took a succession of sales jobs, but the family remained hard up. Partly this was to do with Paul and Lavinia's regular consumption of tobacco and his drinking, but it was also because of some unwise hire-purchase agreements they entered into in order to buy furniture. Under the terms of the contracts, they made monthly payments set at a level that meant they would eventually pay much more than if they had bought the goods outright. Until the last payment was made, ownership of the furniture rested with the hire-purchase company. If they defaulted, the goods were repossessed – and yet they still had to continue the monthly payments. Being my grandparents, they always fell foul of this type of agreement and ended up having their income drained by making payments for furniture they no longer had. These types of contract are more strictly regulated in the present day, but in the 1930s there were plenty of financially illiterate people who entered into them, only to rue the day.

As the person left at home during the day, Helen lived in fear of bailiffs who might come to take away the few possessions they had amassed. It seemed there was no way out of the financial black hole into which the family had tumbled.

Chapter Five

I had never considered that children might love their mother. I always feared mine.

It was traditional in British families in the first part of the twentieth century that the eldest daughter helped to look after her younger siblings and that she cared for her parents if they needed it. Never can this unwritten rule have been as harshly applied as it was to my mother in the 1930s. There was no question of any of the other children missing their schooling to help with baby Edward. Helen's suggestions that perhaps she could go to school for a term, or maybe even attend evening classes, were met with fury and steely refusals, particularly by her mother.

Lavinia and Paul were breaking the law, since all British children were required to attend school until their fourteenth birthdays. When Helen dropped Fiona at school one day in spring 1933 when she was thirteen and three-quarters, she was questioned by a teacher, which led to a visit from a school attendance officer. How her parents avoided legal sanction is unclear, but Helen was required to go to school for the final six weeks before she turned fourteen. Her parents were outraged, but had no say in the matter, and Helen was thrilled. 'It was bliss to hold a pencil in my unaccustomed fingers and to try my wits against the work put in front of me.' The education she had received in her first ten years stood her in good stead and she found she was ahead of her contemporaries in every subject except maths – and that she had a particular talent for art.

There was a scholarship available at the City School of Art, and Helen's art teacher nominated her for it. Her hopes were raised but when she heard nothing, she assumed she had not been picked. Some time later, Alan reported that his headmaster told him Helen had won the scholarship and enquired how she was getting on with it. It seemed her parents had been informed of her success but had decided not to tell her, presumably because they did not want to lose their free babysitter. Helen was devastated, as she wrote in *Twopence*.

> I rocked myself backwards and forwards, as my touching belief that my parents, even if they had not much love for me, would do their best for me, and that they had always done so, died. I was in agony. The research into the ruthless exploitation of the eldest child was still far in the future, and there was no explanation to console my childish despair.

In 1948, psychoanalyst Melitta Schmideberg (among others) wrote that parents who had suffered emotional deprivation in their own youth could subconsciously treat their eldest child as a parent substitute, in a process called 'parentification'. The child thus parentified not only lost out on a proper childhood but also lost his or her sense of identity in a way that could be a hindrance in social relationships in adult life.

Helen's parents were like children themselves, floundering in the financial mess of their own making. While Helen budgeted, tried to save money to replace worn-out clothing, and sacrificed her own needs for the sake of her siblings, Lavinia made ridiculous financial decisions like coming home with a box of cream cakes when they had no meat, bread or milk. Her father couldn't stop himself buying alcohol and cigarettes even as his children subsisted on meals of a couple of boiled potatoes. Helen explained this away, saying, 'Life seemed so hopeless that they snatched at any treat, as if they had only the present and there was no future.'

Her mother frequently sat down to write begging letters to their old acquaintances which, for a woman who used to have a surfeit of pride, must have been hard. It seems most of her letters went unanswered, but the family received the occasional hand-out: once a five-pound note was awarded from a fund run by Paul Huband's old regiment, and another time a packet of second-hand clothes arrived from the mother of Helen's old friend Joan, amplifying the humiliation Helen had felt when she saw them in the street.

Another route out of poverty could be to get the children into work and the eldest son, Alan's, future career was hotly debated in the household. My grandmother and grandfather agreed that he should try to get employment as an office boy in a firm where they would offer training and possibly a chance to sit professional exams. There were shipping firms, banks and estate agencies who might leap at the chance of a bright fourteen-year-old boy, to whom they need not pay much. In fact, he would eventually join the air force and move away from home in 1938. Helen got on well with him, subject, of course, to the usual little rivalries of adjacent children. After they grew up, they led their own lives, separated by their different experiences, but for the rest of his life Helen was closer to him than to any of her other siblings.

Fiona was not asked by her parents to help with the little ones because her health was frail. She and Helen comforted each other when they cuddled up in bed at night, but Fiona did not have Helen's strength of character. Once, when she was left in charge of her younger siblings, she answered the door to the dreaded bailiffs and they snatched all the family's furniture in payment of some long-held debts, leading Helen to feel horribly guilty for not being there.

Brian, whom Helen believed to be her mother's favourite, began singing in a church choir, later joined by Tony, and both of them kept out of the way as much as possible to avoid the arguments at home. Avril had 'such a colossal temper that even Mother was silenced by it', while baby Edward was too small to worry about.

Helen described the dynamic in *Liverpool Miss*: 'As each child grew in strength, it fought quite ruthlessly for a place for itself, giving very little thought to the plight of others. I saw that the family unit was not as tightly locked as my parents were fond of imagining . . . Why could they not help too? I would ask angrily. And the retort was always the same, "You are the eldest."' It was a prodigious burden.

> Nobody asked me what I would like to do. My role in life had been silently decided for me. It was obvious that my parents had no intention of allowing me to be anything but an unpaid, unrespected housekeeper. With all the passion of a fifteen-year-old, I decided that such a life was not worth living.

Helen walked to the docks one winter's day in 1934, climbed over the safety fence and considered jumping into the oily, swirling waters, to escape from an existence that had become 'unendurable'. A kindly sailor pulled her back from the edge and bought her a cup of tea, but that dark moment, when she reached rock bottom, helped to spur her on to start evening school, despite fierce parental disapproval. She would continue to educate herself in this way for seven years, earning scholarships so she did not have to pay the fees, and learning about book-keeping and other skills required for office work, as well as studying languages.

My mother wrote that she felt she had no choice but to have a career since it had long been impressed on her that she was not marriage material. Fiona was the beauty and all Helen had was her wits: "You can't help your looks," our nanny, Edith, used to say, as she scrubbed my face. "Maybe your yellow complexion is from being ill so much."

A rather plain teacher at the evening classes suggested that Helen's parents would be glad of a daughter who brought home a wage and could look after them in their old age, a prospect that terrified her.

> She had put into words something I dreaded, something only a husband could save me from. I could be faced with spending the rest of my life maintaining and waiting on two irritable, shiftless, nagging parents, the usual fate of the daughter who did not marry. Because I was plain and shy and frightened of my mother, I knew I could be bullied into being a nobody, a nothing. Some women with gentle parents found their care a labour of love. Not me. I knew I would be crushed flat as a shadow.

Helen was desperate to work, in order to contribute to the family coffers but also to buy herself a little independence and an escape from the drudgery of eternal childcare, cooking and cleaning for the entire family. A local church deaconess, Miss Ferguson, found her a job as a telephonist working for the Personal Service Society, a charity in Bootle that distributed aid and advice to the area's needy. There was an almighty row about it at home, but for once Helen stood up for herself.

> 'I am going for the interview, whether you like it or not. I may never get such a chance again. I must take it.'
>
> 'Helen, you forget yourself,' exploded Father.
>
> 'Oh, no I do not. For once, I am remembering myself.'

Alan interceded on Helen's behalf, saying that he would lend a hand around the house, and besides, all girls worked nowadays. Fiona also agreed to help, and this time Helen was adamant. Despite the lack of parental consent she attended the interview, got the job and started work.

The Personal Service Society offered advice to the poor, making them aware of any funds they might be eligible for and distributing some benefits themselves. There were long queues every day of men and women desperate for help for their families, families that were just like Helen's: 'They seemed people who had lost all hope, and my heart went out to them.'

Working for the charity was nerve-racking for Helen at first, but it gave her a sense of purpose and of her own self-worth. She handed over most of her salary to her mother, keeping back enough for the odd roll at lunchtime and her tram fares, but more often than not she found that her mother had sneaked into her handbag and stolen any pennies she found there. Eventually she sewed a little cloth bag to wear around her neck in which to keep her money safe. This didn't stop her mother from stealing her new stockings, whenever she managed to find the funds to buy such a thing, but Helen persevered, trying inch by inch to improve her quality of life.

Still she was hungry most of the time. She confessed to Avril, in one of her last letters to her, that during that period hunger sometimes led her to overcome the prohibition on stealing that had been drummed into her as a child.

> The P.S.S. bought a grocer's box of biscuits to serve with office tea, and I used to steal some for lunch! And the Head Cashier swore that SOMEBODY was stealing the office biscuits! But she never pinned the theft on me, thank God. She thought it was the cleaning ladies who came in the evening.
>
> I have always thought it very ironical that the office girl of an eminent charity should be almost starving! And the Committee who ran the charity had a full lunch sent in for all of them on the days they met at the office – mind you, I don't think the P.S.S. paid for the lunch – I think they paid for it themselves. But when I laid the table for the Committee, I was dreadfully envious of them.

The charity had a holiday home in Kents Bank, a small village on the north shore of Morecambe Bay, for the use of its employees. When Helen was sent for a two-week holiday there, she revelled in the blissful peace of a room of her own, hot baths whenever she wanted them, plentiful food, and beautiful surroundings to walk in. She made friends with an elderly man called Emrys Hughes and his brother, Gwyn, who owned drapery stores in North Wales. They enjoyed long conversations on all kinds of subjects: 'If I had been less innocent, I might have been troubled at [their] affability. But as I responded to [Emrys's] good-humoured teasing I knew only a great gaiety and lightness of heart. A liveliness I did not know, began to emerge.'

Emrys was at Kents Bank to recover after suffering a heart attack and he fell ill again while they were there. Two months after Helen's return, she was desperately sad to receive a letter from Gwyn telling her that Emrys had passed away. He had given her a great gift, she mused. 'He revealed to me that, given normal circumstances, I could be a cheerful, merry companion. He gave me self-respect, a belief in myself.'

This would stand Helen in good stead when, in her late teens, she began to have the beginnings of a social life and to test her own firmly held belief that she was unlovable and unlikely ever to attract a husband.

Helen discovered that as well as Kents Bank, the Personal Service Society also had a holiday home in Hoylake – the village across the Mersey where, as far as she knew, her grandmother still lived. By forgoing the use of trams and her lunchtime soup, as well as darning her stockings to make them last even longer than usual, Helen managed to save the money to visit there in June 1938. In her mind was one thought: visiting the woman who had been so kind to her when she was a young girl.

She arrived at the house and was ushered in by one of her aunts to find her grandmother sitting in a chair, 'a tiny, shrunken person, swathed in black', by now in her nineties. Helen wrote in *By the Waters of Liverpool*: 'I had forgotten what great age did to the human frame. To me she was eternal. I was suddenly and brokenly aware of all the years that I had missed being with her.' They sat and shelled peas together, then went out for a brief walk in the fresh air. Helen described her job at the charity and her ambition to become a social worker, but did not tell her grandmother anything about the privation the family had suffered over the last few years, the 'steady hunger and cold' they had endured. She was simply too old to be bothered with it. The visit passed pleasantly enough and Helen said goodbye and returned home.

The following year, in June 1939, they got word that her grandmother had died without ever seeing her son Paul or the rest of her grandchildren again. Lavinia's first thought was to wonder if there might be any inheritance for them, but it had been swallowed up long ago by the interest on the money Paul had borrowed from his sister when he got into financial difficulties. Helen received a gold watch with a black wristband, but by far the greatest gift her grandmother ever gave her had been the lessons of her early years: 'She had taught me more subtle things than reading and sewing, to put on a cheerful face so that one does not depress others, to face with fortitude what cannot be changed, daily courtesies, which always surfaced when I was with people of my own class.'

I never heard my mother speak ill of her grandmother. But I find it disturbing when I read Helen's description of the grandfather clock in the hall, the antique china pieces on a small shelf, and her aunt's 'pink-striped Macclesfield silk dress' – all signs of a life of middle-class plenty – while on the other side of the Mersey the Huband children were starving.

In 2015, after attending the play of *Twopence to Cross the Mersey*, my wife, Dianne, my son, Stephen, and I went to Hoylake to see my great-grandmother's house. By a stroke of luck, the current owner was outside and, when she found out who we were, she invited us in. As I walked down the hall where the clock must have stood, shivers went down my spine.

Chapter Six

I don't think the Germans sank a single ship that did not have Liverpool men on it. I dreaded the days when I walked around the corner to my office, to see a large queue outside. Another ship had gone down, and widows' pensions had to be applied for; money to bridge the time until the pension was paid had to be found. The waiting room was chocabloc with weeping women and howling children.

In the late 1930s, as Jewish refugees flooded into the charity where she worked and the newspapers daily reported the slide towards war, Helen was writing to a German penfriend called Friedrich Reinhardt, a young officer in the Luftwaffe, who was about two years older than she. They had met on a train years earlier when she was on her way to visit her grandmother and had exchanged addresses. Helen did not write to him at the time but years later when she began studying German in one of her evening classes she got in touch with a view to improving her language skills.

The correspondence flourished and it seems she and Friedrich began to think of each other in a romantic light but Helen worried that he would not be allowed to marry an Englishwoman at a time of such heightened tension between their two countries. In June 1939 he sent her an ivory edelweiss on a chain for her twentieth birthday, and it became a treasured possession. Friedrich assured her that the Führer did not want to go to war with Britain, but all around preparations were being made. Gas masks were delivered to every household and local air-raid wardens came to insist that blackout curtains were installed because any visible light at night-time could attract German bombers.

The first wave of children was evacuated to the countryside on 1 September 1939, just as Hitler's tanks crossed the border into Poland. Over the next three days 1.5 million British children were sent to rural locations to avoid the expected bombing, and Edward, Avril and Tony were among them.

The atmosphere was heavy with tension, and it almost came as a relief at 11a.m. on 3 September when radios up and down the country, including one in the Huband household, broadcast Prime Minister Neville Chamberlain's famous words:

> This morning the British Ambassador in Berlin Nevile Henderson handed the German Government a final note stating that unless we heard from them by 11 o'clock, that they were prepared at once to withdraw their troops from Poland, that a state of war would exist between us. I have to tell you now that no such undertaking has been received, and that consequently this country is at war with Germany.

Inhabitants of Liverpool knew the city was bound to be a target because of the docks. They scanned the sky, as if German bombers might appear at any moment, and Helen worried that Friedrich might even be one of the bomber pilots.

A few evenings after the start of war she was astonished to be summoned by the police to an office in Lime Street, and told to bring all the correspondence she had had with anyone in Germany. Her father accompanied her to the meeting at which a young man interrogated her at length about the nature of her relationship with Friedrich, as well as another German penpal called Ursel.

'Why had she studied German rather than French?' he wanted to know. She replied that she studied both. He read the letters she handed over. How had she met Friedrich? She explained. She also told him that she had been put in contact with Ursel after replying to a letter in the *Observer* newspaper asking if anyone wanted a German penpal. It transpired the writer of that letter had been a known Fascist, and that's why Helen was subjected to an intense interrogation that lasted many long hours. 'It was an ordeal,' she wrote. 'The fear of internment, perhaps imprisonment, haunted me. . . At times I thought I would surely faint.' Finally they asked her to sign a statement confirming her testimony and she was released at half past midnight. Looking back, she realized they suspected she might have been supplying information to the enemy!

*

During the early months of the war life went on in Liverpool much as before, except that the blackout every night meant it was easy to tumble in the pitch-dark. Helen wrote in *By the Waters of Liverpool*:

> Only people who have had to walk without a torch or cycle without a lamp through the total blackness

> of a blackout can appreciate the hazards of it. Innumerable cats and dogs trotted silently through it, to be tripped over by cursing pedestrians; pillar boxes and fire hydrants, telephone poles and light standards, parked bicycles and the occasional parked car, not to speak of one's fellow pedestrians, all presented pitfalls for the unwary. Many times I went home with a bloody nose or with torn stockings and bleeding knees.

One evening, after a long walk home because she did not have a tram fare, Helen broke down. She sobbed inconsolably as she contemplated the deprivation of her life, the hunger that still regularly made her feel faint, and the lack of any hope of improving her lot. Surprised by her outburst, since she normally kept her feelings to herself, her mother and father agreed that she could keep more of her earnings for her own use, and that her mother would buy her some new clothes and even treat her to a perm, the fashionable hairstyle of the day. Everyone agreed she looked pretty with the new soft curls, and it was the first time Helen had ever thought of herself as attractive.

'To dance had been the first ambition of my life, and the first to be crushed,' Helen wrote in *By the Waters of Liverpool*. She had been forced to give up ballet lessons just before the age of seven when a large wardrobe had fallen on her, damaging one leg permanently. Now, in the winter of 1939–40, she began to take ballroom dancing lessons at a little school run by dance professionals Doris and Norm, and found she had a talent for it. What's more, she made a little group of friends and gained social confidence through chatting to them as they whirled around the floor.

Among the men she danced with was a ship's engineer called Harry O'Dwyer, who asked her out for a cup of tea after class. It was her first 'date' and the conversation flowed. They each found the other liked reading and both had studied to improve their prospects in life; they discussed their work and what they did with any leisure time. But when Harry told her about a sailors' home where he sometimes went with a friend, and mentioned that they occasionally picked up girls there, Helen became suspicious.

> 'Do you consider that you picked me up?' I asked tartly.
>
> He grinned, hesitated, and then said, 'No. I hope I've made a permanent acquisition.'

When she told him about her difficult family circumstances, Harry listened sympathetically, then gave her a hug and a kiss on the cheek. He confided that he was estranged from his mother; she had wanted him to become a priest and could not forgive him when he refused. He was heading off to sea for the next five weeks but they exchanged addresses and she gave him her phone number at work, asking him to call as soon as he returned.

It was a nerve-racking time as she scanned the papers for any mention of his ship, worrying about the German U-boats patrolling the Atlantic and the mines that were being laid to damage shipping. Because it was on the west coast, Liverpool became the main entry port for food, fuel and raw materials to supply the whole country, transported on merchant ships such as the one on which Harry worked. It also became the hub for the Royal Navy's fleet during the Battle of the Atlantic, and it would be the entry point for the American troops who arrived later in the war.

When Harry returned from that first voyage, he told Helen that his convoy was scattered by U-boats and chased all over the Atlantic, but reassured her that their superior speed got them back safely. He'd brought her a present from New York, a beautiful red dress with a thin leather belt, much the most glamorous garment she had ever owned. It was only their third date, but Helen had to admit to herself:

> I was in love. I knew it. It was ridiculous, absurd, stupid, certainly unwise. I told myself piteously that there was no harm in loving, as long as one did not expect anything in return.

Harry was Roman Catholic while Helen was Protestant and had not even been allowed to play with Catholic children, never mind consider marrying one. In the fiercely sectarian Liverpool of that time marriage would not be easy. However, wartime brought a sense of urgency to relationships and Harry would soon be going to sea again. Helen and Harry weren't the only couple to make up their minds about each other after only a few meetings. Everyone wanted to feel loved, to buoy themselves up against the horrors of war, and remind themselves of the good things in the world. Before he went back to sea again, Harry proposed to Helen.

> 'Love, I know this is too quick. But I want to marry you, if you'll have me . . . I'm askin' you now because I'm away so much that I could lose you to somebody else . . . I've always wanted a wife like you – someone I could really talk to – and so pretty.'

For Helen, this was overwhelming and quite wonderful. She accepted straight away – but she made the decision not to tell her parents. Not yet, anyway. She couldn't bear to have them pour cold water on her plans. She wasn't ready to introduce Harry to them and risk her mother being rude or scornful, from the upper-middle-class snobbery and intolerance of Roman Catholics she retained. For now, her engagement was a delicious secret that Helen hugged to herself.

When Harry got back from his next trip to New York, he brought her three dresses from the Manhattan garment district, and she had to lie to her mother that she had bought them in a second-hand shop. He also bought her an engagement ring, which she wore on a string round her neck to prevent the family seeing it. How sad that she couldn't share her joyful news with them! They planned to marry in the summer of 1940 when Helen would have turned twenty-one, meaning she no longer needed parental consent. Harry put down money on a little house that was still being built, and told her that by the time of their wedding he would have enough saved to furnish it with the essentials they would need to start their married life together. But then he went to sea again, promising that they would be wed as soon as he got back.

In August 1940, Helen was expecting Harry's imminent return. At work, she spent her time helping the widows of men who had perished at sea. They wanted advice on how to claim their widows' pensions. One day she began to take down the details of a new client, an older woman, and suddenly it dawned on her that this was Harry's mother. The woman explained that her son had been killed at sea and that she wanted his pension paid to her. Helen leapt to her feet and rushed from the room, leaving a colleague to deal with her. She was devastated by the news, and furious that this woman, who had been estranged from Harry, would try to profit from his death.

A few days later the *Liverpool Echo* confirmed the news: 'O'Dwyer, Henry, aged 33, lost at sea, beloved son of

Maureen and John O'Dwyer, and loving brother of Thomas and sister-in-law Dorothy. RIP.'

Mourning a loved one was a common experience for women in Liverpool during the war years. There is a memorial on Tower Hill to the 24,000 men of the Merchant Navy and the fishing fleets who gave their lives trying to keep the population supplied with the goods needed for subsistence during wartime. If Helen could have talked about her grief it might have given her some small consolation, but no one knew of her engagement so no one knew of her bereavement and she carried the burden all alone.

Almost fifty years later she wrote to a grieving friend:

When I was staying with my brother [Tony] near London, we were talking of old times, and he mentioned the memorial to merchant seamen in London. He thought my first sweetheart's name might be on it. I did not really believe that he would be listed, because he was the only man who died on his ship. But he was, and on seeing his name I wanted to cry as if I had just lost him. I was again the lonely half-starved girl of that time. Yet I would have sworn that I had got over it long ago. I guess that once bonded to a person, the tearing wound of loss is always vulnerable to bleeding again.

In 1985, Helen related this poignant story to a friend:

> You said idly that you wished you knew what I looked like when I was young. Well, enclosed is a photo of me in 1940.
>
> I am afraid the picture is very dark. I had very thick brown hair with red tints in it, and I still have green eyes. I was very white and I had acne, but so did everybody else have. We were all so poorly fed.

The story of the taking of this photo is rather sad. I wanted a picture to give to my fiancé and I saved up for a professional photo. He was killed just before it was taken, and I was so innocent that I imagined that if one had made an appointment one had to keep it! So I had a photo taken just the same. I am wearing one of the dresses he brought me from New York. It was black with white trimmings, and I wore it for a long time as a mourning dress. The mouth in the photo is smiling, because the photographer said, 'say, cheese!' Which I dutifully did. But the eyes have no laughter in them because there was none in me.

*

The first major bombing raid on Liverpool took place on the night of 28 August 1940 and continued for three terrifying nights, during which 160 planes dropped their load on the city. Over the following three months there would be 50 raids and with each the civilian casualties mounted. On 18 September 22 prisoners were killed when Walton Gaol was hit by an incendiary bomb. On 28 November an air-raid shelter in Durning Road was destroyed and 166 souls perished inside.

The raids usually began about six o'clock in the evening and lasted until eleven or twelve. It was everybody's ambition to be safely at home, or wherever they were going to be in the evening, before the air-raid warning howled its miserable notes across the waiting city. This was usually an impossibility for me, because, as the raids gained in intensity and the bombed-out sought our aid, the load of work in the office increased proportionately.

Helen had many hazardous walks home during air raids: 'when a stick of bombs began to fall nearby, and the whistle of each succeeding missile became closer, I would instinctively duck for shelter in the nearest shop doorway and crouch down, hands clasped over head, until the last resounding bang.' The sky glowed with eerie green flares as the Germans tried to locate targets on the ground and lit up the crowds huddled in doorways. Despite the danger, Helen's mother continued to steal money from her handbag, depriving her of the tram fares that could have got her home more quickly and safely. It made her feel doubly unloved as she mourned the death of Harry.

The nightly explosions and the smell of smoke were particularly hard for Helen's father. They brought back all the horrors of the First World War, in which he had lost so many friends, and he trembled as they huddled on the stairs down to their basement during raids. Helen seems to have become closer to him during the war years. They often went for walks together and he told her more about his experiences in the first war, confiding in her in a way that he never did with his wife. Helen commented: 'Mother and he were never the good companions that older people can become. At best, they carped at each other continually.' He still smoked and drank heavily, neither of which were a great idea for a man who'd had a heart attack at the age of thirty-three, but it was just his way of coping.

Alan was sent overseas with the air force, and Brian volunteered to be an ARP (Air Raid Precaution) messenger boy. It was the job of the ARP boys to rush around on their bicycles telling fire crews and rescue squads where they were needed, and taking messages to hospitals, air-raid wardens and rescue centres, especially when the bombing meant the telephone lines were down. It was dangerous work, as they cycled the streets in the dark, during raids, but at sixteen years old, Brian was still too young to fight and he wanted to do something for the war effort.

There were raids right through Christmas and into the New Year, with a peak in the first week of May 1941 when 681 Luftwaffe bombers dropped their bombs on the port and the city. Over 6,500 homes were demolished, and 190,000 damaged – among them the home of the Hubands, which was not directly hit but was deemed structurally unsound. The family moved across the Mersey to the village of Moreton, where they found a run-down cottage, but Helen still had to commute into town every day to work. Bootle, where the charity was located, had the dubious honour of being one of the most bombed areas of the British Isles. The Germans were determined to cripple the Liverpool docks with these raids and many dock workers' lives were lost. Somehow, through the incredible courage of all who worked there, the port remained in operation throughout the war.

Casualties mounted, of course. Between August 1940 and January 1942, when the last raid destroyed several houses on Stanhope Street, 2,716 people were killed in Liverpool by the bombs. St Luke's church, which stands prominently at the top of Bold Street, was gutted by fire but its elaborate Gothic façade remained standing, a ghostly skeleton that has now become a memorial and a venue for community events.

Helen got a new, better-paid job working on the payroll at the Petroleum Board, which managed the wartime distribution of petrol. Maths was never her strongest subject and she struggled to master the payroll but enjoyed the social aspects of working amongst a group of young people. The camaraderie of this job came through strongly in the stories she told me when I was very little and as a result,

I called it her 'playpen job'. I remember she described painting her legs to look as if she was wearing stockings, and going down to the river with her coworkers to pick up oranges that had washed overboard from ships' cargoes. There were clearly good times but it is hard to imagine a riskier place to work than an oil installation in the docks of a major port during wartime. She wrote about it to the curator of port history at Liverpool's Maritime Museum in Albert Dock.

> I remember the ends of our oil pipes being blown off and my being absolutely terrified of its consequences. We dared not even boil a kettle on the installation for three days.
>
> A quiet employee of the installation won the George Medal for climbing onto the top of a full, huge tank of petrol and heaving off its floating roof a collection of incendiary bombs. By this brave deed, he saved streets of little houses running off Grafton Street from being decimated. I am ashamed that I cannot, for the life of me, remember his name. Fifty years is a long time!

Helen was filling the job of a man called Edward Parr, known to all as Eddie, who was an infantry private. One day in the autumn of 1941, when he came to the office while home on leave, Helen told him off for using bad language within earshot of the girls. He was embarrassed, as he hadn't realized he could be overheard, but obviously took a liking to her as he showed her easier ways to do her job and then offered to walk her to the tram that night. It was pouring with rain but, instead of leaving her at the tram stop, he accompanied her all the way home. The path to the Hubands' bungalow was flooded and, to Helen's consternation, he picked her up in his arms and carried her.

While they were both drying off in front of the fire, Helen's mother arrived home. She was cold and formal with the visitor, snubbing him and sending him straight back out into the downpour, and afterwards she scolded Helen for entertaining a 'strange soldier', especially one who was quite so 'common'. Her snobbery knew no bounds.

A week later, Helen was glad to receive a letter from Eddie, from his posting at Dover Castle where, he wrote, he was supposed to be 'guarding the White Cliffs of England' but was instead providing 'target practice for the Germans'. He and a friend had smuggled in a family of kittens and he wrote very amusingly about their attempts to keep the animals hidden from their superior officers. He and Helen began a correspondence during the winter of 1941–42 that started out friendly but gradually took on romantic overtones.

During 1942 they met whenever Eddie had leave, often just a brief meeting for a cup of tea near Lime Street station. On one such occasion he demonstrated how to kill a man in hand-to-hand contact, but when Helen told him she had been thinking of joining the ATS (Auxiliary Territorial Service, the women's branch of the army), he talked her out of it, saying that the job she did for the Petroleum Board was of more value to her country. In fact, she became a test case whom the Government argued over – should she be doing war work? Finally, the Petroleum Board told the Government that if they lost their new female staff, they would have to close down the installation. This would block off one of the main sources for the delivery of fuel for the country. Helen stayed where she was.

As war proceeded, more and more items became scarce. Bacon, butter and sugar were the first foods to be rationed in January 1940, followed by meat, cheese, jam, tea, eggs, biscuits, rice, and cooking fat. Ration books listed each person's weekly allowance, which was typically 50g (2oz) of butter, the same of cheese, 100g (4oz) of bacon or ham and one fresh egg. Helen wrote about the drudgery of the daily queues for food in her novel *A Cuppa Tea and an Aspirin*. Her character Martha often joined a queue without knowing what she was queuing for, assuming the storekeeper must have some kind of food worth having. Rationing would continue in Britain for fourteen years, until June 1954.

Coupons were needed to buy any new clothes, and soap and coal were hard to come by. Stockings had long since vanished from the shops and girls applied fake colour to their legs (as Mum told me she used to do) or drew a line down the back with eyebrow pencil. More daring women took to wearing trousers but these were banned at Helen's office.

In the winter of 1942–43, Helen travelled across the country to Doncaster to meet Eddie, as he was delivering a prisoner of war to a hospital there. She had to travel overnight and their train was shunted back and forth during an air raid, but she got to spend some precious hours with him. They discussed marriage at one point that day, and he said:

> 'Neither of us will get married while the war is on – wartime marriages never seem to work.'
>
> I thought of my parents' unhappy wartime union, and replied, 'I think you're right.'

All the same they kissed, and over the next eighteen months the relationship continued to deepen. Eddie was a big, strong man: outgoing, friendly and tough. Although he had been an office worker, he was not highly educated; he was, however, kind, good-hearted and sensible, with a quiet sense of humour. My mother clearly fell very much in love with him during the three-plus years they spent getting to know each other.

In spring 1944, Eddie was once again home on leave before heading off to join the invasion of France. As they walked through the streets, he astonished Helen by proposing marriage. At first she didn't know what to say.

> 'I didn't think you had holy matrimony in mind,' I finally responded lightly.
>
> 'Holy or unholy, I've got it in mind . . . I want to come back to you, Helen. Nobody else.'
>
> . . . 'Yes,' I said, and put my arms round his neck. He kissed me again and, though I knew it would be different from all my young girl's hopes, I felt it would be all right.

Eddie promised to buy her a ring and take her home to meet his mother on his next leave, but it was cancelled after D-Day, 6 June 1944, when Allied troops landed on the beaches of Normandy in a vast, meticulously planned military operation.

In June 1983, a fan wrote to Helen reminiscing about D-Day and about how all 'fighting moms' remembered where they were on that day. Helen replied to him:

> I sympathize about D-Day. I always feel a bit low on it. It happens to be my birthday. On that great day I was working on Shell-Mex's teleprinter in their Liverpool storage depot, and the Southampton operator, who knew me well (via the teleprinter) said, 'You have the biggest birthday present you can imagine.' He could not say any more, because it was Top Secret, but apparently he could see the troops gathering and

> the ships from his office window. It was a birthday present I could have done without, because one of my brothers [Brian] was in a minesweeper in it, and though he returned, my fiancé did not.

Eddie arrived in France in July 1944, and joined the British, Canadians and French pushing against German defences around Caen.

Reading the *Liverpool Echo* one evening, Helen ran her eye over what were widely called the 'Hatches, Matches and Dispatches' column – in other words, Births, Marriages and Deaths. I can't imagine how devastating it must have been for her when she found Eddie's name listed under 'Deaths'.

The street parties on VE Day, 8 May 1945, were celebrated with gusto across Liverpool. Tables were hauled into the centres of roads and laden with food. Music played, flags waved, and children wore fancy dress. Three of Helen's brothers, Alan, Brian and Tony, had served their country by war's end, and all of them returned, but 13,000 Liverpudlian men would never come back to their families – among them Edward Parr and Harry O'Dwyer.

To lose two fiancés in one war was cruel indeed. As she watched the festivities, at the grand old age of twenty-six, Helen must have wondered what might have been if either of them had survived.

PART II

Chapter Seven

Avadh being a light brown was not expected to be in the least bit like English people, so he had an advantage. The fact was that he had been so well educated in British schools and came from such good family that his manners were old-fashionedly charming. My parents could not find fault with my choice. In fact, my father was delighted to have an intellectual with whom to talk.

The end of the war brought sheer relief that the physical danger had come to an end and no more lives would be lost to the conflict. Helen's brothers returned: Alan from North Africa and Brian from the navy, with which he had visited ports all over the world. Tony went on to serve in Egypt and Rhodesia from 1945–48. Years of supreme effort and constant danger were over. Helen shared in the national joy but, having lost two fiancés, she felt victory was bittersweet. She was in mourning for both Harry and Eddie, a grief that returned to her on and off for the rest of her life.

When I was ten, Mum and I went to watch a noisy military tattoo in a darkened arena in Edmonton. Over the sounds of pipes and drums, and despite the darkness, I became aware that my mother was rocking herself and sobbing next to me. 'What is it, Mum?' I asked, desperately worried, and she replied that she was thinking of two men to whom she had been engaged during the war, both of whom had died. I was deeply shocked but I reached out my hand to try to comfort her. 'It's OK, lovey,' she said. 'It was a long time ago but I felt dreadfully sad suddenly.'

After that, she would mention Eddie from time to time. Some years after my father passed away, she decided to travel to see Eddie's grave in Normandy, France. She knew exactly where it was because she told me that she had gone there soon after the war's end, walking and riding in rickety, makeshift taxis through the devastated countryside of Normandy. In her oldest photo album there are a couple of tiny black-and-white pictures of hundreds of white crosses, row upon row.

I always listened to these stories sympathetically, but, for me, there was an unspoken awkwardness between us; it came down to an elemental realization that had Eddie lived, she would not have met my father, and I would not exist.

After the war, Helen left the Petroleum Board and took a job with Broadcast Relay, a company that provided a rapidly growing cable radio service on a weekly rental. She was secretary to an electrical engineer in charge of cable wiring all over Lancashire. She travelled with him for about a year, a 'plain thin shadow' who saw that his shirts got washed, the mail went out and his travel and hotels were booked. 'It was very, very boring – the hotels at that time had no heating, no hot water, too little bedding – and one carried one's own soap, towels and toilet rolls. Food rationing was at its height, and hotel food was awful.'

Finally, exhausted, she came home to Liverpool. She had

learned a lot about office work at the Petroleum Board and, together with her night-school education, she was quite well qualified. She took a job in a packaging firm, Metal Box Company, and grew to love it. Metal Box produced all kinds of containers, from tin cans to highly specialized and elaborate metal boxes for biscuits, cosmetics and other luxury items. As part of her job, Helen met representatives of the firms whose products used Metal Box packaging and, through them, she learned about industries such as food and cosmetics.

The combination of the creative with the eminently practical end purpose of its products appealed to Helen. She found the design aspects of packaging endlessly fascinating and, well into her eighties, she maintained a small collection of particularly attractive biscuit and chocolate tins from companies such as Gray, Dunn, and Meltis Limited. The sweet firm Waller and Hartley was one of her clients.

The elements of good design interested Helen throughout her life. 'I am a nightmare to the men who design the jackets of my books – because that is packaging at its worst. I swear my books sell in spite of their jackets.' I remember bracing myself for the onslaught when my mother told me that the artist's concept for a new book's jacket had arrived in the post.

The deaths of over 380,000 British servicemen in the war, and the fact that women had gained experience in the workforce, opened more opportunities for women in the aftermath of the conflict. Metal Box had a reputation for sometimes promoting women but Helen observed that if they did, they paid them two-thirds of the salary of a man. She was not allowed to join the pension fund but she accepted this, along with other inequities, as women of the era had to. While she would always support greater opportunities for women, she viewed her personal career within the context of the day, which was far beyond her capacity to change.

Helen lamented the broader implications of the loss of men to industry in a letter to Avril.

> Schools built after the war, as other buildings, are a shameful monument to get-rich-quick builders and indifferent school boards. Unfortunately, many of the kind of men who would have whipped things into shape after the War, were dead – like Eddie: he was management and he could go through a petrol installation like the wrath of God, and the men jumped to it.
>
> People do not realize that wars are fought, largely by management people, office folk, specialists in seeing things through, and by the unskilled or semi-skilled. Tradesmen, like welders and electricians, are too precious to waste on a battlefield, but tradesmen are only as good as their supervisors make them be – and we were parlously short of supervisors after the war – I soon learned that when I worked for Broadcast Relay and for the Metal Box Company – in the latter, so many of their factories had lost their foremen, charge hands and specialists like tinsmiths and chemists.

Helen continued to live at home because 'nice girls' did not live alone. There are many little indications that her relationship with her parents was improving: now she would describe herself as being her 'father's favourite', while she occasionally confided in her mother, but generally she kept out of their way as much as possible. She contributed financially towards the household, and tried to save a little each month towards her old age. Her great dread was that as the 'spinster daughter' she would be trapped into looking after her parents in their old age, but she had little hope that she would find a husband now. She was twenty-six years old at the war's end and scarred by her lost loves.

All the same, Helen found the strength to start socializing. In the 1990s, she wrote to a Canadian friend describing her efforts to rejoin society.

> One thing I did in Liverpool after I lost Eddie in the battle of Caen in 1944, was to become a 'joiner'. In this I was encouraged by Eddie's best friend, John, who, at the age of eighty – very frail – is my only connection with my lost soldier. I belonged to the Phoenix gramophone club, I remember. About twenty of us used to listen to each other's records and talks by those of us who were fairly musical. I became the Membership Secretary of the Anglo-Chinese Society, before Mao Tse-tung took over [in October 1949] – when it disintegrated. I had chosen the organizations to join very carefully, so that I met well-informed people. And it is not a bad way to wriggle back into society.

In her novel *Thursday's Child*, Helen described a club at which the many nationalities in the city of Liverpool after the war could meet and make friends with English people. There was a canteen, a library and a lounge; English classes were offered and dances were held. There are obvious autobiographical elements in the story of Peggie, a Lancashire lass who has lost a fiancé in the war and volunteers to help at British Council social events, where she meets men of different backgrounds and skin colours. 'I knew very well how difficult it was for strangers to know English families, more especially so if the stranger's skin was not white,' she wrote, and she portrays Peggie as devoid of the racial prejudice that was widespread at the time.

In fact, largely through her clubs, Helen received five proposals of marriage in those post-war years. 'I was the kind of girl men proposed to – I was rarely propositioned. I turned them all down, because the pain inside was still too great.' In more sardonic moments, Helen described herself as a 'Jonah', the nautical terminology for someone who brings bad luck to a ship. She felt her romantic prospects were doomed to failure.

And then, one evening in March 1949, everything changed. A Chinese friend of Helen's, Kun Huang, who was a post-doctoral fellow at the University of Liverpool, brought an Indian friend of his, Avadh Bhatia, to the British Council meeting rooms. Helen struck up a conversation with Avadh, as she had with many other lonely foreign students over the previous year. Very quickly the conversation took an unexpected turn.

Although obviously shy, Avadh asked: 'Would you come to the pictures with me?' When Helen hesitated, he added quickly, 'You do not have to worry, because, of course, I shall marry you!'

Avadh Bhatia was the son of a successful senior official of the Indian land administration. He had been brought up at the large family compound near Delhi with four brothers and a sister. Each of his brothers became successful professionals, but sadly one had passed away recently of a heart attack while walking in the Himalayas. The remaining brothers included a doctor, a lawyer and an expert in ceramics. Avadh's passions were abstract mathematics and theoretical physics.

He had been educated in good schools in both Hindi and English. He attended Lucknow University and then the University of Allahabad, where he worked towards his PhD in mathematics. He was an outstanding student at a good university, but a doctorate from a university in the West was essential to further his career. When the opportunity arose to work under Professor Herbert Fröhlich, a brilliant refugee from Germany, who was then at the University of Bristol, he jumped at it. He arrived in England in late September 1947. When Professor Fröhlich moved to become Chair of Theoretical Physics at the University of Liverpool in 1948, Avadh followed him.

Avadh was kept busy with his research and thesis and spent his evenings alone, until his friend Kun Huang invited him along to the British Council meeting. Peggie in *Thursday's Child* meets an Indian man called Ajit in exactly the same circumstances and describes him thus:

> He was dressed in an old tweed jacket and baggy grey trousers; his white shirt made his skin look very dark but his features were clear-cut and delicate; both in expression and outline his face reminded me of a Saint in an old Indian painting; his hands also, as they invited me to eat and drink, used the gestures portrayed in the same paintings.

When Avadh asked her out, Helen agreed to the cinema invitation, although politely declined the marriage proposal. Their time was limited because Helen had her demanding job at Metal Box and many duties at home, while Avadh had his research, but they met up whenever they could. Despite both being shy or reticent in their own ways, they discovered very quickly that they could talk to each other on a wide range of subjects and in a depth they had never experienced before. Importantly, they both had diverse interests and an extensive knowledge of, and appreciation for, history and culture.

In *Thursday's Child*, Ajit introduces Peggie to a world that sounds exotic and far outside her own experience:

> He told me about the squirrels that lived in the neem trees in the garden of his home in Delhi, and of the lizards that always made a home in the window curtains, no matter how frequently they were shaken out. I shivered at the idea of lizards in the house, but he said they were harmless creatures with yellow bodies and sparkling eyes, and they kept the room free from insects.

It was less than two years since India had gained independence from British rule, after almost three decades of nationalist struggle, led by the charismatic figure of Mahatma Gandhi. The country had been divided by Partition into the separate dominions of Pakistan and India, ostensibly as a way to give Muslims a homeland. Far from being a peaceable transition, there had been bloody religious riots in which as many as a million people had died, and strife continued between Muslims remaining in India and Hindus. Avadh came from a Hindu family, and he had been caught up directly in the violence in 1947 when a train on which he was travelling was attacked by a Muslim mob. His life was saved by a quick-thinking Muslim passenger who hid him from the attackers.

Despite having radically different backgrounds, religions and upbringings, Helen and Avadh were of similar social classes, something that was of much more importance in the 1940s and 50s than it is now. Helen was very clear that she was upper-middle-class, despite the terrible poverty she had endured from the age of eleven, while Avadh came from a sophisticated and well-educated Indian family.

This might go some way to explain the connection they

found with each other but, more fundamentally, they were quickly and deeply in love. Avadh's immediate proposal was funny in hindsight, but came from a visceral conviction that Helen was the girl for him and it was meant genuinely to assure her that his intentions were honourable.

Unfortunately, there were two complications.

First, Avadh was nearing the end of his PhD studies at the University of Liverpool and was due to return to India later that year to take up a post at the newly established Gujarat University in Ahmedabad. Many more Indian universities and technical colleges were being founded in the newly independent country and existing ones were expanding rapidly. An intelligent theoretical physicist, particularly one trained at a good English university under a renowned German professor (so influential that he would later be nominated for the Nobel Prize), had excellent prospects in India.

Secondly, Avadh was already married – a fact I know he would have told my mother very early on, as he was impeccably honest.

Although the actual ceremony came later, his marriage to Kashi had been arranged when he was a teenager. Her father was a friend of Avadh's father and lived in Kashmir, far away from Avadh's family home near Delhi. Avadh and Kashi belonged to the same caste but had different upbringings – hers in the countryside, his in the city – and no interests in common. Attitudes to marriage were quite different in Indian society in the 1940s, with no expectation of romantic love, but unfortunately, it was clear right from the start that Avadh and Kashi were fundamentally incompatible. They simply didn't get along. The fact that Avadh had chosen to spend two years in England without his wife was just one indication of the estrangement. He had left India in September 1947, not realizing that his wife was pregnant and did not meet his son, Vijay – my half-brother – until he returned to India in December 1949.

Avadh did not want to return to Kashi. Even his limited exposure to English society had broadened his outlook further and made him desperate to escape his unhappy arranged marriage. I doubt he had considered the possibility of falling in love with an Englishwoman, never mind marrying one. He was simply depressed and immersing himself in his work. Although she was instantly attracted to Avadh, Helen was a realist. I imagine that, at first, she decided to enjoy spending time with this wonderful man in the full knowledge that their friendship must inevitably be temporary.

As they walked along the breezy seafront at Hoylake, near Helen's grandmother's house, or the Dee Estuary near West Kirby, they talked. And talked. Helen told him about her childhood, although at that stage she probably did not share all the details of her difficult family life. She talked about Edith and her grandmother and all she had learnt from them, and then about their plunge into poverty in Liverpool. She told him how she had slowly pulled herself up by going to night school. She told him about the war and Harry and Eddie. He listened to the stories about her past with acceptance if not full understanding, and he was interested in the woman who had emerged from all that hardship. What he saw was a pretty, still-young woman who was well-read, knowledgeable and very intelligent. It was little wonder she had such a responsible job.

Helen listened to Avadh as well. She found a quietly spoken, sensitive man who valued her for herself. He was also highly intelligent, committed to his work and determined to make a difference when he went back to his newly independent country. He was very unhappy about his marriage but his innate goodness shone through. As the miles unfolded Helen decided that she could trust him.

As hard-working as they both were, and despite the losses and troubles on their minds, they had fun too. Avadh possessed a gentle sense of humour and an ability to make Helen see the funny side of life. He enjoyed light entertainment as an escape from the intellectual rigour of physics and Helen was happy to accompany him to comedy films such as *A Kiss in the Dark* starring David Niven. She would have been tickled pink by Avadh's uninhibited reaction to the humour. They also went to plays, such as Henrik Ibsen's *The Lady from the Sea* at the Liverpool Playhouse, where many well known actors and actresses performed.

My mother was human. As she got to know Avadh better her feelings for him grew. He was very determined in matters that were important to him and at that point, two things were important: physics and Helen. When Avadh explained that Hindus were allowed to take more than one wife and asked if she would be willing to marry him, Helen began to realize that there might be a chance for them to be together if she travelled out to India with him.

In the precious months they had left before Avadh must return to India, at least twice they took a train from Lime Street Station a couple of hours north to the Lake District. There they could walk to their heart's content along the footpaths up the stunning hills and through the beautiful valleys beside deep blue lakes and into welcoming villages. They stayed in a bed and breakfast owned by a woman called Mrs Penny, where roses grew over the walls and a noisy Spaniel barked in the lane. They were alone in paradise, a long way from the past. It was on one of those trips that Avadh proposed again formally. This time Helen said yes.

It was a big decision: to leave her homeland, her family and her job, in order to travel to a foreign country and become someone's *second* wife while the other was still alive, and while there was a child of that marriage. I know she would never have dreamt of breaking up a marriage that had any chance of success, but she had seen first-hand how miserable Avadh was at the thought of returning to Kashi. He had no intention of living with her again, but would have buried himself in his work and become a hermit. So no matter what Helen did, the marriage was over, to all intents and purposes.

How did she rationalize what she was about to do? There is no simple answer. Divorce had long been a taboo, something that brought shame on families, but attitudes in the UK were gradually changing. A.P. Herbert's best-selling satirical novel *Holy Deadlock,* published in 1934, had done much to open up the debate about divorce. After Herbert was elected to Parliament he initiated and helped to pass new divorce legislation in 1937. On a personal level, Helen had seen and experienced so much that had shaken her faith in traditions and institutions. She saw the shambles of her parents' marriage and, looking back as an adult, realized that there had been some pretty wild behavior amongst her parents' friends and associates in the old days before they moved to Liverpool. The poverty and turmoil she had experienced, and the loss of her two fiancés contributed to a feeling that she owed little allegiance to the conventions or institutions of English society. Finally, she trusted Avadh totally and believed him when he said she would be accepted in Indian society.

Helen introduced Avadh to her parents, no doubt with some trepidation. I'm sure she did not tell them that he was already married but racist attitudes were the norm in British society, so they could have objected to the colour of his skin. Her mother's snobbishness when introduced to Eddie did not augur well but, in fact, the meeting seems to have gone remarkably smoothly: both my grandparents recognized that Avadh was a well-brought-up, civilized and extremely intelligent man. They were pleased to see Helen so happy.

In the end, I think the decision to marry Avadh was quite an easy one for her. First and foremost, it was very clear that they were deeply in love and had found a strength and depth of bond that neither had experienced before or ever expected to find. Second, Helen had suffered so much heartbreak in the past that she couldn't voluntarily pass up this chance at happiness. She was thirty years old, which was considered well past the normal 'marriageable' age for women, so this could be her last opportunity. Moreover, life in post-war England was pretty bleak, with strict rationing still in place, so a fresh start in a faraway country, while scary in some respects, was a risk worth taking.

Once Helen had decided, there was never any indication that she waivered in her commitment to be with Avadh, no matter what. Of course, she couldn't tell anyone in Liverpool the whole story but she would only need to keep the secret for a few weeks before she would be gone from England, perhaps forever.

They planned that Avadh would go to India first, in December 1949. He would find a flat and a servant and establish himself in his new research laboratory before Helen joined him a fortnight later.

The more challenging hurdles were, first, for Avadh to break the news to his father and brothers that he planned to leave Kashi for good. They almost certainly knew that the marriage was unhappy but in a close, well-respected Indian family, even a progressive one, a positive reaction was hardly assured. And the news that Avadh would be bringing an English bride-to-be was likely to test the mettle of even the most patient and understanding Indian parents and influential older brothers, not to speak of crotchety uncles. English women did not have a great reputation in

India at the time. In *Thursday's Child*, Helen writes about Ajit's father's reaction to his marriage to Peggie:

> 'I know English women,' he shouted. 'I have seen them – painted, loud-mouthed, immodest. They bare their shoulders and legs so that any sweeper can goggle at their charms. They take all from their husbands and give nothing.'

Might this have reflected Avadh's family's initial sentiments? He must have been more worried about it than he let on to Helen at first.

And then there was the matter of Kashi and her parents. Avadh believed that Kashi was equally unhappy in their marriage and would accept that there was no future for them together. A financial settlement would have to be negotiated between the families and arrangements made for the child's care, but these did not seem insurmountable problems.

In the background, an important initiative of the Government of India was of vital concern to Helen and Avadh. Prime Minister Jawaharlal Nehru was a strong proponent of secularism and modern values. He saw reform of Hindu law governing marriage, inheritance, women's property rights and other important matters of family law as a high priority. After much discussion and debate, both before and after Independence, the Hindu Code Bill was introduced in the Constituent Assembly (the precursor to India's Parliament, which was established after the first general elections in 1951). The significance was that until the bill was passed, traditional Hindu law would apply. Helen and Avadh could be married in India before all the messy details of a settlement with Kashi and her family, and ultimately divorce, were finalized. After the bill was passed, they could not be married until all those difficult negotiations and time-consuming steps were taken. Time was of the essence.

Avadh left for India in December 1949. I can only guess at my mother's feelings of apprehension as she waved him off. They had known each other for only nine months and many obstacles stood in the way of their happiness, but she knew her own mind and felt sure she knew his.

From the day he left until they were reunited once more, Helen and Avadh maintained an almost daily correspondence. The letters provide wonderful images of hope, anticipation, cultural adaptation and sometimes misunderstanding. They also illustrate a fascinating attention to detail, partly necessitated by very limited finances. Above all, they offer a glimpse into the early stages of what would be a lifelong love.

Chapter Eight

With the work of the office whirling round me I could not say a word of what was in my heart today; but you will know I am thinking of you all the time.

Avadh was booked to fly from London's Heathrow airport on 16 December 1949. Heathrow had been in use as an airfield during the war but had only fully opened to civilians in May 1946, replacing an old grass airfield in Croydon. International air travel was still relatively uncommon, and his flight had to touch down in Malta and Cairo for refuelling en route. All this makes it feel like a very long time ago but at two p.m. on the 16th, he wrote to Helen from Heathrow with words that still resonate today: 'From 9 in the morning we have been waiting and I hope we have not to wait more before the plane finally takes off. It is pretty boring. I hear we might leave in about half an hour. I am not ringing you as I have only a few shillings left.'

It sounds as though Helen was nervous about him flying because he reassured her: 'This plane is *now* perfectly OK. It has been passed by the aviation authorities of *this* country.' Perhaps she was anxious about her own forthcoming journey because she had booked a flight on 28 December, just twelve days later. This was timed so that she could arrive in India a few weeks before the earliest date that the Hindu Code Bill could possibly pass. She also had a sea voyage booked for 12 January if there was less of a hurry. One or the other would be cancelled, depending on the schedule for the bill.

On 16 December, the day that Avadh's plane eventually took off, Helen wrote to him in India for the first time.

> My own Dear One,
>
> I shall be counting the hours, the days, the minutes until I can join you, and my heart is already winging its way across the heavens with you – what good is a body without a heart!
>
> If you feel you should meet me, sari in hand, at Bombay, bring some safety pins – it may not be orthodox but I'll never keep it up without!!!
>
> Don't worry, darling, if you cannot have everything perfectly arranged for my coming. As long as you can find a corner in which we can sleep, we'll soon get down to finding somewhere to live afterwards.

Helen was apprehensive about her first encounter with a sari, a long single length of cotton or silk, but she eventually became proficient at wearing them and often donned them for special occasions long after she left India. A few saris with silver or gold brocade were among her most treasured possessions and were handled, stored and cleaned very carefully.

*

Over Christmas week, she began to pack her belongings. Her mother knew that Helen was about to leave for India, but the news had been kept from her father until the last moment because Helen guessed he would be upset about her departure. On 20 December, however, the secret was out.

> My mother has had to tell my father what is happening as he demanded to know what was going on in the house, for example, the packing cases for my luggage arrived and could not be hidden. He has taken it very badly, but has not spoken to me about it yet. I think he is mostly very sad that his favourite daughter is going so far away.
>
> Mother has bought me three summer dresses, suitable to work in the house, and two beautiful pairs of white sandals.
>
> I have been hoping all the time that the journey was comfortable and that you have arrived safely. All my thoughts are with you in these difficult times and it is my constant prayer that we may soon be together.

Avadh arrived in India on the 18th and the next day took the train to Ahmedabad. He tried to telephone Helen at work, likely attempting to reach her after most of her colleagues had gone home, but, hardly surprisingly for the era, the phone system didn't work so he sent a cable on the 21st. Cables did not have punctuation so the word 'STOP' was used for a full stop. There was a charge for each word, so it was prudent to be as succinct as possible. The cable read as follows:

> ARRIVED SAFELY HERE VERY HOT EVEN NOW STOP CANCEL BOTH PASSAGES STOP IF YOU DECIDE TO COME WAIT TILL FURTHER MESSAGE LETTER FOLLOWS STOP DONT WORRY BHATIA

I can only imagine the consternation and dismay with which this cable must have been received. My mother was days from her departure for a new life when Avadh wrote telling her to delay and added the words 'if you decide to come'. *If!* She had planned her entire future around marrying him and now he appeared to have doubts.

They had designed a code for use in their cables, because it was not even a remotely private form of communication. The message had to be written out at the telegraph office for the staff to process. At the other end, it would be passed on by telephone and then followed up with a paper copy printed directly from the cable. Given the sensitivity of their personal circumstances, Helen and Avadh had agreed that ARRIVED SAFELY would mean that the Hindu Code Bill had not yet passed through Parliament but it was not certain whether or not it would pass before the Christmas recess. LETTER FOLLOWS meant that Avadh was not able to go to Delhi immediately to see his family.

In just twenty-four words, the cable threw up in the air everything Helen was counting on and gave her lots of reason to worry. She wrote back immediately on Thursday 22 December:

> My Darling,
> I was simply horrified to get your cable telling me to cancel both passages, since I gather that the Bill has not yet passed and, therefore, it will be all right for me to come to India. The only thing I could think of which has made you decide that I should not come is that you have discovered that the climate is very bad indeed. This fact I had already discovered for myself by the simple process of reading the *Encyclopaedia Britannica*. I have, however, consulted all the men here who have been in India, including two who have spent

> a year or two in Ahmedabad, and they are all of the opinion that I could endure the climate without being ill, provided I was immunized against certain diseases and obeyed certain other health rules.

Ahmedabad, then capital of the western state of Gujarat, is semi-arid, with a monsoon season in July and August. Temperatures in January and February would normally be 28–31°C (in the 80s F), but in December 1949 there was a heatwave with temperatures soaring well over 38° C (100°F) and as high as 46°C (115°F). Helen continued:

> I have cancelled the air passage on 28th December but have retained the sea passage on 12th January and unless there is some very exceptional reason why I should not travel on January 12, I shall come. No doubt I shall have further cables from you tomorrow, Friday, or Saturday, telling me more about it.
>
> My dear, I do not know quite what kind of difficulties you have discovered since your arrival in India, but I do so hope that I can come to you soon. I know life is not going to be easy for either of us in such a bad climate, but I cannot live without you, and I feel that if we live a few years in Ahmedabad you will establish a good reputation and then perhaps you could look for a post in a town with a better climate.
>
> I am all packed and ready to come and prepared to endure a lot just to be with you.

On Christmas Eve, Saturday 24 December, she wrote again:

> My dearest Avadh,
>
> You will have received my cable telling you that I am holding on to the sea passage in the hope that

> I can use it. You silly darling – 'if willing'. If willing, indeed to goodness. Do you suppose I should not come even if we had to live in an African jungle!
>
> I am sure you will let me have definite news as soon as possible and then I will know what to do about luggage etc. I know you must be having a hectic time and I wish I was with you to share the burden, but I shall come as soon as you give me the word.
>
> I miss you desperately and hope this will be our only separation. If deep love, plenty of common sense and years of dealing with difficult situations can help you, then we can make life pleasant together. It will not come without careful building, but what happiness we can have while building!

It would have been understandable if Helen's mother and father were suspicious of Avadh's request that Helen cancel her voyage without giving a good reason. Was he trying to back out of his engagement? The thought must have crossed their minds, although it does not appear to have crossed Helen's.

Avadh wrote on 22 December (a letter Helen received on the 28th) with the explanation that the air passage she had booked was too early and he would not be able to get time off to meet her in Delhi or Bombay because he had to attend a physics conference in Poona. The sea passage was too late because there was a chance that the Hindu Code Bill would pass in late January. He advised her to take a flight in early January, if she was still determined to come. He said he was very worried about the effect the heat wave would have on her, even in January, and saw this as reason enough for her seriously to reconsider. 'I don't wish to discourage you but I wish to impress upon you that heat is quite a good deal and remains so throughout the year – while I get only a month off in the summer.' During that month off, they would be able to escape the heat by going to a hill station where it would be cooler.

Avadh had started work that day and also reported that he had been able to secure a small flat near the laboratory, although he had not yet seen it. At that time, he had not told his family that he was bringing over an English fiancée and he was probably getting more anxious about doing so but there is nothing in this letter that hints at that. There's no doubt he loved my mother with all his heart, but suddenly the difficulties seemed to be piling up.

Helen wrote back on 28 December:

My Dear,

I was so glad to have your letter of 22nd December today and to know the reason for your telling me to cancel both passages. I do hope I can come by sea – it will save such a lot of money and, further, I am at present so very tired that it would be a help to have a rest before trying to cope with a whole new world.

How thrilling that you have found a flat so near the laboratory – I do wonder what it is like. Don't worry if it is not very beautiful – we will soon make it pleasant together.

I am not quite sure what will happen to me in 115° of heat, but we must just hope for the best. You will have to tell me every little dodge you know to help keep the temperature down and keep us well. Between us we shall do it. I believe that October is the worst month – when the earth literally steams with the first rains and the last heat. We shall just have to gargle our throats, swat the flies, disinfect the drains and generally declare a state of war during that time. Is it a malarial district?

> I have a few paludrine tablets from my doctor which will help us at first and perhaps we could get some more, should need be.

Helen told him she had procured a book with which to start teaching herself Hindi, not realizing that Ahmedabad is in a solidly Gujarati-speaking region. Few of the local people would speak Hindi or English, while the university community would generally speak English. It does demonstrate that she was utterly determined to make a go of her new life and was applying all her grit and willpower to this end.

On 23 December Avadh wrote to Helen acknowledging that his cable telling her to cancel both the air and sea passage had upset her. He was clearly under considerable stress. In this letter he told Helen that she should plan to come by sea because it was so much cheaper, but to keep her luggage with her until the last minute. That way if the legal situation changed and she needed to come quickly to get married before the new law passed, he could cable her again and tell her to fly. It seems to have been remarkably easy to book and unbook tickets at the last minute, with none of the cancellation charges we would incur today.

On the 26th, he assured her that coming by sea would almost certainly be fine. The Hindu Code Bill was very controversial in India and the Assembly had decided to establish a committee of supporters and opponents of the bill from both inside and outside the House so it looked as though a significant delay was likely.

Avadh had changed his mind about attending the academic conference in Poona and was now going to attend a different one early in the New Year. In the meantime, he was travelling to Bulandshahr, the small city near Delhi where his family lived in a gracious and spacious house built, as was traditional, around a courtyard. He planned at last to tell his parents and Kashi, who was living in the family compound with them, about his plans. 'But you need not be afraid that I will change my mind. I hope everything will be o.k, although how my father will take it I don't know,' he wrote nervously.

On 31 December, Helen wrote back:

> I am anxious that your father should not be grieved at having another daughter-in-law, and I would do anything to ease his sadness, except give you up. I feel that in marrying you I am not taking away anything that belonged to anyone else – nobody seemed to care very much whether you lived or died whilst you were in England, except me and I cared very much.
>
> I am not worried at leaving England, although I love my country very much. I know at times I shall grieve and want to come home, but surely India is not such a terrible country that I cannot love her too. You are in India, and it is people, not things, that really make a life. We shall make friends and, all being well, will be loved and respected – what more could we ask?

She was understandably anxious about his visit to his family and wrote again on 3 January 1950:

> My thoughts have been with you specially during the past day or two, since you are at home and have to face your family. I hope that you have not been made very unhappy by it all. I wish that I could have shouldered the difficulty with you.
>
> I have thought very deeply about the big change I am making in my life and I feel that the things I shall lose will be outweighed by the things I shall gain. I

know I have a terrible lot to learn, but I feel you will help me to do that learning.

Between us, darling, there will have to be even closer understanding and patience than is usual between husband and wife, but I know in my heart that the foundations for such understanding are already truly laid. Remember, my dear, that had I married an Englishman, my life, at present in England, would have been very difficult. Supposing that I had married an English professor, it is doubtful whether we could have afforded for me to give up my business career, and that means that I should have had to do two full-time jobs, i.e. go to business and keep house. Life for the middle classes in England is far from easy.

The day after sending this letter she received a cable from Avadh, dated 2 January, which read:

SORRY FOR DELAY SEA BOOKING ALRIGHT MAKE FINAL DECISION AFTER FIRST JANUARY LETTER NO ANXIETY

She replied straight away, with great excitement:

The relief of knowing at last that all is well is wonderful. Bahr Behrend's say that the 'Jal-Azad' will arrive on February 3rd at Bombay, but cannot say exactly yet. I will cable you the exact date as soon as I can be certain of it. I am finishing work on Saturday next and will travel to London on the following Thursday, breaking my journey at Leicester in order to see my friend Sylvia before I go. All this, of course, is subject to the contents of your letter mentioned in your cable.

Bahr Behrend & Co. is a Liverpool shipping agent and the *Jal-Azad* was a passenger/cargo ship owned by the Scindia Steam Navigation Company of Bombay. Helen was booked to sail on 14 January, two days later than she had originally expected; because it was partially a çargo ship, the *Jal-Azad*'s schedule could be subject to change. That meant it was only a month until she would see Avadh again and her excitement was palpable. But then on 4 January she received Avadh's letter of 1 January (an unusually quick delivery), telling her of his visit to his parents and her spirits must have plummeted once more.

> I left Delhi last night after spending three days in Bulandshahr with my parents and am still on the train and will remain on it till 12 noon tomorrow. My handwriting is shaky and the paper is hardly suitable to send to you [torn out of a notebook]; nevertheless I must describe what happened in Bulandshahr. I hope you will be able to read it and forgive me if it annoys you.
>
> My father and mother, as well as Kashi, received a very great shock when they heard of my intentions. My father felt very sad but he did not say anything to me except that though he would still regard me his son, and you his daughter-in-law (and invited you to live and wear clothes like we all usually do), yet he would be much happier if I did not marry you. But I had given you my promise and I could not break my promise from my side as they once suggested.
>
> Kashi also feels very sorry but she says that I only have to do that which will make me happy and that she will not expect anything from me. She is not prepared to marry again and she, being what her training is, will probably never do so. She was even

willing to give her good sarees to you, which I did not accept. So here I am in the muddle, not knowing what to do.

You know I love you but somehow I feel hesitant to accept such a sacrifice. In this life we have not much right to accept sacrifice from anyone and yet someone has to suffer because Kashi, with a child, is much more helpless than you are. On the other hand, you have suffered quite a lot in the past and I have not the heart to ask you for more.

Under such circumstances, I am leaving the decision to you. If you think that you will be able to withdraw from me, even at this last stage, without too much pain to yourself and others around you, please do so. For the moment such an action will hurt our hearts terribly but probably this will bring more happiness to all of us ultimately. If you decide to do so, I will naturally pay you all the expenses incurred by you until now in this connection, as soon as I learn your decision, as father will be only too glad to give me the money needed for it.

However, if you feel that you must join me, you can trust me that you will be most welcome because, after all, I do love you. Only sometimes I wonder whether one can be really happy after accepting such sacrifices. However, this is for you to decide; you have a much clearer brain than I have and I shall accept your decision. You must also think of minor inconveniences like heat and changing your outdoor life to a more or less 'secret stay at home life'. If you decide to come, come by sea, as per passage booked, as the Parliament has not yet fixed a date for second reading for the Hindu Code Bill. Even when it comes it will take probably several weeks before it is passed.

> By the time this letter reaches you, there will not be enough time left to consult me, so take your decision and act accordingly. You will find my support whichever way you act. Do not think that I do not love you or that I am in any way letting you down. Only consider the matter once again in view of what I have written above. I am sorry to have put you into this muddle at the last moment and probably you had expected something like this after I visited Bulandshahr.

My father had been naïve in failing to anticipate the pain his family would feel. His parents' initial reaction sounds moderate and considerate in the circumstances. Their son was forsaking the daughter of a friend of theirs, a woman with whom he had a child he had only just met for the first time, in favour of an English woman they had never met. Any parents would be alarmed, even without the cultural and religious implications of a broken marriage in India.

Avadh believed that he and Kashi had been so unhappy before he left India, compounded by their further estrangement during his two years overseas, that she would not be surprised or upset by his announcement. He had written to her expressing grave concerns about the future of their marriage and there's no doubt she knew how miserable he was. Surely, he thought, the dissolution of their marriage would be relatively straightforward? Instead, it had become a nightmare. He felt he had betrayed his family and let down Kashi and his young son, Vijay, whom he had only just met. He was torn down the middle between his family obligations and his love for Helen.

My father was trying to be scrupulously honourable, although, admittedly, he was also shifting responsibility for a decision to Helen. If she decided to pull out of their engagement, at least he need not feel as guilty about letting her down. In this letter, his anguish at being torn between his love for, and commitment to, my mother, and hope for future happiness on one hand, and his feeling of duty to Kashi and his parents on the other is palpable. I can imagine his utter loneliness as he sat on a train in the middle of the night travelling away from the people he had hurt. It was a dark night of the soul for him.

The next morning he regretted the letter but had already sent it. He quickly cabled Helen telling her to book another sea passage and not to worry about the letter, but it was easier said than done. She must have been greatly alarmed and upset by his parents' and Kashi's reaction and his suggestion that she might pull out of their engagement. However, my mother was not about to do any such thing. She replied, on 5 January, with a clear-headed rebuttal of his suggestion and a gentle yet firm reminder to Avadh of his responsibilities towards her:

> I had yesterday your cable and this morning your letter, and I must say that the letter grieved me very much, although I understand the feelings which prompted you to write it.
>
> First I would say that I shall come to you in India and shall land in Bombay about 3rd February. I have taken this decision because I feel that if I give you up and stay at home it will not make either Kashi, Vijay or yourself much happier. Vijay would then grow up in a house which would be divided, the husband against the wife, the wife against the husband. Having been brought up in such a house I know what a bitter cost the child pays in such an atmosphere. He would be better to have his mother only – at any rate his loyalties would not be divided.

I was deeply moved by your father's and Kashi's attitude to me. You are to tell Kashi as gently as you can that she is to give nothing up to me. Even if it means that I must earn my living in India in order that she may have an adequate allowance and that Vijay may have plenty, she is not to give anything up. I do not feel that in marrying you I am taking you away from her. When I first found you she had thrown you away as unwanted – had I not loved you and cared for you, you would not now be in India – you would be dead or near it [since he had been so depressed]. Once the spirit dies, the body follows soon.

To your father say a very deep thank you that he will accept me as a daughter-in-law. It is something I had hardly hoped for and I can understand something of the sadness this must have caused him. I will do my very best to be a daughter he can be proud of, by accepting your customs and your ways of living, and in this you must help me, because although I am well read I have never actually seen India and must, therefore, learn from the beginning.

With regard to what would happen to me if I were to give you up, I suppose that a little more grief added to so much would appear to be merely adding water to the sea, and it is true that by suffering one purchases a certain degree of immunity from further suffering, but I think to lose you would be more than I can bear. Even forgetting what I might suffer inside me, my entire life would have to be altered. It is quite a serious thing to break an engagement with an Englishman; to have been engaged to someone of another nationality and break the engagement would finish me socially in this city, probably, as far as marriage is concerned, in this country. It would mean making a completely new start at a time when I should not care whether I lived or died and without my family to help me. I know that I must start afresh in India, but I will have you by my side to guide and help me and a reason for living.

Darling, in your chosen career you will have many setbacks and disappointments and it is then that a loving wife can be of help to you. I feel that together we can face many things. Single sticks can be easily broken, but tie them into a bundle and they cannot be broken.

If I can help Kashi and Vijay over the stony ways of life at all, I will do so, and I hope that they will not feel too bitterly against me.

Whether the decision I have made is the right one, only time can tell, but I do not feel that I am making any more damage by deciding this way than by deciding not to come. One cannot avoid troubles in life whatever one does, but one can try to balance the unhappiness with a certain amount of happiness and I think we stand a good chance of some happiness in the way I have decided.

You may show this letter to your father if you wish, although the English is far from perfect, but you will know that I am a little distressed at having to decide the futures of four people at such short notice and have had to think very hard. Life has not been very kind to me up to now – Kashi may be suffering now, but she does not know to what depths of misery life can take one, and I feel that any small happiness God may give me from my marriage to you has been amply paid for already and that I should not be asked to pay again.

With this letter comes all my love and the hope that

> you will not think I am being unduly selfish. Also, I send my thanks to your father for being kind to you.

Helen's response has a confident and loving tone that suggests she had thought hard about what she would write and she wrote it with great conviction. Had Dad not sent the cable after posting his letter, I don't know what my mother would have done. Had she made a different decision and not come to India, I believe that my dad's life would have tumbled downhill very quickly and I firmly believe that my mother would have taken her own life. After years of hardship and heartbreak, another loss, of a true soul mate, exacerbated by the social shame she refers to in her letter, would have broken her.

Chapter Nine

> *Sometimes I have such a longing to see you again that I can hardly bear it and lying in bed this morning, I could think of nothing else, but I am so afraid of spoiling our future with hasty action that you need not fear that I shall do anything stupid.*

Helen was greatly alarmed about Avadh's family's reaction to their engagement, but at the same time she must have been relieved to learn that Avadh had finally told them about her. There were no secrets. The choice of whether to come to India or not had been left in her hands and she had taken it, decisively. Her luggage would have been packed and ready for departure when on Sunday 8 January she received a cable, which read:

> UNFORESEEN CIRCUMSTANCES CANCEL BOAT DEPARTURE WILL CALL LATER LETTER FOLLOWS TRUST ME

It was just days before the *Jal-Azad* was due to sail and she must have been devastated. Had he decided she should not come after all?

She had to wait two days for another cable, in which he explained:

> DO NOT WORRY LOVE ONLY THIS DEPARTURE NOT SUITABLE

You can imagine Helen's consternation and alarm at these communications. On the 8th Avadh wrote a letter of explanation, but it would be about five days before she received it: five days in limbo, unsure what was going on. His letter of the 8th told her that as Kashi dwelled on the imminent end of her marriage, she had become increasingly upset about it. Although she had originally consented, she now felt differently and her despair was such that Avadh's family worried the situation was at risk of spiraling out of control. It was for this reason he asked Helen to delay her departure.

> I have this day given you a real SOS and I hope you will act accordingly. It is unfortunate and I cannot express in words how I am feeling about the whole thing. Here are the facts.
>
> I had to fly from Ahmedabad [to see Kashi]. Since this morning we are trying to arrive at some decision. Unfortunately I have not met a more adamant person. I feel that probably she will agree to some better course later on. You will agree with me that unless she changes her attitude, one does not know what trouble she can land us into. It is for this reason that I have asked you to cancel the boat passage. My [Doctor] brother has kindly offered that as soon as the matters are decided

> and if Kashi could be persuaded, he will give us the money to call [bring] you by air, if necessary. He has been so good to me.

Avadh's second-oldest brother, who lived in Delhi, was a physician. My parents always referred to him as 'Doctor Brother'. In India first names are used less than in the West and, indeed, in South India many people traditionally had only one name. In our family, a habit had developed of referring to people using a combination of nicknames and descriptors like 'Doctor Brother'.

On the 9th, Avadh wrote:

> I am extremely sorry that I had to put you to so great an inconvenience, but the circumstances were such that you will understand that that was the only course. Because of Kashi's adamant attitude, my father has said that he will help you and me financially if we stand in need of it. But you should not come before Kashi has been persuaded by her parents or they have been informed of all this. From now on my Doctor Brother has said that you have been accepted by all of us and, even in our marriage, my brothers will participate.
>
> Please take your delay in departure in good spirits. I don't know what you say to all the persons around you [none of her Liverpool friends knew that Avadh was married] because I can't think of a suitable excuse. But you have as good a mind as I have and I am confident that, trusting me, you will act in a way that is best for both of us.
>
> Just at present I cannot tell you how long it will take to get matters decided. The difficulty is as follows. Kashi's parents live in Kashmir – the railroad is closed

> due to snow. Kashi is adamant that she will not go to them and does not want to listen to their advice. But my father has written to Kashmir explaining the situation and it will be cleared up soon.
>
> I love you as I have never done before and if everything fails, I will come to England and stay with you if you will still love me after I have given you a most anxious and hectic time.

On 10 January, Avadh wrote telling Helen more of the reason why he had asked her to defer coming to India – and even to reconsider coming at all. He had met with Kashi and offered her a generous allowance but this was rejected outright. Moreover, Avadh believed that if Helen came at that point, there was the risk of a 'disaster', which he implied might include physical violence, since feelings were running so high. Added to Kashi's distress at the ending of her marriage, there was the vestigial resentment of the English in those post-Partition years and a disapproval of marrying anyone foreign, which meant the atmosphere could be highly charged.

Avadh's family also recognized their responsibility towards Vijay and were trying to determine the best home for him within the extended family. Under Hindu law at the time the father was the natural guardian of a legitimate child unless he was unfit. For Kashi to bring up the boy on her own was not seen as a particularly desirable option – perhaps for the same reason that Helen's grandmother had been persuaded to send Helen's father to boarding school. The belief that boys needed a male influence was widespread. Avadh sounds understandably nervous about what could happen if Helen arrived before the situation was resolved.

He met with Doctor Brother and his sister-in-law in Delhi, and wrote that:

> It did not take more than a minute so far as my brother was concerned – [to say] that if I can support Kashi separately, I should make myself happy by marrying a second time. However, my decision of marrying you (a foreign lady) was not met with so easy an approval. But after 3 or 4 hours of talk and thinking he agreed and now after I agreed to delay your departure and you having agreed to it – they will even participate in our marriage and help you to come by air if need be.
>
> So you should not worry, my love. So long as I am alive I will not say no to you. If Kashi and her parents become adamant and unreasonable and if in that case you will be willing to stay with me in England, I will come to you.
>
> Now also I have to start work. My inaugural lecture is next week and with all the things in my mind, it is appearing to be a great bugbear. But I am determined to try my level best for it and my other work so that no damage is done to the honour of my work.
>
> I am very anxious to hear from you and know that you have been able to do your best with the situation that I suddenly created before you.

It is apparent that my Indian grandfather had already given my Doctor Uncle quite a lot of authority to find a solution to this family mess. While their father would retain the final say, my uncle, who had been partly educated in England, had considerable influence and he was steadfast in his view that Avadh and Kashi could never be happy together. Another of Avadh's brothers, Kailash, the lawyer – who was also referred to as 'Lucknow Brother' – wrote to Avadh trying to dissuade him from marrying an Englishwoman, but he finished his letter by saying that whatever happened they would always remain brothers and friends.

In the next letter I have, dated 17 January, Helen wrote of her delayed departure, playing down her disappointment while gently reminding Avadh of quite how difficult it has been for her.

> The days drag by and it grieves me to think that had all been well I should have sailed tomorrow. Having no special work to do, but just helping in the office where I can, gives me no outlet for my thoughts and they go round and round in my head like flies round a sugar bowl. Mr Wilkinson [her boss at Metal Box] is very good to continue employing me, because it is a terrible inconvenience to him not to have from me a definite date of departure, and I shall be boundlessly thankful when I get a date of departure from you – however far ahead, so that I can make some plan of action and so can he.
>
> Has any move been made at all over Kashi? Is there any reply whatever from Kashmir? Any news you have would be welcomed.
>
> The weather here is now getting very cold – I wish I could pack some up and send it to you in exchange for some more heat. At this time of year one never manages to get really warm – the wind is bitter, but there is no rain and the sky is a beautiful duck-egg blue all day long. I always move quickly, as you know, but the last few days I have literally run around to keep warm. We shall have some snow I think in the next fortnight. It would be lovely up in the Lakes now, despite the cold. The snow would be on top of every hill and catch the evening light. Didn't we have a lovely time up there? This last year has been the happiest in my life despite all the worry and I pray that we may soon be able to add to that happiness.

In response, Avadh commented drily that, 'There is very little hope that the cold of England could be imported here because though it would be welcome to the people, the Government has strict restrictions on all kinds of imports.'

On Wednesday 18 January, Helen wrote a little more about her feelings about the delay. It put her in a very difficult position.

> I cannot put into a letter all my fears at the present time, but you will know your own feelings and can, therefore, guess at mine. I am very lucky that up to now I have been able to earn my living and in consequence I eat and sleep in comfort, but once I get past the 1st February [when she was due to leave work] I do not know what will happen to me and I do hope your father will be able to give me word to come before then.
>
> I am trying hard to get some extra rest but although I have the time now in which to rest, I cannot. I wander around like something lost.
>
> I have finished reading a translation of the 'Fugitive' by Tagore, and cannot honestly say that I understood it in its entirety, but much of it was very beautiful, but awfully sad. Even in the translation his words touched one's heartstrings – the original must be very fine indeed – I presume that original is in poetry, although the translation is in prose. I will keep on reading – I have discovered a whole new literature.

Avadh seemed concerned to reassure her and on 14 January he wrote her a four-page letter that began:

> I have only a few minutes back posted an air letter to you, but I find that my thoughts are still running after

you and I am reading your letters again and again, so I thought I might as well write to you again. My whole heart wishes to say to you, times without number, that I love you and yet you are not here to hear the thumpings of my heart. I am being sentimental but so far as you are concerned I cannot be anything else. Sometimes I do wish I had not left England at all – at least I would have been with you then and that is probably the only thing I want now but somehow destiny was determined to lead us otherwise lest

by getting that or this (a little early)
I might grow proud a while.

As well as protestations of love, and with this elegant near-quote of 17th-century poet Robert Herrick's 'To Electra', he told her that 'the storm in Delhi and in Kashi's mind is subsiding now – as I hear from brother – and in due course I hope to be able to call you again to come.' He also said that he planned to take Kashi back to her family in Kashmir just as soon as the railway line was operational again.

Helen's response to this letter, written on Thursday 19 January, is glowing:

My dearest Pussycat,

Today I received the nicest letter I have ever received in my life. You said you would not read it a second time for fear you should disapprove of it and tear it up. It is a lovely letter and I shall treasure it all my life. Do not think to be sentimental is a profession of weakness – the English are a sentimental race and I do not think even now they could be called weak, but we are afraid to show how we feel sometimes and the result is brusqueness and rudeness on our part quite frequently. But who in the world minds being told they are beloved – certainly I love to be told so – it gives me strength to face each day and encourages many another virtue.

There is a saying that there is nobody so politely rude as the English and it is very true. It is perfectly clear that everybody here thinks I have been jilted and am too proud to say so. They take the attitude that it serves me right for daring to marry a foreigner.

Although they were all quite pleased that I was getting married they expected that it should go off without a hitch, and the fact that something has obviously gone wrong, as I cancelled my passage at such incredibly short notice, makes them look round in their minds for criticisms of me which, alas, they can find all too easily. If I would admit that I had been jilted, they could patronize me with pity, but since I have certainly not been and have a boundless trust in you, they think I am snooty and proud.

I love you intensely and nothing can shake that but my letters may have inadvertently conveyed some of the suppressed fury I have felt against people here, and I do not want that to happen. I could not care less if I was snubbed by people I did not know, but to be snubbed and sniggered at by people I do know (most of whom have some healthy skeletons in their own closets) reduces me to a rage beyond reason. 'Owever, we are crawling through and will doubtless survive until we eventually land in India.

To speak of something a little more cheerful, has your brother, who has been, so kind, any children? If he has, please tell me whether they are boys or girls and how old they are. I should especially like to come to Delhi armed with a little gift for each of them. I can remember as a child watching grown-ups unpack and the incredible joy and wonder when at the very bottom of the case there was a present for me and I would like to do the same for them. It will have to be a light parcel because of the limit of my luggage, but our toyshops are full, as you know, and I should love to bring them something. I suppose I dare not bring Vijay anything??

We have a funny saying, 'dreamin' of my darling love of thee', and that is what I am doing this minute!

Much love, dear,
Immer Deine [The Lucky One]
Helen

On 20 January, Helen wrote with sympathy for Kashi: 'If there is anything I can do to help her in her predicament, you must tell me and I will do it. I hope she will not shut herself away from life, but will go out amongst people.'

Her letter continued:

I am going to dance at the British Council each Sunday until I can come to you, the reasons being that it is a form of entertainment which costs me nothing and in dancing I can completely lose myself, forgetting my miseries completely. Afterwards my mind is refreshed and clear. I do not dance with anyone very long but flit from partner to partner, so as to avoid any embarrassing entanglements. The dance makes me go out whereas otherwise I would not.

I am thrilled to pieces at the idea of sorting out the flat and making it a happy home for us, but first I must take a peep into one or two Indian homes to see what they are like – otherwise you will find yourself with an English home and that will not do at all.

Perhaps your Doctor Brother's wife would show me round her home?

I am not worried about Ahmedabad not being westernised – as long as the fly population does not invade our flat!!

Avadh replied that he was quite happy for Helen to continue attending the British Council dances: 'I have no objection if you go out a bit more only please let no one else fall in love with you and you with someone else otherwise, well, it would be a disaster for me.'

On 17 January Avadh wrote describing the life Helen could expect to find when she arrived in India:

Ahmedabad city can be described as one which in certain ways has remained completely untouched by the Western ideas – for example, literally there is not a single restaurant (except at Railway Station) where one can eat anything – unless of course you try to eat the local food – which I must say is not very interesting. The Railway Station is 3½ miles [5.6 km] from our place and on bus it takes about an hour to reach there. Vegetables and all vegetarian things one can get very easily, even at the door of the flat, but meat is scarce and hard to get – eggs can be had from town (2 miles [3.2 km], ¾ hour on the bus) and also western bread.

Of course, I have asked for a power plug but I cannot say if it will be fitted because the characteristic of the people here is to never say 'no' to anything and do things only at their own wish.

However, my only worry is how you will employ yourself or your time. So far Dr Vikram Sarabhai's (Professor of Cosmic Rays) family is the only one

> where ladies know English and then he and his father are millionaires, being the owners of the finest cotton mill in India, and live at a distance of no less than six miles [9.6 km]. I do not find anyone going to his place except when they are invited.

Dr Sarabhai was a native of Ahmedabad who had studied physics at the local college and then at Cambridge University. He had founded the Physical Research Laboratory in 1947, initially in his own residence, with funding from the Sarabhai family, who were wealthy mill owners, and some well-to-do friends. While another scientist, Dr Ramanathan, was in charge of the laboratory, Dr Sarabhai and his family were clearly very influential in the university community. Dr Sarabhai went on to play a major role in the Indian space programme. My parents often referred to Dr Sarabhai as Professor Cosmic Rays as that was his field of study at the time.

Avadh continued:

> Probably you will be able to get some job at the University as a stenographer or teaching English, although I don't think you need earn because my income will be sufficient for us. All this might mean that for some time to come you may have to become a Sweet Stay at Home! Of course there is a Lady Lecturer in the flat adjoining to mine (Christian) who will I presume to some extent be your company.
>
> Every Sunday at 10:30 AM or so we can go to see an English or American picture provided we start from our flat at 9:30 AM which is easy enough since the sun rises at 6:30 AM.
>
> My mother does not mind you coming provided you will adopt as many as possible of our ways. You can try to learn a little more Hindi when you come so that

> when any member of my family comes to stay with us, they will appreciate it very much.

On 18 January Avadh wrote with more information on domestic matters in Ahmedabad.

> I have settled in my flat and have got a man to cook for me. Last night was his first. He does not understand Hindi and I do not understand Gujarati and so there was a good deal of a humorous scene with no one to enjoy it – what a pity. Anyway I am now beginning to learn the language of the province [Gujarati] – so that I could enjoy when you will have to explain to him anything.

He added: 'I have received information from Brother that Kashi's mother has come from Kashmir and is with her. I do not know what decision has been taken but since my position is quite clear in their minds; i.e. if they insist on their way, I shall simply come to England.'

Avadh described his Doctor Brother as having become his friend through this turbulent period, and said he wrote to him twice a week. He told Helen that his brother was well aware of the humiliation she was experiencing and was doing his best to resolve the situation. I met my uncle a couple of times when I visited India in my early twenties and heard much about him over the years. He struck me as a kind, strong, unflappable man, equally capable of dealing with the complexities of his impoverished patients in old Delhi as with difficult family matters. The mutual respect between him and my dad was obvious and I am glad that he was there as a moderating influence during this terribly difficult period.

*

Money was tight for Helen and Avadh, and Helen had borrowed against the value of a small life insurance policy, which was not an uncommon arrangement. Even the poor sometimes had a policy with a premium of a few pennies per week to cover funeral expenses, and, if they were slightly better off, to be used as a form of savings. In *Twopence*, Helen describes beautifully the elaborate funeral procession of a rag-and-bone man, paid for with insurance.

Helen had also borrowed from a friend. John had been Eddie's best friend and was an old colleague of Helen's at the Petroleum Board who had generously lent them £100 to help start their married life. Helen had agreed to pay him back at a rate of not less than £4 a month.

On 24 January she wrote to Avadh outlining the state of her finances:

Borrowed on [life] insurance policy	£ 47.0.0
Borrowed from John	100.0.0
Saved	20.0.0
	£167.0.0

I have had to spend as follows:

Sea Passage	£85. 0.0
Inoculations	1. 1.0
Luggage to London	1.17.6
Insurance of Luggage	2. 5.0
Luggage to Ahmedabad	8. 8.9
	£98.12.3

This leaves me with £68, out of which I must pay a further £45 for air passage, £2 to London, further luggage by sea, say, £5, and incidental expenses on the journey. I think I shall just manage nicely. I hope to

> save a few more pounds. I have not saved any more up to now as you will realize I have paid for all cables and £5 for telephone calls out of my weekly salary.

She said she was 'rather concerned' to be starting her married life in debt but hoped that if they were careful they would manage. She added: 'It is good to have one's married life on a sound financial foundation.' There speaks the girl who had managed to feed seven children and two adults on one shilling a day in the early 1930s!

There were complex and difficult negotiations to be undertaken before Helen could set sail and it must have been horribly frustrating to be stuck in Liverpool with so little influence over events. But she was dogged in her determination. It was only a matter of time before they would be together again. The Hindu Code Bill had been deferred until at least August, so there was plenty of time for Helen to get to India and be married under the old law. I expect she wished the bill would pass sooner because then they would have had to act more quickly. As it was, Helen waited, more or less patiently, at home in Liverpool for news of when she could rebook her passage to India and begin her new life.

Chapter Ten

> *Sometimes I get so appalled at the thought of all that I must learn and at all the mistakes I shall inevitably make that I am reduced to despair and your letter reminded me that I shall have someone to laugh with and someone to tell me. It will be your turn to say, 'Hush', or 'Don't do that' and I shall simply die laughing because I shall know just how you feel!*

As they waited for a settlement to be agreed with Kashi and her family, Helen and Avadh wrote almost daily about their forthcoming life together, in letters that are often amusing and always affectionate. They shared a similar sense of humour and entertained each other with their lively descriptions.

On 25 January 1950, she wrote:

> Your descriptions of Ahmedabad [in his letter of 17 January] made me laugh and wonder if it would shake the town to the foundations if I rode a bicycle too. If it would not be considered absolutely unpardonable, that is what I shall aim to do, even if it takes all my

> pocket money for two years to buy. I could always wear slacks so that my legs remained covered whilst on it. If both of us had bicycles we could sometimes – when the heat was less – get away from the city for a day. Anyway I'll soon see how other ladies deport themselves, when I arrive.

Avadh replied that a bicycle was practically a necessity because of the heat. It was a twelve-minute walk to the laboratory where he worked and bicycling was much preferable.

> There will not be the least objection from my side of your having a bicycle, and ladies do go on bikes; if not so much in Ahmedabad, it is common in Poona, Bombay, Delhi and Allahabad. So don't worry on that account – when you get here, the first priority will be your bike. I never thought of a bike for you – being a fool as I am – at least till the time we are in a position to get a car.

On Saturday 21 January, Avadh wrote applauding Helen's attempts to learn Hindi.

> Even though it will be no good with the servant [who spoke only Gujarati], it will carry you further, for example when my mother comes here. I am afraid that, as matters are now, she, as well as sometimes my father, are bound to come to see whether you are adequately taking care of me and I hope that you will welcome them and take care of them when they are here, as anyone else in your place would have done. That will give us also a feeling (probably specially me) that I have not been dismissed by them. They have been

> grieved very much by the situation that I have created – but they have accepted it as well – the rest will be in our hands to keep their love on us.

This letter must have caused Helen some trepidation since she knew that his parents were vegetarian and many of the ingredients she was used to cooking with would not be available. When Avadh first arrived in England, he had been a strict vegetarian. His landlady, Mrs Lewis, presented him with a poached egg but he refused it. She told him that he had to eat it because under the rationing system still operational in Britain, he would starve if he did not eat eggs and meat. He duly slid the egg down his throat whole.

How could Helen impress her parents-in-law when she was not familiar with either vegetarian or Indian cooking? The chasm between the food Helen was used to and that served in India was far greater than it would be today, now that Indian food is very popular in Britain and many upper-class Indians eat meat dishes. She replied, bravely:

> Of course they will be made most welcome and everything will be done to make them feel comfortable. I only hope they do not come too soon after I arrive, as I am so ignorant and will possibly offend them with my western ways until you have taught me the more obvious things. Also we shall have to buy a few more things for the flat before we can entertain visitors! However, you can be quite sure I shall do all I can, not to let you down.

Avadh replied with a little more detail about the foods that would be available.

> Your food at least to some extent will have to change for the simple reason that we might not get certain things – but milk, eggs, even your type of bread, rice, mutton, vegetables, potatoes, carrots, peas, and other vegetables, bananas and other fruits, good fresh butter – will be available and in plenty. Sugar is rationed (½lb per week) and so is wheat and rice (10oz per day per person).

He added that the servant he had hired would be responsible for much of the cooking and continued, as if trying to reassure her:

> Yesterday all wheat flour was finished at the flat [so the cook could not make rotis, a staple of daily dinner] so I had to go for a meal out and by luck I found a place only two miles [3.2 km] from our flat which serves English food, and I had soup, fish and chips and bread pudding. It was not very good but it was not bad as well, though charges compared to Indian food were higher (4s/6d) – but Ahmedabadi food in hotels – well I better not talk about it.

Helen replied:

> Darling, I hope the cook you have acquired is tempting you with all kinds of good things so that you are eating properly and keeping well. I am thinking constantly of all the things that ought to be done to make the flat comfortable and are probably not being done. 'Owever, I must just wait until I arrive. It completely mystifies me how you managed to tell the boy what to do. I visualise you, dictionary in hand, resorting to drawing all over the kitchen wall in a despairing attempt to be

> understood. Reminds me of Father who, whilst in Russia, wanted to buy an egg. He squatted down, clucking like a hen laying an egg. A delighted Russian, thinking he understood, promptly showed him to the lavatory. After that, father managed without eggs.

Avadh often wrote to Helen about his work, beginning a lifetime habit of sharing with her his professional concerns.

> I have both plans for developing my section of the Laboratory and fears that I may turn out to be a failure – only God knows how much I shall succeed. My first research student is arriving on Monday, though unofficially one of my colleagues has taken on a research problem from me to work on. I shall battle on with my work as best I can – so that my section is not disgraced – rest must be left to God. From the first week of February, I am starting two courses of lectures on Relativity and Wave Mechanics – lecturing part, I am not so afraid but the research part – well I shall try my best and even if I produce trash, I hope you will love me. The one difficulty is that in theoretical physics, no one here knows more than I do – and I know so little – so that I cannot get much benefit except by my work alone.

On 29 January, Helen wrote with a piece of news of her own, foreshadowing the career in which she would later be so successful.

> Do you remember that about three months ago I wrote a little article on how a shorthand typist should <u>not</u> behave at an interview for a job? It was such a small article that I did not even bother to send the magazine

> concerned a 2½d stamp with which to return it to me, but last night when I got home a letter was waiting for me with £1.1.0 in it as payment. I was terribly pleased because it is the first article I have ever written for money. On Monday I shall bank it and it will be a little more to help to straighten out our finances. It is encouraging to try again. I am so anxious that you should not have to bear the entire burden of what we must do and if this can be a way of helping you, I shall write everything I can think of.

Avadh replied, obviously proud of her:

> I was very glad to know that your article was accepted for publication. I congratulate you on it and assure you that I will see that you write more of them – don't think I write this because of money – but because – well one does many things for pleasure – it will be a pleasure if you write something – detective novels say.

As far as I know, Mum had not considered writing novels at this time, but my dad obviously appreciated the quality of her writing. Was it he who originally put the germ of the idea for her future career into her head or did she already have ambitions in this direction? Much later she commented in a speech that it was taken for granted that a well-educated person of her generation would be capable of writing a book.

Before long their thoughts were once again preoccupied by the delicate negotiations with Kashi and her family. Helen wrote:

> I am finding it a little nerve-racking knowing that our future is being decided for us by people I don't even

know 6,000 miles away, knowing that they can do all sorts of things to you and I shall not know and shall not be there to take the blows with you. Sweetheart, I am always behind you to love and take care of you whatever happens. I do not fear the future if we are together. Neither of us is exactly helpless and we can make our way together.

Dear God, I hope I can come to you soon. I am not starving or anything – it is just wanting to be with you, to sort our lives out, to build together like birds. Roll on the great day.

Avadh replied:

First of all I must say that you can trust my people that they will bring about a settlement in our favour – one of the reasons is that only yesterday my mother had written to me – asking me to be only patient and take care of myself – the rest she said they will look to my happiness. But a settlement is not in their hands alone, so it may take some time.

We know now that the Hindu Code Bill will not come before the Assembly before August. Since it will be difficult for you to get a week-to-week employment, either I can send you some money £20 to £30 every month, which I must say I can afford to share from my pay. I think this will be enough for you and I shall begin sending it to you, whether you need it or not, so that we can get rid of our debts as quickly as we can.

What I am arriving at is whether it would be possible for you (of course in the event of things not being settled just at this stroke) to postpone your departure for here at one stroke for a month or six weeks or even two months, and get employment there. I am

> certain that things must get settled in that time and if they are not then the only course left will be my coming to you. From my point of view this procedure of delaying your departure has certain advantages: i) we will clear our debts much quicker and then when you come we shall be able to spend more on ourselves; ii) in case I have to come to you, you will get enough time to secure a permanent employment. iii) when you come after that time and you decide to come by sea, it will just be time for summer holidays (May) and we can spend the entire days at a hill station – of course, the heat otherwise would be rather too much for you.
>
> But, Love, you must not think I am asking you to do this as I do not exactly know in what position you are there and all the above arguments have counter arguments.
>
> Rest assured that whatever you do will have my unreserved support because I know that I have put you in a completely strange situation by my follies – for if I had only guessed what Kashi would do at the last moment, I would have asked you from the beginning to make your departure at a later date but it was a genuine mistake and I am really sorry about it.

Helen wrote back sympathizing with all the stress he was going through. She was mindful, however, of the need to avoid being a financial burden on her parents. Her father, Paul, was still working for the City of Liverpool at this time. I am not sure if Lavinia was working or not, but certainly money was not in abundance.

> When I think of the effect it must have had on you I feel for you and am amazed that you had the courage to stick to your guns and insist that you would marry

me – I feel I have a champion indeed and that you will never fail me if you did not fail me then. Sometimes I feel very wicked at all the grief I cause to you, but I feel that the world would take every mortal thing away from us if we did not fight tooth and claw to keep it, and also particularly you and I have earned a little happiness. I may have been inconvenienced at this end, but I think you have gone through hell at your end and I do appreciate that it was for my sake – makes me feel proper humble, as they say in Liverpool.

I still do not know what is to happen to me at the office but I know I can be sure of employment for this week. Actually I am very anxious indeed to avoid leaving the Metal Box Company because if you were to return here I must have a good job until you are able to work. For this reason, I have asked you to let me have a cable if you decide you must return, so that I can make arrangements with the company to take up permanent employment with them again. I hate asking you for money, but my parents cannot unfortunately afford to keep me for nothing, as they already have to keep one adult, my brother Edward, who is not earning, while he goes through school and university. I should be most unwelcome were I unable to contribute anything to the home, although of course they would never actually let me go hungry.

I appreciate your suggestion that I should time my arrival for May, so that I will land when holidays are due to commence, but I have such an overwhelming desire to be with you, no matter what the discomfort, that I hope you will let me come as quickly as it is humanly possible for me to get an air passage. The thought that we may be able to spend a little time in May in the hills will make me endure the heat, knowing

> that I shall have some break from it, no matter how short. The fear in me that we might be parted forever by some malignant fate haunts me throughout each day and nothing short of being actually with you will cure it. You know also that feeling I always have that I must act quickly or I may lose the opportunity. The feeling is only a residue of the war, but it is very real to me. When we never knew whether we would live to see the next day, we tended to hasten everything!

Two months before, it had all seemed quite simple. She was in love. She was about to join her husband-to-be in India. Now, my mother had been separated from the man she loved for much longer than the two weeks she had expected, and there was still no certain resolution in sight. Given the difficulties of coming to a settlement with Kashi and her family, she must have worried that it could still go wrong – and she was determined to do all she could to prevent that happening. She was under a lot of stress and I can sense her frustration.

Many years later my mother would once again be a very resilient and selfless person but, at this point, she saw serious obstacles on the path to happiness that lay in front of her. The strident tone of some of her letters betrays her anxiety mingled with sheer determination not to lose this wonderful man she had fallen for. She *would* find a way through all the practical difficulties and challenges the uncertain delay meant for her, but she couldn't help reminding Avadh from time to time that he was not the only one who was suffering.

At least she had some beautiful love letters from him to sustain her. He wrote: 'You must wonder whether it is not someone else who is writing to you, for in my writings in England you had always seen me in very matter of fact style, but I can assure you that it is the same person writing only somehow I find that when writing to you my whole heart begins to crave for you and then my mind and brain retire.' They are long, rambling letters and at one point he said he was trying to make his correspondence more structured and answer Helen's points more directly but then he gave up and decided to go back to his 'happy-go-lucky' style.

The latest news was that Kashi's mother wanted to come to Ahmedabad to talk to him directly but Avadh's Doctor Brother managed to persuade her not to. Instead she went to Avadh's family home near Delhi. His brother wrote advising that it would not be prudent for Helen to come to India until Kashi's mother had returned to Kashmir. Adding that he agreed, Avadh forwarded the letter to Helen.

Helen wrote on 31 January:

> Darling,
>
> This is in reply to your letter of 24th, 25th (enclosing your brother's letter) and 26th January, but before I say a blessed thing about them I want to tell you that I love you terribly and that loving you grows with me each day – that is, if it is possible to love someone more than with every bone in one's body and every thought in one's mind.
>
> Your letters made me realize that I could not go on in my present situation any longer and that I must, both for my own sake and Mr Wilkinson's sake come to some sort of agreement over my work which would enable me to continue to work, if necessary, for many months to come. I have agreed that, if I do not receive definite news from you by the end of this week, I shall take up a post which he will offer me in this office at my present salary, on the understanding that I must give him at least one month's notice before I leave –

> that is the snag. It means it will be a whole month from receipt of news from you that I am able to come, that I shall be able to start on my journey, and if possible he wants more than one month's notice. The fact that I should have to wait so long even if I have good news from you hurt me almost to tears but it was the only way in which I could be sure of earning my living until you send for me and the only way of being sure of a good job should you have to return to this country.
>
> Thank [Doctor Brother] very, very much for the offer of help. The way your family have helped us touches me to the heart. Thank you, too, for the way in which you consider my wellbeing.

She then offered advice on the forthcoming visit to the laboratory of a prominent Swedish radio astronomer, Dr Rydbeck. My mother was always very astute when it came to the murky, dog-eat-dog world of academic politics and Dad was grateful for her realpolitik insights.

> I would, if I were you, snatch every possible opportunity to get to know well as many of these important mill owners, or scientists of any nationality, who may cross your path, even for a moment.
>
> Many a man has saved his life by having only the faintest acquaintance with the right person. Even if you only meet for a moment in a corridor, or hand a person his stick, make sure he knows who you are if you possibly can. You may not realize it, but you are very charming and you should cultivate all the important people you can – snatch every small chance that comes. By so doing you will slowly make your position more and more impregnable.

> When I come you will be in a better position to offer hospitality to any visitors, so you can then quickly jump in with an invitation yourself. Also, where any Europeans are concerned, you will have the advantage of having a home in which they will not feel completely strange and a wife who can at least speak good English. When I come out, I shall seize every opportunity of getting to know the right ladies in the town – a few old female battleaxes on our side who will nag their husbands to death if anything detrimental happens to us, will be worth their weight in gold. Even if I have to walk 10 miles with fresh flowers (or whatever one takes to old ladies in India) and on top of that have to eat things full of red pepper, I'll do it to help you!

Mum would later be an incredible asset to Dad, not only in her endless emotional and practical support, but by hosting many parties and dinners in order to advance his career, although she found them rather boring and a lot of work. For the moment, she sounds resigned to the delays in their plans and relieved that her boss, Mr Wilkinson, was prepared to be so flexible: 'I think I must be a damned nuisance to him, but it does him credit that he has continued to employ me although he is bound to be censured by Head Office due to the cost. He is indeed a good friend.'

Around this time, Mr Wilkinson and his wife invited Helen to spend a weekend with them at their house. They gave a party and Helen told Avadh how proud she would have been had he been with her.

Mr Wilkinson thought very highly of Helen and she had enormous respect for him. In the 1980s she gave a talk about the development of characters and she cited him as an example of a person who compensated effectively for a weakness.

I once worked for a man 4'8" tall. His wife, incidentally, was just under six feet – and they adored each other. That man was a big executive in an enormous business. When he wanted to speak to his workmen he had to send for a chair to stand on, so that he could be seen. Once he started to speak, you could see how he dominated the hulking types who worked for him. His eyes flashed, his arms flailed. He was tremendously clear and exact in his instructions to his men, and he delivered them with such wit that the place would be echoing with laughter before he had done. In sixteen years of rule, he never had a strike.

I once said to him when I had stopped laughing myself, 'That was a marvellously clever way of telling the men something unpleasant.' He grinned, and said, 'I was always the smallest boy in my class at school – I couldn't fight anybody. So I had to learn how to make a quick joke and divert them without causing further offence.'

You see, a little man, who was physically lost in a very muscular world, compensated beautifully.

On 1 February, Helen was delighted to receive a request that she bring out to India some surgical instruments that Avadh's Doctor Brother had ordered. Surely it was a firm sign of her acceptance by the family?

I don't think anything could have cheered me up more than your brother's request that I should bring with me the surgical instruments he has ordered. I really and truly felt that he was quite certain in his mind that you would be able to arrange for me to come to India. I will certainly bring them and take great care of them – when they arrive at my house I will write your brother a little letter – it will give me an opportunity of saying 'thank you'.

The flat sounds awfully nice – we are lucky. I think, sweet, you had better get some curtains as soon as you can conveniently afford them, as it will do more than anything else to make the house look pleasant. I do not know what kind of curtains it is usual to have in India, but patterned curtains always make rooms look more 'furnished', so do you think we could have some with a pattern of flowers or something with a formal design all over them? If the builders have left the walls of the rooms just white or pale yellow, a soft blue would look cool and pleasant in the living room, and I should like something pink or yellow in the bedroom. In the kitchen, something in gay red or green stripes – or anything which looks gay and clean. Perhaps the Lady Professor [who lived next door] would advise you on buying material which does not fade. Have them made 6" longer than the window bracket unless this makes them drag on the floor (in which case, don't). This will give the curtains a better chance of fitting the windows of any other house we may move to. I should love to have made the curtains myself, but I do want the flat to be pleasant for you.

I am counting the days, the hours, the minutes until I may come to you. God grant it may be soon – the time is so long without you.

Your own adoring devil,
Helen

The delay was also preying on Avadh's mind. On 27 January he wrote:

> I feel that I can no longer bear your separation and I agree with you that if after four weeks, there is no settlement either I shall come to you or you come to me. I feel that I am losing all interest in work and it is no use bearing something to such an extent one has very little left. But anyway though I sound depressed and am so, I am made of enough steel not to crack, so you better take care of yourself.

By the 28th, Avadh's resolve to force the issue with Kashi had strengthened and he wrote that he would leave for England if there was no settlement within a month. It would be much more difficult for her to get maintenance if he was out of the country. She would likely have to force it through the courts.

Helen replied on 2 February saying that she thought he was right to force the issue with Kashi but warning: 'Do not act too hastily about giving up your job – that is something to be done only in the last resort. As you see, I can keep myself going for a while now, and that will give you breathing space.'

She reassured him that she would manage financially, and that he should not berate himself for the difficulties in which they found themselves.

> You say you have given me nothing but worry up to now but that is not true. You have already given me untold happiness. This last year, despite all its worries, has been the happiest year of my life. I often think of all the nice things we have done together and I dream of adding to this precious store of memories. You are not to think that because I write long letters all about the practical things we have to do, that I do not think of the mental and physical good things of our future

> life together. You and I are a perfect complement to each other – like coffee and cream. We shall be together soon.

There was little that Helen could do to speed the resolution of the situation. However, she wrote to Avadh's Doctor Brother in Delhi, assuring him that she would take good care of his surgical instruments. She explained to Avadh: 'I thought it might bring it home to him that I am a very real person, waiting for word, and that he might bestir himself again on our behalf. I know you are doing your best and I do trust you most deeply.'

She then reassured him: 'I am taking care of myself, because I want to be lovely for you. This thought makes me go to bed, eat my food and keep myself neat more than anything else. And I want you to do the same for my sake.'

And finally, she wrote with a request that was of paramount importance to her.

> Darling, if I have to stay in England several months (which I pray may not be so) would you buy me and send by air an engagement ring. It need not be a valuable ring, but it is advisable that I should wear the usual symbol of a woman about to be married – it would save me quite a lot of embarrassment. It is usual to give a ring with a stone in it, or a silver ring with engraving on it – I should imagine it could be bought in the bazaars.

Later the same day, she wrote another letter in which she demonstrates that she is doing all she possibly can to prepare herself for their new life.

> I have found a shop which has a book called *Teach Yourself Gujarati in Three Weeks*. It costs four shillings

so I am going to buy it. Of course when the author said 'in three weeks' he had not met me – undoubtedly it would have been 'Three Years' otherwise!

I have just done an hour on Hindi and have learned the colours and a few birds. The book from which I take the lessons is not terribly informative, but it does give me some idea so I keep on trying.

I am going to see if I can buy a parasol and coloured spectacles, as you suggested. I shall have quite a bit of fun, going into shops to ask for them – the shocked look on the faces of the assistants will be as good as a pantomime.

The book I obtained from the library on Hinduism is finished. It actually had about half a page in it on the Arya Samaj – which sounds a reasonable sort of religion to me, which is not incompatible with what I already believe in.

Arya Samaj is a reform-minded movement within Hinduism that has been progressive on women's issues. One of its core beliefs is in the equality of all human beings, and the importance of equal opportunities for all. Avadh was a follower of this sect and it would provide Helen with a route to becoming a Hindu before their marriage.

Helen continued:

Some sides of Hinduism must be rather embarrassing to highly educated and well-informed people, just as some sides of Roman Catholicism are here, but I do appreciate the complete honesty of thought of the philosophers who hammered out the fundamental truths of Hinduism and I feel that with complete honesty myself I shall be able to really respect people who believe in those truths – which points may not mean much to you, but are things on which I have had to ponder very seriously – you have no idea how earnest your memsahib can become!!

*

Avadh wrote to Helen with great relief that he had managed to secure the support of both his bosses at work for their marriage.

> The fact that something has been making me depressed and worried did not escape attention of Professor Sarabhai and Dr Ramanathan and they asked me if they could help. Their knowledge was more due to their opening cables from you by mistake and my sudden departure to Delhi for a day. Anyway, I thought fit to tell them just now that I wanted to marry you to which they said that so far as they were concerned, their relations with us will not alter at all. It was very kind of them, indeed.

This must have come as a great relief to him, but still he sounds depressed in his letter of 30 January.

> What I have done today is merely nothing because I have been feeling so lifeless. Today is a holiday; as you know two years ago on this date Ghandiji was killed [Gandhi was assassinated by a Hindu nationalist who shot him at point-blank range]. I am pretty certain that things as they are in this country – black marketing and all that – he would have wondered whether this is the country where he preached non-violence. If you think that I have gained anything from his preachings, you had better get disillusioned now, for in the situation in which I am, with you so far away – had he been in my

place – he would have worked day-in and day-out – and I just wander round here and there, feeling as lonely as a lonesome cloud in the sky.

At this point in the letter, there was an interruption and when Avadh returned his mood had lifted.

I had just got the trunk call through. My brother and father are trying first to persuade Kashi to either join a college of nurses or a graduation college and as soon as that is done, you will be able to come. Since it is a question of only a few days, I think as brother suggested, I shall give you the word of coming only after everything has been settled. According to brother, it will be settled in about eight or ten days. If it has to take longer, I don't think it will take much longer than a fortnight. I am considerably cheered up because from the trunk it appears that soon everything is going to be all right. You better not say anything just now to anyone because I am afraid something might turn up again and then it would be again awkward.

Love, now cheer up and take care of yourself and write to me a lovely letter so that I could also cheer up. I feel with you I could go through everything – even the heat of Ahmedabad – and you must have a reciprocal determination, at least about heat.

Helen was, of course, ecstatic to hear this news and replied on 5 February:

I was thrilled by your letter giving the result of your telephone call to your brother; Oh darling, darling, it would be so heavenly if we could get things settled in a fortnight. It would mean that you could stop worrying

> and I could too, and we could just happily count the days until we are together again. If I came by air it would mean six weeks, or if I got a sea passage in two months I could be with you. I don't know about you, but I am not afraid of waiting just a little while once I know that quite definitely on a set date I shall see your dear face again. I have played around the house today like a kitten in the breeze I have been so happy at your letters. I just feel I want to sing at the top of my voice. I do hope Kashi does agree to your father's proposals, not only for our sakes but because it will be good for her. She probably thinks at the moment that her life is finished, but as long as she goes out and lives and does not sit at home, she may well find that God has much in his ample storehouse for her. I thought my life was finished till I met you and realized it was only just beginning.

Unfortunately, this was just one of many instances of false optimism. Kashi and her family were not going to be satisfied easily.

*

In the midst of all his pressing concerns, Avadh wrote on another matter: 'I wonder whether when you are coming you could bring a dozen or two pipecleaners – they will cost only a few pence, and would form a nice birthday present for me in August, though I shall certainly utilize them much before.' I can sympathize with my father here: there is nothing worse than a dirty pipe!

Helen replied: 'Sure, I'll bring some pipe cleaners. Might I suggest some feathers in the meantime! What happens if I use the pipe cleaners for hair curlers on my way out to you? Do I get shot down??'

And on 7 February she wrote: 'To go from the sublime to the ridiculous in one swoop, I don't know how many pipe cleaners you want, but I have bought you a dozen bundles, which will keep you going for a while – you old chimney! The tobacconists thought I was buying them for hair curlers and actually recommended another kind because they produced better curls! When I said I wanted them to clean a pipe with, he knew I was mad.'

She also responded to his pessimism about Gandhi's waning influence.

> You say that the black market is rife and India has forgotten Gandhi's teaching. In that case it is all the more reason why we should set an example of true moral integrity, if we can find the strength to do it. I do not mean that we should be slaves to orthodoxy, but try as best we can to be honest in the true sense in all we do. You probably saw Gandhi, which I never did, but his example of industry and forbearance, of understanding and honest thinking, is a model to us both. We could do worse than do as he did. Put your worry on one side now, my heart; we are going to be together come what may – you can work in peace in this knowledge and, in building a good name for yourself, will build something worthwhile for India. We both have talents which, well used, can be of inestimable value, and remember that nearly all good ideas and reforms have always started with a single person.

*

No sooner did it feel as though the situation with Kashi was moving towards a resolution than Avadh began to complain about his job. When he took the role of head of theoretical physics at the laboratory, he had been promised two research assistants and a seat on the governing body. These promises had not been kept and he complained that hiring him as a professor because they could get government money for it and then only being willing to pay his research associate a fraction of what others were getting was like 'begging the gift of a car and then not being willing to pay for petrol'. He and Dr Ramanathan also shared concerns about the influence of the wealthy mill owners who funded the laboratory.

He said his work was 'to teach some elementary Physics to the "Experimental blokes"; ¾ of them won't know, and what is worse will not care, what I am talking about'.

He continued that he felt 'very England sick and I somehow want to come to England and stay there – rather than this country – provided of course, I could get some post in England which I am sure I would get. People in England are more courteous than here and, of course, in Ahmedabad people do not know what courtesy is.'

Helen must have been frustrated by this letter, and worried that it could throw all their plans up in the air once more, but she replied calmly.

> Dearest Avadh,
>
> Thank you for your letter of 30th January, telling me something about the laboratory. I was deeply interested in what you have to say and can understand that it must have caused you a lot of headaches. I am very ignorant of such things but proffer the following advice, most of which will probably have occurred to you anyway.
>
> Most important, I think, is to get hold of whoever promised you membership of the governing body and a research scholar, and be very awkward indeed about

the non-fulfillment of these promises, because undoubtedly you do not stand much chance of being able to do a lot unless you are on the Governing Body. Naturally, Ramanathan [the head of the laboratory] and Professor Cosmic Rays [from the wealthy mill-owning family who funded it] will not wish to share their throne but they must. If fulfillment is not forthcoming, a few personal letters to Sir Krishnan [a member of the University's management council] and any other important person you can think of might help. You could write on the lines that you feel sure they will be interested to have your impressions, etc., then praise what can be praised and go on to say that the greatest of stumbling blocks is that you are not on the Governing Body and can they suggest how this could be arranged – you have already approached Dr So and So or Prof That without success. In other words, get pressure brought to bear from several directions. Since Ahmedabad does not understand courtesy [as Avadh had said in his letter of 30 January], dispense with it and hit out hard, but if you can avoid deep offence do so.

Another thing I think you must do – and I may be asking more work than is possible – and that is, do some hard thinking yourself and try to publish as much work as you can possibly turn out, even if it is not very great work – people are impressed by publication and your value will go up. This must seem like absolute sabotage of true research, but believe me it is practical politics and you may well stumble on something really great.

If I were you I would keep in very close touch by letter with Fröhlich and Huang [Avadh's PhD supervisor and a colleague respectively in Liverpool]; write

> them fairly frequently and find out what they are doing. Don't forget this job puts you on an equal footing with a great many important people, with whom you are possibly already slightly acquainted. Keep in touch with them – ask their advice, and so on. You can always dictate letters to me to save time and I can type.

All of this was very sound advice and probably helped Avadh think about how he could manage his career more actively. Helen told a friend later about the central role of Professor Fröhlich in Avadh's career: 'I don't think that Professor Fröhlich ever understood Avadh's complete devotion to him. To Avadh, he was his Guru, his great teacher, a person who, in Hindu lore, was to be respected and served even more deeply than one's parents.'

He also had a deep bond with his Chinese friend Huang, based on intellectual honesty. They had to break off their friendship, however, when Huang returned to China. At the time, both worked in nuclear physics and any contact between nuclear physicists from opposing nations was far too risky.

Helen finished her letter by saying:

> We can aim eventually to come to England if you like (naturally I would like) but what you do in the next year or two largely depends on how good a post you could get here – you never know, it might form a recommendation for something pretty good here.
>
> I have written so much and yet no word of love, but it is all love because all I am thinking about is you and how you can best order your life to do the best you can with it. I am full of joy to think we may soon be together.

On 7 February, she wrote again about Avadh's problems at the laboratory:

I realize how complicated is the problem you have to solve of your position in the laboratory, but unless you fight for what you want, I can quite see that you will be hopelessly squashed by the weight of Prof Cosmic Rays. Domineering people have to be very sharply dealt with, but it is surprising how they shut up when they find someone really tough opposing them. Of course, apart from any ability of yours, your position must be rather like that of a Londoner in the provinces – the provinces think that the Londoner is sophisticated and affected and the Londoner thinks the provinces are boors (which they often are). You have been brought up in a capital, which means you must have seen a whole lot more than Ahmedabadites, and I expect they view things in the same light as a Londoner. Wot a life, but never mind, love, we will walk up the avenue [a Judy Garland lyric] together and make them step in the gutter to let us pass before we are done! We shall hardly be able to complain that life is dull.

Except to see some Chinese films through the Anglo-Chinese friendship Society, I have not been to the pictures since you left. I can never sit long if I am worried and naturally I have been worried, but now I am more relaxed as I know that it is likely that we shall soon have a settlement, and even if we don't get one I can keep you if you come back here until you get a job, so perhaps I shall go one of these days.

It seems a dreadfully long time since I last saw you, although it is only seven weeks. I was thinking only today of our last evening together and the terrible fear in my mind that I would never see you again; that

> fear, at any rate, has gone from my mind. I know that I may have to wait, but one day I am going to be able to look at you again and feel my heart leap with the joy of it, and hold your hand and stroke your hair. To me these things are well worth suffering for and worth waiting for. You have given me so much happiness that you have made me greedy for more!
>
> Darling, if there are any formalities I should observe in the shape of gifts to people at our wedding, will you let me know. In this country a gift is given by the husband to his bride and to his bride's maids, and by the bride to her husband only. The bride also supplies at least some of the linen for the new home – which I shall do, although I am sad to say not very much. I hope your father will not be involved in a lot of trouble in the arranging of our wedding – I am touched that he should even interest himself in it.

On Thursday 2 February Avadh wrote again about his growing disillusionment with India.

> In certain ways, after seeing life in England, I feel in India, even though it is my country and I should do something to solve some of its problems, there is so much of peculiar relationships that, well, one has to do so many things which a really free-minded person will not do. I wonder whether my doing things at times which I do not like, will not produce in you some sort of hatred for me. As far as it is possible I must keep my head straight – but you know there is a proverb in our country that one might walk as carefully as possible through a coal mine but one is bound to get some black spots.

He was thinking more and more about leaving Ahmedabad and having his former professor in the United Kingdom help him find a job there. Helen sounds near breaking point with the stress of all the uncertainty but she replies on 8 February with a very well-reasoned argument.

> I think, Darling, that we should definitely come back to England as soon as you can get anything to do here. We can return to India in a few years time when all this has been forgotten. I had been told by Dr Chico [an Indian medical doctor and friend in England] since I sent the cable that I should find it hard to work because I was English, but another Indian told me quite casually that when he left India three weeks ago the Indians were so busy hating the Pakistanis that they would never bother their heads about an English woman!!
>
> If you think we could safely live together in Ahmedabad until September, perhaps I could find some work to do so as to swell our banking account. Don't spend much on clothes for me and don't buy another thing for the flat unless you feel we cannot live without it.
>
> Dearest, dearest I feel we must be married – that is why I am coming. If I come back to England with you, that will be all right in the eyes of my family and of the people amongst whom we should have to live in England. I adore you and I can't live without you.
>
> So now you are going to be quite a busy man for you have to do the following:
>
> 1. Try to make a reasonable settlement with Kashi.
> 2. If you can't, arrange for our marriage to be done quietly, so that Kashi's people do not know about

it, but tell your father – he has a right to know.

3. If we can live together in Ahmedabad, buy the least possible of anything. If we can manage without going to the hills, all the better.
4. See if you can arrange provisionally two cheap passages to England in September.
5. If in a last resort I must stay away from you, find me the cheapest clean accommodation you can in Bombay, and I will try and get a job there – but marry me first!!!

Dearest, don't you think it is time you wrote to Kashi's father direct, ignoring Kashi and her mother, and ask when he could see you? Also, would it not be best to talk to your father yourself instead [of through your brother]?

Avadh wrote a long and gloomy letter on 4 February. A settlement with Kashi and her family seemed ever more remote, he said. Kashi's mother had made it very clear that she did not want the marriage to break up and the atmosphere was highly charged. He remained concerned that Helen might face prejudice in India because of the situation, and perhaps even violence against her.

Avadh's family continued their support, including his sister and brother-in-law, who lived a thousand miles from Delhi and were not otherwise very involved in the events at the family home in Bulandshahr. They offered their home as a temporary refuge for Helen until things calmed down, if necessary. Avadh's brother-in-law also agreed to lend Avadh £45 and Avadh's father gave him a gift of £30, which Avadh planned to forward to Helen. His Doctor Brother in Delhi was continuing the negotiation on Avadh and their father's behalf but thought that their father needed to be consulted again before Helen left England.

Meanwhile, Avadh's resolve was growing stronger: 'Don't think that I am getting fed up with the fighting – I am prepared to fight with all my might.' At the same time, he had never expected the situation to get this bad and wondered if he had blundered in his approach. He knew of another similar situation that had gone much more smoothly. He told Helen again that if matters were not settled within a month, he would start looking for a post in England, taking British citizenship, if necessary.

Of course, the problem was that he and Helen could not be married in England while he still had a wife in India. She replied with a long, thoughtful letter, dated 9 February.

> I am glad you told me precisely what has been happening, because although the news is bad I would rather have accurate information than none at all. I am sorry, darling, that you are having such a rough time trying to get me to India, but I think we shall manage it in the end.
>
> Darling, don't be in too much of a hurry to resign from your job, because life will be very much easier for both of us if you can keep it. Don't think I am trying to avoid my promise to work for you in England if need be, but I do not feel that we should give in to the enemy too easily. I am sure Fröhlich could find you a job at pretty short notice, if need be and the Ministry of Supply are always looking for physicists of one kind or another. Moreover, as I said before, we should not starve if I had to be the wage earner for a little while, so I would say to you, 'Carry on, making the best success of your job that you can, for the time being.'

She then commented on what would happen if any harm came to her in India; this letter would cause considerable controversy when Avadh received it.

> It would not be quite the same thing as hurting an Indian lady. I do not lose my British nationality when I marry you and can demand protection from the British government if I am hurt whilst in in India.
>
> If a Conservative government gets into power on February 23, my father can pull endless wires to bring intolerable pressure to bear on the Indian government if his daughter is hurt. This means that the Indian government must, to save their face take some action, which means that what might have gone through small courts in Ahmedabad as an ordinary case of assault, becomes an insult to the British Crown to be wiped out by the Indian government with blood, sweat and tears – they would not get away with small fines. They might succeed in hurting me, but by God, they would wonder what had hit them if they did. England still has far too much power indirectly over the Indian government, but in cases like this it is extremely useful. Perhaps this small point has not occurred to their hot heads. An English Conservative government would simply rejoice at such an opportunity to show up the inefficiency of the new Indian government and prove how dreadful a state India is in since the British Raj ceased to rule. They would know perfectly well that the Indian government is doing very well, but such pro-British propaganda would never go un-neglected!

It is interesting that Helen thought that her father had so much influence. Because he worked for the City of Liverpool, albeit in a junior position, he may have had some contacts that at least would have helped him get attention and he might have been able to contact some of his very old friends as well in such a situation.

Avadh was a keen supporter of Indian independence, achieved just three years earlier, following two hundred years of British domination, and, while hardly a radical or even a very political individual, he had taken part in the peaceful protests led by Mahatma Gandhi. Helen assumed there would be some residual British influence in India but Avadh was quick to defend his new nation. As he explained to her in his reply of 14 February, this was a very sensitive subject.

> Well, darling, you have said something in your letter about what one could do to protect and avenge if on your coming there was some unpleasantness. One could do these things no doubt, but for that even Indian law will be most sufficient. And, once we have been hurt, all the revenge combined will not help us out.
>
> Of course you did not mean to create such a situation. But you know I love you so much, yet I was grieved a bit when you talked of British hold over India. I know that British might have some indirect hold over us, but I would hardly like to invoke that influence in India as an individual either for you or for myself. Because that would only mean that people in India would hardly like us. I do love you in a way as I have never done before but love could foster only in equals, as you yourself had said once. I know that I have harassed you and troubled you, and you must be feeling terribly upset, but I could do only my best, and that I can assure you I am doing. I hope you will forgive me if I have given you my reaction but it did grieve me very much, the idea of working the nations for our personal purposes.

Helen was quick to retract in her letter of 15 February.

> I must apologize for my remarks regarding protection from the British government. I did not intend them to be read quite in the sense in which you read them and if such remarks hurt I am terribly sorry. All I meant to convey was that I have, in addition to the protection of one government, also the protection of the second, my father being able to influence the second. The result would be bound to be a lot more fuss if I was hurt than if an ordinary Indian was hurt, since two lots of police would be demanding explanations instead of the usual one. Since father could influence governmental quarters here, they are bound to ask the Indian government for an explanation, just as they would do so if I was to marry a Frenchman and was injured in France. The fact that England is more closely tied up with countries in the Empire than outside of it means that her requests receive more attention in the Commonwealth countries than even say, a Spanish or Portuguese request would have. I did not mean to be hurtful in the least, and I hope you will forgive me.

It was a rare misjudgment by her of the cultural and personal sensitivity of Indians in general, and Avadh in particular, towards the lingering role of Great Britain in India, but both ended up apologizing to each other once they had explained their mutual positions.

*

On 10 February Helen wrote about more mundane matters:

> I have caught a cold from Avril and lost my voice. I am not very ill, don't think that; anyway I looked

> round the house for some medicine to help my voice and found a big bottle of black stuff of which I drank a tablespoonful. I thought I had been shot – I could feel it burning inside and fled to Mother, thinking I had drunk weedkiller at least. She roared with laughter. I had just taken a far too big dose of quinine and licorice, but in about five minutes my voice literally boomed out – I sound just like a boy of about 15 years whose voice is breaking, and every time I speak people giggle. I laughed so much at myself that I am nearly speechless again. I thought, 'this will be the day Avadh will ring me up because my voice is a dreadful roar and I shall not be able to answer him!'

On 12 February, she wrote:

> I've read over again this morning your letter of February 4th in which you tell me how Kashi's people do not want a settlement. I feel sorry for Kashi because, in a different marriage, she might have been very much happier but there is not much chance of really deep happiness where a marriage is 'arranged'. How can God's Laws of natural selection choose to possibly act in such circumstances? However, nobody wishes her to be happy more than I do and anything I can do to help her I will do – except lose you!

Helen's comments on arranged marriages are perhaps not surprising for an Englishwoman of her generation but later she accepted the idea and came to think of them as an equally good way to find a match as Western methods.

In a letter dated 6 February, Avadh reported:

> It is just today that I have heard a bit of hopeful news from Delhi. It appears that Kashi's mother threatened legal action to which my brother replied that I will be prepared to grant to Kashi whatever maintenance was in law. I do not know how much it is, but my brother is consulting my younger brother Kailash who is a lawyer and it is likely I may have to go towards the end of this week or early next week to finalize the settlement. But don't begin to have too much hope till the matters are finally settled. The terms of the settlement will be that I will pay the maintenance set in the terms provided they create no untoward scenes on your arrival or afterwards. I hope everything comes off all right.

Helen replied on 13 February:

> It would be as well if I could earn until we have paid our debts, but I will see what the situation is when I arrive. I do not want to have to work all day, if I can avoid it, as it will make me tired and old and irritable, none of which I want to be, but I will do it if it does not look as if we are in a pretty sound position. If all goes well and I come to you, I vote we do a couple of years in Ahmedabad, pay our debts and try and save some money and then you look for a post in England or America, because having held your post for a couple of years you will have gained in experience and it will sound well when applying for a post in the Occident, so that you will stand a better chance.

Avadh complained about the corruption and inefficiency in the Indian Government and the thriving black market and he wrote: 'I will tell you an example of the black-marketing here. Wheat, sugar and rice are rationed. You go to ration shop – you will be refused at times because they say they haven't received the quota. You go out in the open market, know a few people, and get things in any amount you like – if you are willing to pay double the price.'

Of course, this also happened during rationing in England, where black marketeers (commonly known as 'spivs') helped to supply goods that were rationed or in short supply. Such stock was said to have 'fallen off the back of a lorry'. Helen expressed concern about the impact of corruption.

> It seems rotten that such a big country should have such corruption, but it is bound to be so in these beginning days; only many years of government will make it any better and the government will have to be much stronger than it is before it can start stamping it out. I only hope that we can survive amongst it with some moral principles still intact. Of course, crime flourishes in England at present, but we have a fairly incorruptible police force which is a great help. Once the police are corrupt one is really sunk. The courts, too, are largely not corrupted.
>
> The news in the papers here is absolutely horrifying – all about poisoning all life on earth, hydrogen bombs, murder and sudden death – makes me want to start living quickly, but it is surprising how one survives to live again.
>
> On Wednesday I start my new job. I shall be dealing largely with the food trade and we'll be talking to canners all over Lancashire and Cumberland, so I hope to find some interest in it. It is one of those jobs where a mistake may cost hundreds of pounds, so for heaven's sake keep your fingers crossed for me and whisper any spells you know – although the best

spells you know will have to be whispered when I come to you!

I hope your brother was not offended at my writing him – I am apt to forget that he is not an Englishman and it might be rather shocking to him, but if he is anything like you he is pretty good – you scamp.

Ever your loving,
Chutney

This is the first of many letters in which Mum referred to herself as 'Chutney', a name my dad coined for her since, he said, she brought sweetness and spice into his life.

Chapter Eleven

Sometimes I wonder how on earth I lived before I met you. To every day have a sweet letter in my hand and the knowledge that someone loves me enough to risk all they have for me is a very marvellous thing to me, and I do hope that all my days I shall not be a disappointment to you.

In his letters of early February 1950, Avadh sounds more confident that he can deal with the politics at the laboratory and that if he does sufficiently valuable research, all will turn out well professionally. He also makes a valiant effort to lighten the tone of the conversation with Helen, talking about the cinema and his efforts at teaching the new cook he had hired to prepare meals. While reading P. G. Wodehouse's *Carry on Jeeves*, he muses that Jeeves, the resourceful butler, might have been able to help him sort out his problems! All his life, Wodehouse would remain one of Avadh's favourite authors.

On 9 February, Avadh wrote, 'Round about this time must have been the day when I had the pleasure of first seeing you, though probably not actually talking to you.

That was about 20th March last year. You had asked about a ring – well if the matters don't get settled soon, I will send it to you – the cheapest that could be available – because I might be wanting money for other purposes.'

For all his love for Helen and the romantic way he often expressed himself, he did not appreciate the importance of an engagement ring in the West. She reminded him on several occasions, and even explained to him how significant it was. On 14 February, she wrote:

> People still think I have been jilted and some are not too kind about it. Their opinions are confirmed by the fact that I do not wear an engagement ring, which means that in law I am not engaged at all. This absence of a ring means also that any man is free to ask me to go about with him (which they do ask at times) and are quite hurt when I refuse, since apparently there is no reason for the refusal. You will think me quite crazy that I ask you to send me a ring all the way from India when I could easily buy one myself, but an engagement ring must be the gift of the man and it is always an Englishwoman's most treasured possession because it is his gift. She will cling to it when all her other goods are gone, as it is the visible sign that someone loves her well enough to marry her.

She also explained to him about the significance of the date 14 February, which he would not have known.

> Thank you for all the kisses in yours of 9th – it was appropriate that it should arrive today, as it is the feast of St Valentine, patron saint of lovers, and on that day a man may express his affection of a girl he hardly

knows (or a woman affection for a man) by sending a pretty card with little verses of love in it. It is a nice custom, so having all those kisses today was very nice indeed.

Dearest one, I am hoping every day for news and yet I don't want you to feel that I am harassing you, because I am quite safe really for the moment. It is only that I want to be with my favourite devil, and that I have intolerable memories of seeing my loved ones go away and never come back, so that the fear is with me all the time that something might happen to you. Take care of yourself, my own love, my true love, my one love.

Ever and ever your beloved,
Chutney

On 18 February, Helen wrote about her daily routine, and for once her loneliness spilled over:

Here I am actually by myself for once and it is almost too much for me. There were no letters yesterday and none this morning, but I had such a spate of them at the beginning of the week that it would really be wrong to expect any, but such is woman that she is always hoping for more! How on earth you manage to express so well all you feel in a language alien to you is beyond my comprehension – I hope for the day when I can say to you all those things in Hindi, but in the meantime you must put up with English.

After I had posted it, I thought my letter yesterday sounded very depressed, but you must forgive me if it did, because I did not mean it to be so. All the uncertainty makes me depressed, but I'm really not coming to any serious harm as my days are absolutely fully occupied and I am earning my living all right. You will see what an iron circle of activity I am bound up in when I tell you how my day is spent. I get up at 6:45 AM, wash and dress and have my breakfast and sometimes do some odd job for mother. At 7:50 AM I go to work where I arrive at 8:30 AM and I work from then until 12:30 noon without a break. 12:30 to 12:45 wash and make up my face, 12:45 to 1:00 PM lunch, 1 PM to 1:30 write to you (half a letter). 1:30 PM to 6 PM work without a break. 6 to 6:30 finish letter to you. 6:30 to 7:15 travel home. 7:15 to 8 PM dinner, 8 PM to 9:30 PM wash dishes, wash or iron clothes for the family. 9:30 PM fill hot water bottles, make tea for family, wash myself, put clothes ready for the morning, brush my hair and into bed at 10:30 PM.

This never-ending circle goes on without a break, except on Wednesday when I go to Mrs Lewis's [Avadh's former landlady in Liverpool] for the evening and on Sunday evening I generally go to the British Council dance. On Saturdays and Sundays, of course I work in the house or go on duty at the British Council. You will see that I have no time of my very own, but I try and do a little Hindi if I am quicker at a job than I expected to be and sometimes I do a bit in bed, but this week I have not done a damn thing, but I might get a chance tonight. Sometimes I simply long to sit down in front of the fire and read without interruption or just sit and do nothing for a little while – in India I think I might get a chance to do so just occasionally. You can imagine with an itinerary like that outlined above what trouble I used to get into when I dropped my work to come out with you – I used to think I should never be able to go to bed at all some nights,

> but it was worth it and the time with you was doubly dear because it was stolen time.

She continued, reminiscing about their stay at Mrs Penny's bed and breakfast in the Lake District the previous summer:

> I often wonder if we could ever live in such a beautiful place – perhaps when we are old, we could buy a little tiny house in a beautiful place and make up for the years one has to spend in ugly places. It is funny, you are the only person I can possibly imagine living the whole of my life with and being happy. The thought of being young with you is full of joy, of being middle-aged and having children is full of charm and of being old and welcoming our grandchildren and our old friends to some little home of ours is surely something delightful.

The vision of their future that Helen outlines in this letter is heartrending for me, particularly with regard to welcoming grandchildren, because Avadh would miss meeting his first grandchild, Stephen, by nine months. She continued:

> I always have a feeling that when the passions of our lives are over, we shall still love each other intensely and be strong in our unity. Now you will think I'm being solemn and that won't do it all – I'm sure chutney was never meant to be eaten solemnly, but to be so hot that it made you jump – well I am sorry I am too far off to make you jump, but I hope I shall be with you soon and we can share our pickles forever after.
>
> By dint of reading on the buses and trains I have

nearly finished the four Indian books that I got from the library and I shall go next week and get some more. I can honestly say I have enjoyed them all and hope to read a lot more, now that I've found out where to get them. I feel the more I read the better I shall understand people when I get to India and the less likely I shall be to let you down, but I wish I could get some translations of up-to-date Indian novels and other books, but Tagore seems to be the limit of the fiction side of our libraries.

Take very good care of yourself, my treasure, and whatever you do, do not neglect your meals. Napoleon said that an army marches on its stomach – and that applies to us too. A man with an empty tummy is no good to anyone.

*

Around this time Avadh began formulating what he called a 'wicked plan' that Helen could come to India and they could get married in a semi-secret way with only one of his brothers present. Helen could take a job in Bombay and they would live apart until the issues with Kashi were settled. However, in his letter of the morning of 15 February he wrote in despair that there was still no news from his brother and he felt utterly trapped. Of course, Helen coming to Bombay was a flawed plan because it would mean both of them would have to find new jobs if they subsequently decided to live in England, whereas at that time she already had a good one.

Moreover, he wrote that his father, who had been so supportive, seemed to be wavering: 'In a very subtle way, my father has suggested that it would be welcome if I changed my mind. Of course, he only harps on Vijay and says that if he lived with me (at this time) he will certainly bring some life into my otherwise dull life. Well, I don't know what he means by it. Because of all this I feel so stupid that I can't even write good letters to you.'

At this stage, Kashi and Vijay were still at the family home in Bulandshahr, near Delhi. In the afternoon of the 15th, Avadh received a letter from his Doctor Brother saying that Kashi's mother now appeared to be amenable to an agreement. His heart 'leaping with joy', Avadh wrote to Helen outlining a detailed financial plan. When he was absolutely sure of the settlement, she was to come to India by sea, the cheaper alternative. He would send her the £75 his father and brother-in-law had given him, with which she could repay John. By the end of February, he hoped to have £98 in the bank out of which he would send £13 to Kashi, leaving enough that he could perhaps send a further £25 to England and still maintain an emergency reserve. If Helen sold a radio he had left behind as well, she could pay down her life insurance debt.

At last my dad could see light at the end of the tunnel, and thought he could see a path through their financial minefield as well. Helen replied to him on 20 February:

Dearest one,

Today came three letters from you, a love letter of 14th, a proper wail of woe of 15th and your later one of 15th telling me the good news. The first one delighted me, the second nearly made me weep with utter despair and the third one filled me with hope again. (I always look at the postmarks on your letters and read them in datal order!)

I feel as if I have suddenly woken up after a most horrible nightmare and can see the light peeping through chinks in the curtains to comfort me. I know we have got lots of battles to fight yet, but slowly we shall get ourselves into a strong position, so that we can take a strong financial blow without worrying very deeply and then we will get a little home together. I feel we can do quite a lot once we can settle this sad business over Kashi. Although it means that I shall not see you for another fortnight, I shall be so glad to get onto a ship, go to my cabin, lay my head on the pillow and rest for several days. At this moment I do not feel that I have any strength left to cope with any change in my life without first resting a little. I have kept on my feet and have not been taken ill, but the strain has been so great that, like you, I am feeling the effects. We shall have to be a little patient with each other at first and, although you will not have the rest of the sea voyage, I will try and make you well when I come.

I will have an orgy of stitching on your clothes as soon as I've got the flat into some semblance of order – it is a thing I always itched to do when you were here, but could not really do it – short of stripping you in public and sitting down there and then with my needle! I hope very much my sewing machine has not been broken in transit.

All my love,
Your favourite trouble and strife,
Helen

The phrase 'trouble and strife' puzzled Avadh so she had to explain in a later letter: '"Trouble and strife" is just London slang for "my little wife". They always talk about "my trouble and strife" or "my old Dutch" when they mean their wife. It is a peculiar rhyming slang about which I must tell you one day.'

Negotiations continued to the point where Avadh believed

there was some sort of agreement, but his father and brother had not yet given a green signal for Helen to come.

> I think all my family can be trusted now. They will act only in our best interests. So, darling, be patient, just very patient, and in the meantime, take best care of yourself.
> I am sorry that I have given you a slightly wrong notion of the attitude my father is adopting and will adopt. He will help me financially or otherwise – in anything – though he will have every sympathy and love with us, he does not want to show that he has been, in any way, instrumental in forcing Kashi out. I think we should not grudge that, because he feels that he brought Kashi for me and this is the only way he can remain friends with Kashi's people. Well, I suppose it is all right. Do not write to him just at present – there is not enough space here to explain – but he does not want to have any proof against him that he conspired with me to have you – although no doubt without his active help things would have been much more difficult. Of course, once you come, you become as much a member of our family as anyone else.

*

On 21 February, Helen wrote about women in the world of work. Millions of women had worked during the war and although many were laid off when men returned to take up their old jobs again, a substantial number remained. Some companies had what were known as 'marriage bars', which prevented women from working after marriage: it was assumed that the husband would support them so they did not need jobs. Lloyds Bank had a marriage bar until 1949 and the BBC had one from 1932 to 1944. However, the times were changing fast, and women were beginning to enter higher education in greater numbers than ever before, and to expect a certain amount of career satisfaction from their jobs. It was 1970 before the Equal Pay Act was passed in Britain, stating that men and women who did the same job should receive the same remuneration, but Helen sometimes complained about inequities she encountered in 1950.

> My present job is keeping me very occupied, but I like it. The customers are on the whole very pleasant with me and give me the same respect that they gave my predecessor, who was a man. Even now in England one has to fight quite a lot of prejudice against women in the business world, although it is getting less every year. Indian women have yet to really start going through the mill in this respect. There is a great deal to be said for the complete freedom of women and I do firmly believe that they should be free to earn their living as they wish, if they wish to, but one does have to pay for it by taking responsibility, accepting insults and losing something of one's feminine gentleness.
>
> You will wonder why I am talking about this, but really I am only gossiping to you and it is something which has come to the front of my mind during the last few days since having to handle big businessmen. One can tell in a minute by the way these men treat you whether they are men who got rich quickly during the war or whether they had been in business for generations. The latter ones are always courteous and polite because they are very proud of their firms and the old names these firms bear. The others don't care twopence.

Left: Elizabeth Ann Huband, Helen's grandmother, wearing her widow's cap. Below: Helen, aged 6, with her doll. *Bottom left:* Helen's father, Paul Huband. This was the photograph of him that Helen always had on show. She did not display one of her mother. *Bottom right:* L to R. Helen's Grandmother, Helen, Fiona and Alan on a visit to Ludlow racecourse.

Right: Helen, 1940. This photograph was taken shortly after the news that her first fiancé, Harry, had been killed: 'the eyes have no laughter in them because there was none in me.' *Below:* Helen around 1943 possibly in Princes Park, Liverpool. *Opposite:* Helen around 1943, now with some of the laughter in her eyes returned.

Top: Helen arrives in Bombay; the grainy photo conveys the sense of anticipation. *Left:* Avadh 1949, the Lake District, near the spot he formally proposed. *Bottom:* Helen and Avadh, May 24th 1950, their wedding day.

Left: Helen, laughing, at home in Ahmedabad. *Below left:* Helen, cleaning lentils in their Ahmedabad flat. *Below right:* Avadh, at home with his beloved pipe.

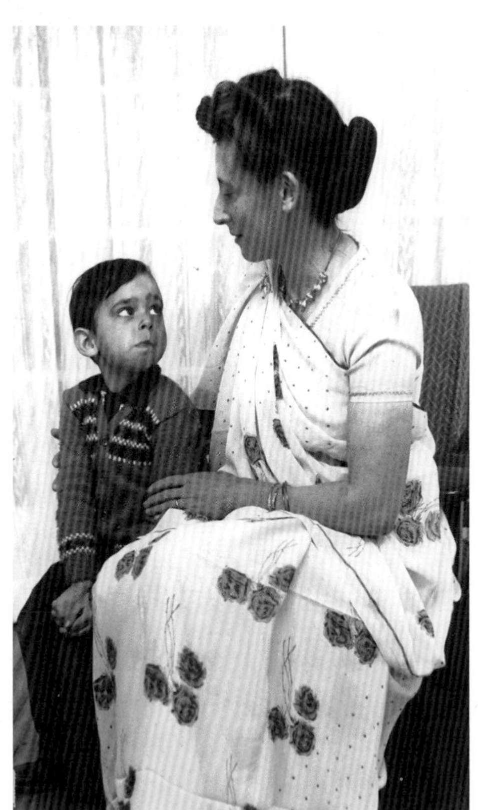

Left: Helen and Robert, 1959, at home in Edmonton. This photo was taken on first publication of *Thursday's Child*. Helen wears the traditional Indian sari. *Below:* Robert 1962, almost seven years old. *Bottom:* Avadh and Helen at home in Edmonton around 1982. Avadh would pass away two years later.

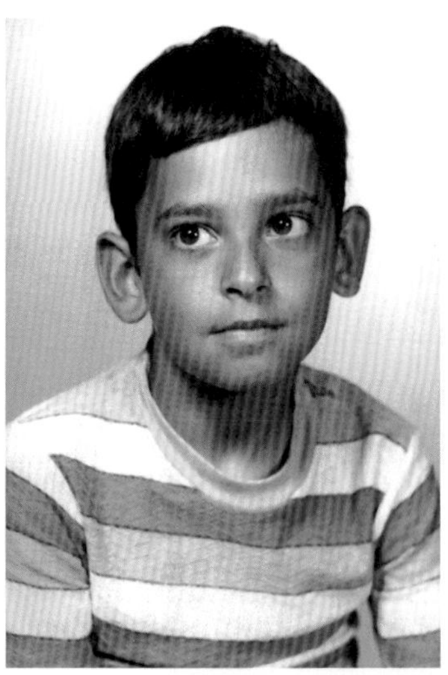

Above: Helen at her desk, Edmonton 1987. *Below:* Helen with her grandchildren, Stephen and Lauren, 1993.

Helen, at the University of Liverpool, receiving her Honorary Doctor of Letters, 1988. Helen was particularly proud of this honour.

> Although I find interest in this work, I shall drop it like a hot brick the moment I can come to you, because then I shall have a job to do in which my whole heart is – I only hope I can do it well.
>
> I was awfully pleased when you said you had started to work seriously – I felt that you were not worrying quite so much. I know you can produce some very creditable stuff, given peace of mind to work with, and I am positive that you are by far the most knowledgeable man in India at present on your subject. I do hope I shall get to India in time to type your thesis, but if I don't manage it, do have it typed by someone good, even if you have to pay a goodly sum to have it done well. A beautifully set out paper always gathers more approbation then a messy one and I know what a mess some typists can make of papers.
>
> Mother asks to be remembered kindly to her future son-in-law. I might add that you meet with her approval. I am going to get into trouble with [her] tonight, as I shall be so late home from work, but I could not write any of this letter during my lunch hour as I was too busy to take a full hour and just stopped to eat a little and wash my face. Mother has forgotten the days when she used to write reams to my father when he was fighting in Russia!!
>
> Darling, what fun it would be to have a really good giggle and laugh together. I feel as if I have been solemn far too long and need a jolly good spanking.

It's obvious that Helen's relationship with her mother had improved markedly since the old days. Both of her parents genuinely liked Avadh and treated him with respect, although they must have shared in Helen's frustration over the delays to their marriage plans. When she did finally leave for India, Helen wrote regularly to her mother for the rest of her life.

*

On 17 February, Avadh wrote as usual despite having little news. He said he was going to try to have an informal discussion with the director of the laboratory about his ongoing professional concerns and he professed his love for Helen: 'My love for you is as great as the Himalayan mountains – though I wonder whether I will give you that much happiness and protection as it does to its people.'

She replied on the 23rd: 'You say you cannot always manage to say in English the words of love which you would like to say, but nobody has ever written to me such beautiful letters as you write to me and I treasure them – I have them all – yes I have.'

In this letter she wrote about the general election in Britain, which was taking place that day:

> Nobody in this country really wants the Conservatives to rule us again, but we are so afraid of the Labour Party opening the door to a Communist regime, which is completely against our way of life, that it is almost certain that the Conservatives will form the next government. It is better to have a Conservative government which we can bolt out of office again in five years than to have a Labour government who might change the constitution and make way for a Communist dictatorship. This is written on polling day and as soon as this letter is finished I shall go and vote; it will be interesting to see if my forecast that the Conservatives will get in with a narrow majority is right. We shall know tomorrow.

In the event, Clement Atlee's Labour government was re-elected by a majority of just five seats over Winston Churchill's Conservatives. In office they continued the campaign of nationalization that had seen the creation of a National Health Service in the postwar years, but Helen's fears of a Communist dictatorship, common to many in this Cold War era, were not realized.

On 19 February, Avadh wrote in response to Helen's explanation about the significance of an engagement ring, but the message was not yet getting through to him.

> Darling I am sorry that sometimes you are embarrassed when someone asks you for an evening out. I do not know the English ettiquette [*sic*] (I don't know the correct spelling) but if you know such a person fairly well to be your friend, you can go out with him. I mean as a friend, without the word 'boy'. I would not mind it, though, of course, if I saw and knew, probably I would feel it; but then I am a reasonable person. Do as you please; all I tell you is that I still love you and need you.
>
> Darling, if you like I can buy a ring and send it to you – or you can buy it on my behalf and put it on. Don't buy a very expensive one, but one which could serve your purpose.

She replied on the 24th, spelling it out for him in black and white:

> It is really very trying with one's heart in one place and one's body in another but I hope that Dr Bhatia will be able to sew them together again one of these days – what do you think?

> The English etiquette about engagement is this. When a couple agree to marry at a future date, the man gives the girl a ring to wear on the third finger of her left hand. Seeing this, no honourable man will ask any favours of her, such as to go out with her, although he will, of course, talk to her quite freely if he knows her. In law, she is engaged and has a definite status in court. If no ring is given, she is not formally engaged. She has no status in law and any man who can persuade her away from her fiancé, should he wish to do so, is quite at liberty to try. Of course, it would be a waste of time for any man to try and persuade me away from you, but occasionally people do ask me out, etc. I do not want to go out with them – nobody is of any interest except you, so, of course, I do not go. If John and his wife or Ronald [Helen's second fiancé's brother] and his wife asked me it would be different as they have wives with them. But enough of that. I don't need a ring yet. One day, when we are out of debt you shall buy one for me, just for the love of me.

When she finally arrived in India, Avadh presented Helen with a beautiful gold engagement ring with a ruby and two small pearls. She treasured it always.

*

On 25 February, Helen wrote about her continuing experiments with Indian cooking.

> I am writing this letter with one eye on the oven. I am having a second try at making bread without yeast. I think one cannot buy yeast in a country like India where no beer is made to produce the yeast. The first loaf I made was so flat that even the ducks to whom I fed it

had difficulty in eating it! Next weekend I want to try and make an Indian lentil dish of which I have the recipe, but it is not easy to experiment in a house full of people like ours!

You have no idea how concerned I am about keeping your tummy full. Is there, do you think, in Ahmedabad a really clean shop where I might buy meat or fish occasionally until I have learned enough Indian dishes that we need not bother? I have to think that I must know a minimum of 14 Indian dishes at least, to be able to give you at least different meals every day for a week, meals that are nourishing too. I am so thrilled with the idea of keeping house for you and of having you snuffing around the kitchen to see what's cooking. I want to be a good cook. I have just taken the bread out of the oven and I think it is right this time!

On the 26th, she reported the unfortunate, but not surprising, results. Indian bread cooked in a Western oven is doomed to failure.

You will be amused to hear that the bread I turned out yesterday was not right but I know one can make it without yeast so I shall try another method. Father teased me dreadfully about it when I fed it to the ducks. He swore that their stomachs were dragging along the ground with the weight of it!

Once she was in India, Helen learnt to make excellent *rotis* on a brazier and, later, a gas stove.

Avadh, too, wrote about food. First he reassured Helen:

Is it possible that I will not be eating to my heart's content [when you are here]? I am all the time

> instructing the servant to cook things without putting any hot stuff so that you may find the least difficulty with coping with Indian food. In fact, the cooking of vegetables in this flat is hardly any different than English cooking. There is some difficulty about the English type of bread, as I do not know how to make it. But we shall get it from the market so long as you are not in a position to make it at home. Eggs also we can get in plenty, there being no ration on them and they cost only two shillings and threepence a dozen [in England they were four shillings and a penny, almost twice the price]. The only point on which I have not been able to make any headway is meat, since I do not know how to cook it and the servant does not take it. But I know that one can get mutton (goat's meat) which they say tastes similar to beef which of course is difficult to obtain [because Hindus believe cows to be sacred animals]. In summer months, one should try to take meat only occasionally. We will always be able to make several types of English sweets which as you know I like much more than Indian types. We will have to get an oven.

In reply to her letter about the difficulties of breadmaking without yeast, he wrote:

> What do you mean when you say in India we don't get yeast – everything rots here, even the human brain – and so yeast is plentiful. Your ambition to know 14 Indian dishes is very high. All you should aim is a) to be able to occasionally make chapattis, b) Lentil Soup, c) Any vegetable soup (Indian style), d) Frying vegetables (All vegetables are cooked in the same style.), e) pancakes, (f) poached – fried – eggs, (g) some types

> of English sweets, and then you will find me dancing around you in a mood to kiss you. You can get meat in Ahmedabad – I don't know how they keep it – but I won't advise you to go alone in that market; either we could go together sometime or the servant could bring us.

And on 27 February he wrote to Helen about a stroke of luck.

> You know my servant, I asked him in joke whether he will bring meat from the market and whether he eats it. I had expected that he will jump simply – but he said that he has cooked it before and knows how to cook it (only he does not eat it). Of course, we will have to be miles away from egg or meat when my father or mother come – but otherwise I am much happier now that the servant will be able to bring it from the market and cook it, if necessary, for us. The market is 2½ miles [4 km] from here; and though all the other provisions one can get nearby, not meat.

He worried that Helen might find life as a housewife boring, and described his own domestic strengths and weaknesses:

> I forgot to write something very, very, very important that I have not yet polished my shoes a single time since I left England; it is a complete victory of mine – howsoever reluctantly you may admit – but my other clothes are pretty tip-top. Up till now I have been using winter clothing, but from about a fortnight, I shall have to use summer clothes. Unfortunately my younger brother robbed me of almost all cotton trousers, except

> four of them. I will have to get a few more soon, also some shirts.
>
> The second thing important is that besides keeping the lavatory, kitchen etc. clean, I also keep the flat practically free from flies by using Flit and DDT which I spray fairly often. You see, if once flies begin to sit, they make the ceilings and walls look very dirty. You see I am trying to keep the flat in such order that no damage is done to it and it is in a ready condition to be made comfortable by my expert, when she comes. All these things that I write to you are often trivial but beneath them my heart simply rages with the desire of seeing you soon.

DDT was widely used in the 1950s and it was only in 1962 that Rachel Carson's book *Silent Spring* began to raise the alarm about it decimating wildlife, particularly bird populations, and being implicated as a cause of certain types of cancer.

Avadh continued to waver on whether it would be better for him to move back to England. He still thought that there was more scope for career advancement in India and that if he moved back, he would 'have to give up the wild dreams of going "uppish"' but he added that it would be worth it so Helen could be in the environment in which she was most comfortable. He also commented, 'You seem determined to become a scholar of the Indian Religion, history and culture – rather awkward for me – never mind so long as you will not ask questions the answer to which you will get, "the day is glorious".' In other words, if she were to ask him too difficult a question, he would merely comment on what a wonderful day it was.

He also wrote in response to a question of hers about

whether kissing in public was frowned upon in India – it was, and still is. She replied:

> I should be tickled to death if when you meet me in Bombay you kiss me in public, because unless I remember I shall automatically lift my face to be kissed and you will automatically want to do it, but I will do my best to remember not to tempt you!
>
> Don't worry, I am not going to become a scholar of Indian religions, as you put it, only you will have learned so many things from childhood about which I know nothing at all, and only by reading about the beliefs in India, her fairy tales, etc., can I pick up the background which has surrounded you all your life. One example that I have learned is that asceticism is considered the thing which will bring you nearest to God and is, therefore, one of the highest virtues, whereas here we believe that good works will do more for you than anything else. By understanding this, quite a lot of pieces of the jigsaw puzzle suddenly fell into place, so for a little while, if you will forgive me, I shall read as many of your classics as I can lay hands on. I am very anxious, for example, that I shall not give an opinion in public which perhaps damns the dearest held beliefs of more orthodox Hindus – for the simple reason that I do not want to hurt their feelings or make you unpopular in consequence. The things I do for love of thee!

*

Throughout this period, Avadh's Doctor Brother was negotiating with Kashi's mother in Delhi. He tried to convince her to summon her husband in the hopes of finalizing a settlement around 4 March, when Avadh planned to visit for the festival of Holi. On 23 February Avadh told Helen that it would be best if she were not in 'daily waiting', but that he expected to have news around 6–8 March.

He wrote: 'I am going to Delhi on the eve of Holi – you know the festival in which we play with colours by throwing it on each other. I will miss you very much specially then, for I would have loved to see you in all coloured clothes from top to bottom. But that is impossible – but even in the entire gathering of my family, I shall feel lonesome and my mind will just run to you.'

Helen regretted missing the Hindu festival: 'I should simply have loved to have seen the Holi Festival – and now I have to wait a whole year – blow it. I hope your family dragged you out and made you have some fun. We shall be quite busy keeping the Hindu festivals and perhaps very quietly and unobtrusively the Christian festivals as well, although unless you wish it we will not keep the latter ones.'

Avadh wrote on the 24th that if no settlement could be reached at this meeting at Holi, either he would come to England where they would have to live together without being married – a fairly radical suggestion for the day – or Helen should come to India to be married under Hindu law and then they would return to England.

In a third letter on the 24th Avadh complained about life at the laboratory. He had received somewhat grudging approval to hire a student to help with his research but he complained:

> To get a thing done one has to go on asking shamelessly hundreds of times. Even to get books for the library, I had to ask one thousand times till I was fed up and I told them very frankly that this is not the way in which work is done. And then I was told very

apologetically that the list of books that I had given to them has been lost. And so here I am preparing a fresh list. I might not be very competent but if other people say a thing, they might as well see that it is done. Due to the adamant attitude of mine, I am sure to get the books for the library.

On Saturday 25 February, Avadh apologized for his suggestion that they could live together without being wed.

Darling in one of my earlier letters, I had implicitly asked you whether we could not live in England without proper marriage. That was in the sheer spirit of desperation and I do hope you will forgive me for it. I did not mean to hurt you by it.

My dearest love, I simply dream of the time when we could be together. For living with you, I have always dreamt of living in cooperation with one another in all aspects of life. For example, if you think I shall leave you alone in all the house affairs, you are grossly mistaken – of course you will have more time for it and aptitude but when I will come home from work, I shall always be with you poking my nose in everything that you will be doing – darling as I told you there will be no secrets between us – no watertight compartments for anything – of course subject to you having the same opinion. We shall both help each other in everything we do to the best of our ability. To give you an analogy, if you are cooking, say, anything, one hand holds the vessel while the other hand stirs it. Somehow my Indian mind would like to live with you in that sort of cooperation – but, of course, as I have said, if you will want to be left alone with any part of your work items, I will gladly

> (not really though) leave it entirely to you so far as I am concerned.

It's a lovely, very romantic analogy, and I wonder why Dad sometimes worried that he was not as loving in his letters as my mother deserved. He continued:

> Darling I love you in every aspect of your life, where there is love, there is poking of noses – for every affair belongs to one and the same heart. Everything is subject to your approval my love – but we should never try to draw barriers between us. If I do a thing that annoys you or makes you uncomfortable, you will tell me. I will do the same – otherwise there may arise a misunderstanding. This is particularly important between us for even though we love each other, trust each other and are determined to make each other happy and also understand each other – nevertheless, our minds at times because of different backgrounds may be working on different lines, and even though they may be working for the good of each other – yet at times it might become difficult to understand each other – unless explicitly mentioned. I hope you will remember this my darling – I bet you know all this – but I have just said it as it came in my mind.

Helen responded on 1 March.

> The only reason that I am anxious to marry you in law with all the legal trimmings is the fear that somewhere in the future, in this dreadfully disturbed world, we might get separated and, although governments are quite kind about getting husbands and wives put together again, they are not kind about people who

are not husband and wife. For example, if in England I am legally your wife you would never be turned out of England, even if all other Indians had to go, but if I could not prove I was your wife you could be turned out and I might not be allowed to go with you. It is that kind of thing of which I am afraid, so if no solution is reached at Delhi with Kashi's people, perhaps you would talk to your father and brother about how we could most cheaply be married and what it would then be best for us to do. When they have given their opinions we could have a good think about them and make a decision ourselves. But above all, you are not to distress yourself, because we will get out of this muddle, even if we are paying debts for three years to come. Mercifully none of our creditors would press us for the money, so that if we pay a little regularly every week, we would gradually get ourselves straight. If both of us were working in England, we could pay at least a pound a week in debts and probably much more, depending on rent, salaries etc.

You say perhaps you write things that hurt me, but you never do. The letters you write are the most beautiful expressions of love any woman could wish to receive and I treasure every one of them. No Englishman (at least very very few Englishmen) would ever bother to write as you do, and as I read your letters I am more and more glad that I'm going to marry you and nobody else. I love you for so many things that words cannot express them, but life has not been very gentle to me and Englishmen have forgotten how to be gentle to their womenfolk, so I appreciate your gentleness most. I also love the wickedness of you too! I am sure our lives will be full of the most peculiar situations and hazards, but being together I think we shall have a good joke over all of them no matter what happens to us.

Now to get down to business. You scamp, you scally-wag, you devil. Never cleaned your shoes in two and a half months! Oh you are naughty – just wait till I see you – I'll make you walk around with such a shine on your feet that all your friends will remark on it! I can see I shall spend my life chasing after you with a clothes brush, a needle, a flat iron and a shoe brush. You are incorrigible! Whatever will your mother say when she sees you?

Now I hope you will go to Delhi a little comforted and don't be afraid to tell me the worst if need be. If there is no other way of doing it, we shall just live together in England, but I hope that we may somehow be married. My heart is with you all the time – you stole it, you wretch – and only the body is not there.

Ever your adoring,
Helen

*

On 22 February, Avadh wrote again about domestic affairs.

Today I have spent some time in cooking – but I must warn you that you will have to learn to control your temper while explaining and taking work from the servant – he is providing me with a good exercise on control of tempers. Well, one thing I have cooked – I don't know how it will taste – take 1 pint of milk and 2 ounces of cornflour. Mix cornflour in 2 tablespoon of milk, thoroughly. Boil the rest of the milk, etc., etc., (Blancmange) you must be knowing how to make it. I wonder how it is going to taste.

Helen replied: 'We make blancmange exactly as you do only we put some sugar and vanilla essence in as well to make it tasty. It is very good and not easy to get just right, so I was surprised that you could make it.'

In a previous letter she had asked him why October was said to be the most dangerous month for catching illnesses in Ahmedabad when it was not by any means the hottest month. On 28 February Avadh explained:

> The weather mystery is like this – May is the hottest month – and very dry – in this season, what to say of human beings, even germs can't live. But from middle of June, temperature lowers a bit, rains set in and in September and October, it is moist heat – which is the root of all disease. We will have to be damned careful how we eat things. We cannot rely on servant but see ourselves that everything – vegetables etc. are washed properly with potassium permanganate – if eaten raw. Rules are not difficult to follow but they are essential in order to remain O.K. In Ahmedabad, the weather remains pleasant only in November, December, January, and February. But evenings say after 9 p.m. are usually always cool.

In order for Avadh to send the money he had promised Helen, he first had to satisfy the Bank of India that it was necessary to send the money abroad. Accordingly he asked Helen to follow a rather convoluted procedure:

> a) Give me the address of John. b) You impersonate yourself as John and write (typed letter on air sheet) stating that I borrowed from you (John) the sum of £75 (this is the amount I can share) in December and that you (John) will feel obliged if a speedy

> return of the loan is effected. This air letter will be from John although you might as well send. There is no use troubling him. But if you like you can ask him to do it – and tell him that it should be written to me as if I borrowed the money.
>
> I will get the permission for sending the money to him. If the permission is not granted, then we shall send the money by collecting British Postal orders of £2 every day for which no permission is necessary.

When Helen replied to this a couple of weeks later, she was obviously tickled by all the complications.

> You will have by now received a letter which I wrote as if I was John – I hope that sounds right! I was laughing all the time I was writing – I had to write it myself as I tried to get John on the phone three times but he was engaged. I will, however, just tell him that I had used his name because you want to send me some money and it will be quite all right. He is a good scout and as long as we don't land him in jail, he will not worry.

On 2 March, Helen wrote, knowing that Avadh would not receive her letter until after his return from the negotiations with Kashi's mother in Delhi. The wait must have been excruciating, but she managed to write in a positive tone.

> This letter will reach Ahmedabad after you have left for Delhi and when you come back and read it our future will have been decided, for better or for worse, but whatever the verdict is you are not to worry unduly because there are ways out, even if they are

somewhat expensive! It is when there is no way out that it is time to worry.

I was interested about staying at the hill station as long as possible. I do not know whether you must take all your holidays in May or whether they can go on into June, but I think I would like to see how long I can endure the heat and then go to the hill station when I cannot bear it any more (with you if possible). In other words, I would rather spend the end part of the very hot period in the hills than the beginning and have to come back before it starts to get a little cooler. I can often endure things quite a long time if I have something to look forward to and a definite date, so that I could say to myself, 'next week or the week after we shall go away' and so endure the interim period. Dr Chico said I should try to get a bit fat before I come to India and I will try to do so. On the voyage I will eat and rest a lot, and once I know I can come I shall be able to eat better here and will rest better. How about you in the great heat – do you think you will stand it all right?

Don't think I do not understand how a man's love of a woman is made up both of body and mind and spirit. I understand very well, my darling, because I love you too. You never hurt me darling and as for wanting to punish you – good God, do you think I am a sadist? All I ever worry about is not being able to share with you the immediate troubles that surround you, because I keep thinking to myself, 'I could have saved him that', or 'he should not have had to bother with this or that'. I appreciate how you are trying to take care of the flat – how good of you to wage war on the flies and other creeping things.

You know, it would be fun to try and write a book

together, even a detective novel!!! I am sure that in both our lives so much has happened to us that we must have the material for 20 books, never mind one. We could write one about India for example and sell it in England, and about England and sell it in India! I should like to do something that, when we were finished, we could say 'we did it together'.

A kiss on the tip of your nose.

All my love and devotion,

Ever your,

Helen

Chapter Twelve

> *I am thankful that my new job keeps me occupied to the utmost and I have no option but to concentrate really hard on it which means that at least 11 hours out of 24, I can't think much about what is happening to us, except sometimes it hits me suddenly.*

It was now two and a half months since Helen had seen Avadh, and her fate rested upon the crucial meeting between Kashi and Avadh's families in Delhi over Holi. Would Kashi's family accept a reasonable settlement? Would she soon be able to join her beloved fiancé in India? She wrote on 5 March:

> My own Darling,
>
> Today you will be home and I am wondering so much what sort of reception they have given you. I do so pray that they are being kind to you – somehow the fear of what you are going through far outweighs the fear I have of the decision which has to be taken. You are so precious to me that the fear of your being hurt either by word or deed troubles me greatly. Also

> the thought that I cannot write to you at Delhi. Still this torture will be over soon and then we shall be free to decide what we are going to do without consideration of people who do not deserve consideration.
>
> I was touched to the heart by the words you wrote about growing together until we were almost one person. I did not know a man could feel like that about his wife – I thought only women dream of these things, but I'll love being treated so and having someone whom I can trust. I have lived so many years inside myself that I can hardly believe that I shall soon be living with someone to whom I can talk freely. Usually such trust in this country is ruined by the criticisms of the families of both parties, but we shall be fortunate in a way that we shall be a fair distance from our people and can largely evolve whatever kind of life or thought in our home which makes us happy. Also we are both old enough not to be greatly influenced by other people.

She added a P.S.: 'I bet you did not even honour Delhi with clean shoes???'

On 2 March, the day before he was to leave for Delhi, Avadh received a letter from his father:

> in which for the first time he has mentioned that he himself has impressed upon Kashi's mother that she should come to an agreement and that she appears to be in a reasoning mood. This means that Father himself has spoken about it and I feel now that things will brighten up. Don't be angry if I write to you that it has really moved me seeing how my father has taken it and helped us. I had never expected it from him and I only hope we both are able to serve him a little and

> bring him some comfort, when he comes and stays with us.

Indian fathers had great authority, and Avadh's father commanded particular respect from his sons. His help meant a lot to Avadh and gave him hope for the days ahead. 'Don't worry about my Delhi visit,' he wrote to Helen. 'I will come out unhurt and probably with success. If I do succeed, of course, you will hear in two to three days after this letter reaches you.'

On the 3rd, Avadh wrote from the train, apologizing that although he had originally bought an ordinary second-class ticket for two pounds he had upgraded to a sleeper for an extra pound since it was so crowded. The 860-kilometre journey would take twenty-eight hours, so I'm sure Helen didn't blame him for the extra expenditure.

On the morning of the 4th he started another letter from the train and reported feeling much better after sleeping all night but the jolting of the train made his writing virtually illegible and after the first page, he gave up. He had already read two detective novels, he wrote, and the train was running an hour late.

Back in England, Helen was getting increasingly anxious:

> These waiting days while I know you are in Delhi are the longest days you can imagine. I do love you so and the longing to see you and touch you again is very great – sometimes I feel that even one more day is too long to have to wait! Mother has promised to telephone me if you cable home – she is very good. The whole family are anxious to see us happily settle – they realize the strain of being parted, but of course do not realize the further difficulties under which we are labouring.

She continued:

> I found one or two Indian recipes in a magazine, so I spent about a quarter of my lunch hour buying suitable spices, so that I could try them. The only two I lack now are cardamoms and cumin seeds, both of which I may be able to buy at Boots [the chemist] tomorrow. I shall not know for sure when I have cooked them whether the dishes are right or not, but I shall know if they are very badly wrong! It will do me no harm to experiment.
>
> If you don't hear from me for a day or two you will know that I have gone up in smoke with the hotness of the dishes which I am about to try and cook – see above. Looking at the recipe, it seems hot enough to need a fire extinguisher afterwards!
>
> It is funny how when you love somebody very much and are away from them, there is not much fun in anything you do – normally I would have loved experimenting with cooking these dishes, but I feel I want you behind me to pull my leg and tell me how horribly wrong I am and to stick your fingers in things and lick the spoon, etc. Cooking is not cooking without these embellishments! Anyway, if you have good news for me I shall be running round like a cat with two tails trying to get a passage, etc., so I shall not have much time to cook, and if the news is bad I shall still be running round looking for a place for us to live in here, because even if you did not come for several months, I should like to move in and get things started – I shall be a great deal happier if we can get married first though!
>
> Ever your adoring plague, nuisance and general entertainment,
>
> Helen

However, the next day she wrote of the lentil dish (dahl):

> Mother and I had it for supper and thoroughly enjoyed it – but this morning the fun began. The family nearly stuck us in a room by ourselves – because we simply reeked of garlic – I've laughed myself helpless today, they have been so funny about it, so we have decided that whilst in England – NO GARLIC! I shall have to find a Frenchman to dance with tonight – they are always bathed in an aura of garlic, so we shall not upset each other! The fact remains, however, that mother and I liked it very much. You are right when you say that frying the spices takes the bitterness away. Do people in India mind if you smell of garlic?? I hope not because the flavour is extremely good.

Avadh later replied with a piece of folk wisdom.

> Some families do use garlic in their cooking – in our family, it has never been used – e.g. my father etc. never take it. I have taken it several times; if one does take it, there is no doubt, everyone knows that someone has taken the garlic – if no antidotes are taken after the meal. After meals, one takes either betel or one other stuff – whose English name I do not know – which kills the smell of garlic in mouth. You naturally do not know these tricks – but if you have to take garlic or onions, you have to take antidotes – after the meal – a teaspoonful of *saunf* (Hindi name) [fennel seeds]. So much about lentils.

By 10 March, there was still no word from Avadh, and Helen was sounding desperate.

The dreadful silence of today – no letters, no nothing! I am praying that you are all right and that things are going smoothly for you. I keep imagining all kinds of awful things happening to you and yet I know that today is only the first day on which I could reasonably expect news, and yet I am tortured with fear for you. Being so far away makes it so difficult because I cannot lift up the telephone and enquire what progress is being made as I could if we were in the same country. Since all I can think about is your dear self going through hell on my behalf, I had better find something mundane to talk about, or you will think I have lost my nerve – which I haven't – but you know what it feels like!

Have I told you that Tony (my brother whom you met) is to announce his engagement to Anne (whom you also met at our house) on March 25th which is Anne's 21st birthday. All the family is very happy about it and I think they will be a happy couple. They cannot be married for a couple of years, but they can save and prepare for it, so I think they will be happy. [Her brother Alan had been married during the war and Brian the previous year.]

Dearest, I remember how [a year ago] this month you first asked me to have coffee with you at the British Council and afterwards we had our first date and how happy I have been since. Come what may, this has been a lovely year and I hope next year will be lovelier still. It is not a great deal to ask, to want to share one's life with someone whom one loves, but nobody is helping to make it very easy for us.

At last, on 10 March, Avadh sent a cable, which reached Helen on the 11th:

YOU ARE WELCOME BUT ACT AFTER RECEIVING MY LETTERS OF NINTH AND TENTH MARCH STOP WORRYING

It sounded positive but did not answer any of Helen's burning questions. She wrote immediately:

> I gather that no settlement has been reached but that I am to come – however, I await with anxiety your letters of 9th and 10th, as from the tone of the cable I feel that there are some difficulties. I am doing my best to stop worrying as you tell me! I am dying to know what is happening, but curiosity killed the cat and it might kill this little cat too, so wait with patience I must. But gosh, I shall be glad to have news.
>
> My own darling, all I can say is that I love you and I love you and I pray you have not been too much hurt at Delhi. I can't tell you how much afraid I have been in this past week, for you (if this letter sounds more than usually insane, it is because people are talking to me incessantly, although they can see I am writing!) I thought of everything from a train smash to a knife in your back and I don't read detective novels! Never mind, it will all be good exercise when we write our novel.
>
> I hope so much that I can come to you soon.

Finally, on 16 March, Helen received Avadh's letters of the 9th, 10th and 11th describing the negotiations in Delhi. He wrote long, rambling letters, as if trying to work out the solution to their problems as he wrote. All three of his brothers had been present, he said, as well as Kashi's mother. 'She now says that whatsoever my father will decide, she will accept it' – but he added that Kashi and her father would have the final say.

In a section that must have been difficult for Helen to read, he wrote that his brothers had made one final, last-ditch attempt to persuade him not to marry her.

> They said several points but one of them which I want to mention to you is that some people may not accept us in their society – of course a few always will. This I wanted to mention because this can occasionally mean a bit of company of ourselves alone for days, and you should be prepared for it. It may not happen but to some extent it will. Then the three brothers said I should think it over again but if I decided to call you, they would stand by me. I have told them that I have no intention of changing my mind.
>
> So we have to decide what we have to do. My Doctor Brother advised me that if I wanted to call you now I could do so and the matters with Kashi's people will get settled in due course. Of course, this has a disadvantage for if Kashi's people tried to be awkward, it will be very inconvenient to us, but I don't think they will be awkward.

Once again the decision was left in my mother's hands and once again she was quite clear about what she wanted to do. On 16 March, she wrote:

> I have thought all day about whether I should come to India or whether you should come to England, and I have decided that fundamentally I have no choice but to come to India, the reason being that it is the only possible way in which we can be legally married. If we are not married in India during the next three

or four months, we can never be married [unless and until Kashi granted Avadh a divorce]. I have made my decision and I hope it does not distress you very much, because I realize that you would like to come back to England and that you do not like your job very much.

With regard to all the various things we shall both have to face in India, they are all things which I have long since considered and feel we can get over them. The fact that some people will not want to know us fails to make me quail, as long as we can have a few friends, and we know we shall have at least one or two; in one's life one has to face many, many snubs. We are fortunate that moving in university circles there is always hope of meeting people of more advanced ideas than, say, in the business community. Secondly, the very deep change in my life I feel I can bear, as long as I can at least walk out each day a little. I should go mad if confined to a form of purdah.

When you consider my life in India, you work firstly on an assumption – you as a scientist should know that nothing should be assumed! You say you do not know how you are going to provide me with a life such as I have in England. That assumes, my heart, that I like my present life in England. Well I don't. I shall thank heaven to put up my legs mentally and physically a little, not to have to tear around, to be able to wear loose clothing, experiment with strange dishes, and learn a new language, watch a new world go by and try doing things I have never had time to do before, like spending an evening doing nothing but gossip idly, drawing, writing – and 101 other things.

The curious, the unusual have boundless fascination

for me and you will be surprised what interest I shall find for many years in a lot of things which you have taken for granted.

With regard to the heat, I shall endure as silently as I can, but if the language sometimes gets a bit 'Dockside' you will have to forgive me! If I get the April passage, I should arrive towards the end of the first week of May.

Ever your loving,
Helen

On 13 March, still awaiting receipt of Helen's confirmation that she was coming, Avadh wrote that he was in a balanced state of mind and trying to do some work. He was, however, dealing with another irritation. 'My servant who left four days before I left for Delhi, and though he was to go for a week, he has not yet returned. I wonder whether he intends to return and I had given him (on his request) two weeks pay in advance. It is damned inconvenient to me but it can't be helped, I suppose.'

> This evening I shall again write to you a long letter – yesterday (being Sunday) I spent almost the whole day in bed and that could be the reason I did not actually write to you – the true reason being that I had fallen temporarily in love with a 'Lady with Lucky Legs' [actually *The Case of the Lucky Legs*], a crime story by Erle Stanley Gardner right about the time I should have written to you. It is a very good story and I shall keep the book for you; though I think it will be suicidal for me – for you to get hold of the detective book, you will forget all about me and that is the situation which I cannot bear.

My dad was a huge fan of the Perry Mason mysteries written by Erle Stanley Gardner, as well as Georgian mysteries by Jeffery Farnol, and the prolific output of Edgar Wallace, the first British crime writer to regularly use policemen, rather than amateur sleuths, as protagonists. He found detective novels the perfect escape from physics.

Helen wrote on 17 March, rejoicing that she had managed to secure a passage on the *Jal-Azad*, which would be sailing on 21 or 22 April. That meant she would arrive in India around 3 May. It would be almost five months since they had last seen each other, and she cautioned Avadh that she could not cope with any more changes of plan.

> The thought that I am coming out to you has acted like a tonic and I feel a new woman – it takes me all my time not to positively dance along, but to maintain that decorum required in an office.
>
> I hope the family realize that now I have committed myself a second time, there is no question of postponing my coming again. That is something I could not face, and I should sail even if you had decided you did not want me (which I hope to God will never happen) and would work in Bombay. Nothing would persuade me to go through again all the difficulties of the past few months.

She responded with scepticism to Avadh's news about his servant's disappearance:

> Something tells me that you have been 'had' by our respected servant – he has probably been working happily these last two weeks for another employer, rejoicing happily at having two weeks unearned pay

in his pocket – if they have such things as pockets. Probably by now, he will have shown my judgment of human nature false and have turned up with apologies for being late – I hope the latter is the case. If not, do try and recruit another for your own sake – it is too much for you to keep house and work as well, particularly your kind of work which is liable to overflow into the evenings, etc.

In the night I was thinking that perhaps you would think I would be shocked by seeing a lot of life in India which is carefully hidden in England. For example all our lunatics, cripples and diseased people are in hospitals and one never sees anything deeply revolting in the streets, but I realize that some countries are not so fortunate. I shall probably be a little shaken at such things, but they do not repulse me, only I know I shall wish I was clever enough and rich enough to help all those in such troubles. I have seen a lot of the cruder side of life and it did dull my sensibilities a little, so that smells and dirt and dust, as long as I can keep them out of my home, will not sicken me, although I shall probably moan much as many Indians probably do about them. I suppose a lot depends upon where one lives, just as in England, as to how much one sees which is not pleasant. When you said you were afraid life in India would shock me, I am not sure whether you meant the kinds of things about which I have written or not but you need not be afraid. The only thing you have to watch is that I do not start dabbling in business which is not mine in an effort to put right everything which would possibly appear wrong to me! I'll do my best not to.

If this letter is to catch the mail I shall have to stop, and I haven't said a word of love – what a to-do. But you know I live for you and love you and I am as excited as hell coming to you at last, so wrap yourself in cotton wool and save yourself for me.

Dearest, I do love you.

Ever your,

Chutney

Chapter Thirteen

> *Never fear, we shall have some fun, even in Ahmedabad, even if we have to start a secret society of Hearty Laughers and Gigglers with you as President and I as the Secretary, Member, Chairman and Lord High Executioner.*

With her passage booked for either the 21st or 22nd of April, Helen could relax somewhat and start to look forward to her new life. On Saturday 18 March 1950, she wrote:

> Darling, have you any idea what we are to do when I first come to India? Am I to go to your brother's house at Delhi and will I enter the Hindu religion on the same day as I am married, or will that have to be done beforehand? No doubt you have these various arrangements in hand. I will follow whatever you decide to do. Can you see that I have some form of written word that I am married because that has to be shown to the English passport authorities, my parents, my insurance company and goodness knows who else in years to come. In England one can usually

> swear a thing before a commissioner for oaths and the document to which you swear is acceptable in a court of law. It costs about 10 shillings. Doubtless your lawyer brother will be kind enough to advise you on this. Also very quietly and unobtrusively the English government will just check that all is well with me – they try and do this to avoid white slavery, so it might help if I had something to show the consular authorities. I am just living for the day when I see you again – I keep looking at your picture and thinking 'not very long now!' I am sure, my heart, that we shall have some marvellous good times just doing small things together.

Living on his own, miles from the family home and without Helen there, Avadh said his life was:

> as dull and monotonous as the scenery in the middle of the desert of Sahara. My only oasis is my writing letters to you. I think a person ought to be a thousand years old before he can settle in Ahmedabad – at a stage when his only ambition is to just be left alone and die. Even Mahatma Gandhi, who has made his abode in this blessed town, could not stand it for beyond a few years and changed it for a more pleasant place. But we are not so lucky and I think I must have committed an untold number of sins in my previous life, so that I have to live in this town. Don't get from all this that I am in a very cross mood today, for with Ahmedabad I am always cross, but otherwise I am in quite good spirits.

During the dry months of the year Ahmedabad resembled a desert. It was hot and uncomfortable in March 1950.

Avadh wrote: 'Because of the heat I get sometimes irritated – but I shall try to be serene, when you get irritated.'

Not knowing whether his servant was ever going to return, Avadh tried to hire another but 'dispensed with his services after exactly 20 minutes' because the servant refused to clean Avadh's utensils after they had touched egg. 'Servants are a bit hard to find these days at a reasonable pay. Because of the servant's absence, the flat is getting demoralized, and so is its occupant at times.'

'I cook my egg breakfast daily, and also my afternoon tea and the rest of the two meals I take with Venket [a friend he had made while at Allahabad University]. He and some other students of the Laboratory have jointly offered the mess and I have to go there. I would have much preferred to have cooked my meals – cooking is easy – but the cleaning of utensils is a dread to me. Even in making tea – first in one vessel, then in second, then in third – till finally none are left clean. I just have to clean them, like I have done this evening.'

On 17 March, Avadh told Helen that he had written to Professor Fröhlich asking if he would have a reasonable chance of getting an Imperial Chemical Industries (ICI) fellowship in England. He explained that he had heard that applications were due in London by 30 March so he felt he had to enquire right away without consulting Helen first. He also asked whether she would be able to get a good job in England once she was married.

She replied on 22 March, sounding not unreasonably frustrated:

> Frankly I was a bit shaken by the news that you had applied for an ICI fellowship – not that I do not think it would be a good idea, I do. I think it is excellent and I have no doubt that if your application gets in

in time, you will get a fellowship. The thing that floored me was that only about three days ago I had a letter from you in which you said you felt you would really prefer to settle in India, and not long before that you said you wanted to come to England. I know you will have, and are having, a rough time, my dearest, and all sorts of reasons must have made you change your mind, but perhaps you don't realize the desperate mental torture through which I go every time you do change your mind.

First of all, I had to get used to the idea of going to India and since then it must have varied about 20 times. Each time I have to make a great mental somersault and I thought last night my brain had snapped and I would go insane. However, even after a completely sleepless night, I feel a bit better this morning and determined I would write and tell you about it.

Dearest one, I love you so much. Surely it is possible for you to confide in me and tell me what you really <u>want</u> to do. I am not asking you to do the impossible and predict what we shall do. I only want to know what, in the bottom of your heart, you wish to aim for. Do you want to eventually settle in England or in India? All I want to do is to help you and love you, but I cannot bear this constant changing of mind – it is driving me in a straight line to a lunatic asylum. Let us have an agreement between us that we will aim eventually to settle in one country or the other, and then we can work together to achieve that, even if it means a temporary stay in the country in which we do not intend to settle.

You ask me if I could get another good job in this country – I might – it would depend where we lived. Liverpool is a very bad place, but I think I could

> guarantee to earn £4.10.0 (less taxes) a week anyway. I could not do a job as heavy as my present one and keep house as well, unless I was the only wage earner and had no option, but I might in London or any of the Midland or southern towns earn the same for less work. A married woman is always at a great disadvantage in seeking a job, but I would, I am sure, earn as indicated above.

In a letter the following day, she had calmed down somewhat and wrote:

> Darling, I am sorry that yesterday I wrote such a distracted letter, but it was unfortunate that your letter about the ICI came on a day when I had already been tried beyond endurance at work, and I just thought my mind would crack under the added strain. I feel better now, but I shall be glad to know what in the bottom of your heart you really want to do. The only thing I would beg of you not to change is my coming to India to at least be married, because it is our only chance of marriage and we must take it. I think I should just die if I had to cancel this second passage.

On Sunday 19 March, Avadh was longing for some communication from Helen.

> I wonder why you are so silent; you could easily have sent me a cable if nothing else – what about, I don't know, but I assume you are busy making hot lentil soup so when you come to India, you could blow me up in smoke. My dearest, why are you trying so many cooking experiments? All I am afraid is that the more you have experimented before you came here, the less

> I would have the pleasure of pulling your leg. Anyhow you seem to be determined so I shall try to find something else to pull your leg about.
>
> For some time past, I have been feeling a perfect beast when I think of the odd and depressing letters I have written to you and I hope you will forgive me for it. I hope you did not get too disturbed by them. Darling, I love you very much and with this admission, I think I could get your forgiveness. I stand in need of it.

Helen wrote on 25 March that she had found a new leisure activity.

> I have to tell you that today I have been gambling! Not threepence like you did at cards, but a whole three shillings. It is Grand National day and I have a shilling on Ackton Major (a big Irish horse) and a shilling to win or get a place on Wot, No Sun. If by any fluke – and it will be a fluke –Ackton Major wins, I stand to win nearly £5. With the other one I should get about 30 shillings. I shall not know until 3:30 PM whether I have won, but I should like to because it would be an addition to our Exchequer. I chose Ackton Major because Mr Winterburn (for whom I work) is really Major Winterburn and came here from Acton, and Wot, No Sun because here I am still in England in the cold with no sun! If you can think of a crazier way of picking horses I cannot.

Wot, No Sun was placed second and Helen won 4/7d. She continued the letter with more about her brother Tony's engagement.

Tonight Anne is holding a 21st birthday and engagement party and all the family has to attend for at least a little while since Tony is announcing his engagement. Tony has bought a beautiful ring: he has been saving up for over a year for it, and I am afraid the poor lad will be completely broke after it, but as he is marrying a high-class girl, the ring must match the girl! They are both quite young and not likely to be married for a few years, but they will have quite a lot of privileges now they are engaged and will both save hard for their home. I am very glad they are happy, but I still think I am the happiest woman in the world because I am marrying you.

The days are creeping by and it is less than a month now until I sail. Never did days go so slowly. I suppose your people will be making some small arrangements for our wedding. I do not want to put them to much trouble and hope that it will not mean a lot of work or money to them. As far as I am concerned, there will only be you and I at the wedding – I certainly shall not have eyes for anyone else! I wonder if it would be possible to have one or two photographs taken that I can send home to my family, because my father and mother are rather sad that they cannot be present at my wedding. I do not know whether this is customary, but if it is, perhaps some kind friend would take a few snaps with your camera for us.

Always your adoring,
Chutney

On 20 March, Avadh sent a typed letter in which it is obvious the typewriter ribbon was almost completely worn out. It switches between faint red type and faint black type twelve times. It must have seemed to Helen that the typewriter was changing its mind as frequently as Avadh was. In a paragraph that is breathtaking in its swings between the vitally important and the trivial, Avadh says that he would be happy living in either England or India.

> When I suggested to you that I come over to you I meant only to avoid all these changes to your life since I find that I am happy either way. But I think I have said enough of this song. As far as the finances are concerned we could manage to travel back to England in October. By the way, can you tell me why it is that sometimes the typing has the ink in it and at other times it has not? Has the ribbon dried up? You never wrote to me how you fared at the Sunday dance when you were carrying garlic in your mouth by the dozen. Leave all this specialized cooking experiments. Otherwise you will have to unlearn all this. When you are here I will show you how to make the lentil soup without any hot stuff or garlic in it and yet I can assure you that you will like it.
>
> In my earlier letter, I asked your measurements. Please send them. You must have something Indian to wear when you come, especially since you will not have any summer dress, suited to Indian conditions. Don't be scared that you will have to observe Purdah; nobody in our family does, and even if there was, we could do as we liked. You could, for example, go to market, or to see any of our friends, by yourself, leaving apart, of course, certain notorious localities, and at times when there is trouble in the city. Such troubles are not uncommon, for at present there is a good deal of tension between India and Pakistan, and that means an explosive is always there between the Hindus and

> Muslims to explode. This town is peaceful apart from one or two stray stabbing cases.
>
> Our programme immediately after your arrival I shall fix up when I know your date of arrival. Would you mind staying a day in Ahmedabad before going to Delhi? On the shortest route to Delhi [from Bombay] one has to pass through this town. Most likely my sister-in-law will be with me to receive you.

Helen did not respond to the rather alarming report of 'one or two stray stabbing cases' but in her next letter (of 27 March) she wrote about clothes:

> I do not know what is the minimum of clothes on which I can be a presentable wife, but I have sent you my measurements and I suggest you buy just one set of clothes – not expensive and something which will wash easily – and that we might go shopping in Bombay or Ahmedabad together. Of course we can go to Ahmedabad before Delhi – anything to help us out financially. I do hope my coming and all the travelling you will have to do will not take every penny you have – you poor child. If saris are cheaper than the other clothes you mentioned, I can probably manage in them, since I have blouses and petticoats already, but if they are the same price I would prefer the something-or-other Kamiz [a shalwar kameez] you mentioned. Once I can get my sewing machine unpacked I can probably buy material cheaply and make my clothes in future – and some of yours as well.
>
> Dearest Darling, it is exciting and so lovely to be coming at last – I can hardly believe it. I shall be able to rest on the voyage and should arrive quite well and

> bonny. In the meantime you are to take good care of yourself – until I can do it for you.

In another example of cross-cultural misunderstanding exacerbated by physical distance, Avadh reacted negatively to Helen's request (in her letter of 18 March) for written proof of their marriage. He took it as a sign of mistrust and replied on the 24th:

> I have not yet made arrangements about our marriage but I shall do so. I cannot tell you the programme just now unless it is settled. The point is I am worried about so many other things and you write about getting a legal document of our marriage. You know very well that in Hindu marriage there is no written legal document and yet the marriage is legal. If you say, I say and my brother and the priest say we are married and if it is otherwise valid, there is no further proof required. Do you think you can trust me only after you have legal documents of our marriage – in which case we will have to wait until after the Hindu Code Bill passes etc. etc. However, if you trust me well enough and that if you feel that I shall stand by you whatever happens then only you are welcome to come – for you know India at present is a melting pot and the conditions go on changing and I can promise you only that I will not betray your trust, whatever happens.
>
> If I ask my brother about legal documentation, my entire family will withdraw whatever support we have – because they live in India – they regard Law Courts with greatest suspicion. However, if and when the English consular authorities themselves raise this question – I think they will be satisfied by your telling – but if they are not then we shall see about it.

He finished with all the usual endearments, but the tone of the letter as a whole is rather abrupt, and Helen apologized in her reply of the 28th.

> My own Love, I am dreadfully sorry if by asking for some proof of my marriage I have made you feel that I do not trust you. I took it so much for granted that you knew that I trusted you implicitly, that such an idea that you might think I did not trust you, honestly never entered my head! The only reason why I wanted something written is that we are likely to travel to countries other than India and it is so uncomfortable if one has no proof of a marriage. In England, for example, even to get a ration book in my married name I must produce something to prove my marriage. However, if the English Consulate will agree to alter my passport, that will probably be enough. I know there is no written proof of the Hindu marriage – that is why I asked specially. Don't be angry, darling, because if you look at it from an English standpoint, it was not a very unreasonable request, and to me it was a very big thing.

On Sunday 26 March, Avadh wrote a reflective letter in which he describes with considerable insight the struggle that is reflected in his vacillation about where to live.

> To decide now into which country we should ultimately settle down, is very difficult. I know that both of us feel the same way about each other, i.e. both of us are prepared to do their best to make each other happy, and yet one cannot overlook the inner conflicts which always go on in one's mind. I mean that I will always prefer to settle in India (it will not be actually preference

> in action). What I mean is (it is no doubt difficult to explain) one will always have a sort of craving in the innermost of one's heart for one's own country. Maybe this feeling may die out in years to come and one becomes perfectly international minded – if not, this inner conflict will prevent us from being happy and other circumstances of our lives will either aggravate it or if God is kind, and we are geniuses in sensibility, we may be able to overcome it. Darling, do not think that I do not love you, for that's not true, but by virtue of the fact that our period of trial has been elongated, these feelings which were at one time in a suppressed state have come on the surface – and since you asked me to write about my mind, I have done so.
>
> I do not know how you feel about this; you are capable of making your quick decisions, but I do feel that you must be getting at times when you feel less enthusiastic about coming all the way to India, the same type of feeling.
>
> Truly one can be happy in the long run only if one is able to harmonize the innermost conflicts.

Helen was so keen to escape her past in England that, if she had any doubts, she did not express them. She just wanted to be with Avadh and felt confident that once they were together they would make it work, one way or another. She wrote on 31 March:

> Your loving and gentle letter of last Sunday arrived today and I would say first how very much I appreciate the real effort you have made to tell me what is in your mind and believe me, my heart, I do understand now very much better. I only wish that you had written me about it all before, because it has been in my mind

too. The only difference was that I had rather taken it for granted that although we might visit England our real home would be in India, and therefore, I would have to do most adjusting – which I think I can do fairly all right.

My biggest enemy is going to be a damp heat, but I don't suppose we shall have to live all our lives in Ahmedabad – India is a fairly large country and I think maybe we shall have a chance of living somewhere nice one day. I am very used in my life to having to make drastic decisions and sticking to them, even if the result is not as good as I thought, so I shall do my very best, Dear, to make a happy life even if at first, it is a struggle. You know that many things are worth a lot of bother. In other words, compared to the many sweet and good things which my marriage will undoubtedly bring me, the drawbacks will be worthwhile. The only thing that I really fear is that you might one day regret marrying me because I am English – but I will try very hard to give you all the things that an Indian wife would give you.

Secondly, I would say that my letter should not have sounded angry because I was not angry. I was only terribly afraid of having a nervous breakdown. As you know, I have had to learn an entirely new job and at the same time carry on as best I could as Mr Wilkinson's secretary, because his secretary was away ill, and also do half Miss Hunt's work as she was ill. This strain was so great that, in that alone, I was nearly at breaking point. Then I was worried to death about you and thirdly I had, on a day when I came home nearly reduced to tears, your letter about the ICI Fellowship. I expect it is this sort of piling up of trouble which has made your poor head so tired, and I shall be so glad to get to you so that, at any rate, if I do nothing more constructive, I can make your home pleasant.

Now I think I shall write to you something of the good things I think this marriage will bring at any rate to me but first I must tell you that all my life, except the last two or three years, I have been tossed about all over the country with no continuity or feeling of safety. There has hardly been a moment of peace except on two or three holidays – apart, of course, from the lovely holidays we took [in the Lake District]. I have always held jobs which demanded infinite work and, on top of that, my miserable education had to be supplemented by night after night of night school for years.

My last engagement was spent in a mental cold sweat knowing that if Eddie survived the fighting I was hardly likely to survive the bombing; so that you will see I have never been able to relax at all. So many other things have happened too. When I marry you I shall be able to relax just a little in the company of one who loves me very much, with someone who will help my mind to flower along lines it never had time to explore before, will encourage me to take care of my body as it has not been taken care of before, who will teach me the gentleness of life like sending a little English girl balloons and saying my prayers at night.

No marriage of any kind is ever built without slipping and sliding along a narrow path, each hauling the other up when one partner falls, enjoying the good times and struggling through the bad ones with as much good humour as possible and, in a little leisure, doing together something which is of interest to both. I don't think our marriage will be any worse than any other and, it may be, if we try hard, one of the loveliest of unions. We cannot know for certain, but we can have a very good go! This must sound very unromantic but I have tried not to let my bubbling affection for you colour the picture too much.

She continued on the same theme in her letter of 1 April.

It is true that if we live all our lives in India I shall sometimes long to see England again, but I would not mind betting that if after, say, five years in India, I spent quite a long time in England, I would begin to remember all the good things about India and the friends I had made and would come to realize that, like a transplanted flower, my roots had dug deeply into their new soil and there was my home. After all, I am by no means the first Englishwoman to live in India or the first woman to marry an Indian and live an Indian life! If you can get used to having me about the place, I think with thought and care and time I can do the rest! If, as you say, I can have enough physical freedom to be able to potter round and shop, it means that my mind will be always a little interested in all I see, and, as you know, my favourite occupation is to observe small things as I trot round – how many nature talks have you had to endure already!

As for the Indian mode of thought and ways of looking at life, that will come slowly to me, I feel sure, from being with you, reading Indian authors, and listening to discussions among your friends. I am afraid my thoughts will tend to always be a little solidly practical, but that is my nature, and I suppose there must also be practical Indian women otherwise no children would ever get properly brought up. You know, our life in England very often is in opposition to our natural instincts and I think this accounts for the terribly high number of nervous breakdowns here, so that it is quite possible that once I have got used to the Indian outward forms of doing things, I may find many of the fundamental desires of living far better satisfied than I have ever had them satisfied in my life. It is, for example, against nature to stay single and chaste for 30 years of one's life, to have to control men at work – it is very difficult when you are a woman, to have no religious belief and not be able (to jump from one end of the problem to the other!) to eat meals regularly, and so on, many of which things will be settled for me by life in India.

'Owever, as the Lancashire people say, I feel I can have a jolly good smack at it and for your sake I'd do more than that.

On 28 March, Avadh wrote:

I am afraid I have revealed to you my most unwholesome side of character in the last few letters – but I am less sorry for exposition than for the fact it must be hurting you a lot. I hope you will forgive me for it and tell me that you still love me. Darling I promise you I will bear almost anything to be able to love you.

My dearest sweet, I will not ask you to cancel the passage – you need not be afraid – unless I win a prize of £300 or £400 on a crossword puzzle – in which case I shall ask you to fly – but that is a wild dream, but I do want to see you as soon as it can be arranged.

On 2 April, with just over two weeks to go until her departure, Helen wrote:

> You asked me in one of your more recent letters whether I had not sometimes got to the stage when I felt I must give up the idea of marrying you, but I must tell you that, despite all the difficulties which have beset us, I have never got quite to that stage, because the thought of life without you is, and has been, so intolerable that my mind refuses to contemplate the idea. I freely admit that I have felt like cussing everything and everybody from here to kingdom come with the frustration of it all, but wash my hands of you – never!
>
> [I] heard of a girl sailing to India in November to marry a man from Lahore. Two girls sailed last week to marry Egyptians. It is no wonder that our first export is often said to be wives for the rest of the world. It is very true that our girls do go all over the place, so I am merely following in the footsteps of many.
>
> I am quite sure, however, that none of them will have a more dear husband than I. I look forward terribly to living with you and sharing all your ups and downs and having a good laugh over most of them. Do you remember Christmas shopping with me once – that was something I simply loved – no Englishman would have done it except under the most terrific persuasion. I was so happy to have you with me – I could have hugged you in the street. How good it will be to do small things together again, never mind the pleasure of being married to each other.

She sounds blissfully happy as she looks forward to seeing her husband-to-be in just a month's time. However, nothing had been straightforward in their courtship to date and more problems were about to emerge before she was due to sail.

First of all, on Wednesday 29 March, Avadh wrote that Professor Fröhlich had said it would be a pleasure to have him back in his department at the University of Liverpool and that he would, at once, write a letter in support of Avadh's ICI fellowship application.

> [Professor Fröhlich] has put me in a great pickle, or rather, due to my own actions, I have put myself in the pickles and chutney. From his letter, as far as I can see, I stand a good chance of getting the ICI fellowship. I suppose, if I get it, I shall risk this job in Ahmedabad, but in three years time if we wanted to come to India, I should surely get some job. But living on the ICI fellowship will mean that you will have to do both housework and at least part-time work, for I will never be happy if I did not send something to Kashi. That's a responsibility which we cannot shirk; I hope you will agree with me. My father will, of course, be a bit angry with me and particularly with you for he will naturally think that it was you who has uprooted me – how true?

After that Avadh did not write for several days because bad news was piling up. He confessed he had started many letters and let them remain unfinished and unposted, but finally he wrote a letter over a few days, finishing it on Sunday 2 April.

> In question hour in the Indian Parliament on Thursday, the Prime Minister of India replied to the effect that an Indian officer [civil servant] has to take permission from the Government before he can marry a foreigner. Technically, I am not a Government Officer, but indirectly I am, for the post in which I am, is the one

sanctioned by the Atomic Energy Commission which is a Government Body. If for one reason or another, they try to do something against me, they may.

Under normal circumstances of our marriage, the British Authorities would have said nothing but the fact that you will have to become a Hindu first and then marry me, I do not know what attitude the British Consul in India will take.

India is in a very sort of explosive atmosphere where its rulers, in theory, have very high minded principles – what they do in practice – they are able to keep it hidden – an ordinary middle class man cannot even feel secure if he does what he thinks to be the right thing.

He was also concerned because Doctor Brother reported that Kashi's family had dug in their heels again over a settlement and her father was refusing to engage.

[I am worried] about the possibility of Kashi's people trying to put a case in the court, in which case, the court, which will consist of some old crony, will in all probability grant a maintenance to such an extent that we may become financially crippled. Many a marriage has turned out to be a failure because of financial difficulties. I am not talking to frighten you but the situation is nothing better than this – Kashi's people are much more adamant than I ever imagined – and at a time when the feelings in the country are so much roused – that anything like what we are going to do might have more serious consequences than in normal times.

Darling do not think that I don't love you, for I do love you, only under the circumstances, I somehow

> feel that our marrying you just now is not advisable. Of course, I know that you have made so many arrangements – and these too for the second time but if you can bear being pickled for a little while – we might save the situation. Do not think that I shall leave you, for I will definitely come to England, and as you will say, either live with or without you; and then I shall try to get a divorce from Kashi.

He also said that he had told Professor Fröhlich that he was willing to take any work in Liverpool just to sustain himself, until such time he could get a better post, and continued:

> I know that I am writing to you at the last moment, and you may think me a cruel ass, but I cannot help it. I love you so much and yet I am afraid, for one reason or another, our financial liability may become so great and unbearable and then of what use shall remain our marriage?
>
> I promise to you that this is my last letter in which I am going to say anything about changing decisions, for I realize fully that it must be getting on your nerves. If you feel, in spite of my letter, and my sense, that you should come, you can come, and we shall make best of what we can. However, if you can do the other way, I think we shall in the long run be much more happy.

Unfortunately the first page of Helen's response is missing but the tone of her letter of 7 April suggests that she was not going to be distracted by Avadh's last-minute panic, no matter how distressing it must have been for her.

> My only love, please do understand that it is not lack of money which is driving me to come to India but the utter ruin of my own life here. The only way I can ever hold my head up in Liverpool again is with you by my side married to me.
>
> Of course, things may not turn out nearly so badly as we think, but we will try and plan out for both eventualities, and in the meantime just do the best you can with [marriage] arrangements and don't worry yourself sick.
>
> You will know best if the following is the right thing to do, but if I were you, I would at least write and tell your father that for my sake you are having to take action, if you have no opportunity of seeing him personally. Do make it clear to him that it is not just that I shall be without money, it is that my whole life is completely in a hopeless mess, and, quite frankly, I am not prepared to go on living without you here – I just must come. I cannot go on living like I am.
>
> I know you love me, my heart, and I simply adore you, and it grieves me to go against your wishes and against my better judgment, but I think, if we take refuge in England for a few years, that the tumult and the shouting will die down and, if you wish, we can then go back to India. In the meantime, I beg of you to let me come and marry you – I will do all I can to minimize the damage that my coming may do. It is possible that someone you know might be able to give me accommodation in Bombay or might suggest where I might start looking for work.

The whole situation must have been incredibly difficult for everyone involved. Kashi faced an uncertain future with her young child, my half-brother. For my dad the stress must have been nearly unbearable. For my mum, it must have been desperately difficult to deal with my dad's worries by letter and cable without being able even to speak on the telephone, never mind her own troubles, as the days ticked by until the sailing she had booked. On 8 April she wrote:

> I looked so awful today – because I was worried as you will understand – and my mother asked me what was the matter, which made me weep. I told her that I was afraid of being stranded in India if something went wrong and I wanted to get back to this country, and she told me that in a last resort I could come back as a distressed British subject, paying my fare back to the authorities as best I could after I got home. This did comfort me a little because it is possible that you could get here having your fare paid by some organization like ICI but if I was left I could not make it home.
>
> My mother says if we come home suddenly, she will give us a room in which to stay until we can find a room or flat near the University. Mum would not charge us much, if anything, for our room, as long as we did not stay too long.
>
> I can almost hear all the various people attached to you telling you why you should not marry me and, of course, there are sound reasons for not doing anything – even eating!
>
> I am 6000 miles away, but I feel if I was with you, nothing people could say would deter you from your purpose. Darling, Darling, please don't be put off from your purpose.
>
> Dearest one, please write to me even if you are angry with me. I'd rather be poor with you than middling

well-off without you, and I will try not to grumble when things do not go well.

Always and always your adoring,
Chutney

She wrote again on 9 April.

As long as I have you by my side and it is apparent that I really have been to India to be married, I can soon re-establish myself in Liverpool and could get a job. If I put off coming to India again, I shall be looked on as a woman of 'doubtful character' – someone who tells lies and associates with foreigners and, therefore, is not fit to associate with other girls in an office. It is funny that one can marry a foreigner, but if you just go about with them and then are left alone by them, you are socially damned. Even Mr Wilkinson, knowing all of the facts of the case could not reinstate me in the eyes of head office. That is why I am so desperate to sail, even if I come back in September with a load of debt round my neck.

If we are prepared, my love, and I certainly am, to battle hard for a year or two with our finances, we can establish ourselves quite firmly, but it means we must be very close to each other and a little patient and we must not in the meantime lose our heads and be stampeded into actions we do not want to take, unless we are of course absolutely cornered – as I am at the moment.

My love, do write to me and tell me I have not damned you utterly by coming to India. My heart is nearly breaking at the thought of the damage I may be doing, but I can't help it – and it may not be too damaging anyway – I pray not.

On Monday 3 April, Avadh penned a short note on one of the airmail letters that he had started and abandoned the previous week. These letters came with a printed stamp so they could not be allowed to go to waste.

> All I want is to go on saying, 'I love you, I love you'. I am sitting in the laboratory and there is a radio in the adjoining room which has been put on BBC and some band music is filtering through the walls to my room. I do not know what has happened to me but at times I just feel sad and I cannot even explain why for I do not have any reason. But I am quite well; you should not worry about me. Depressions are my hobby, which God has granted me as a special gift. This was one that I received in a steel box, while the rest in a sieve, so that by now they have all drained off.

On the 11th, Helen replied:

> Thank you for your funny little letter of April 3 – with a bit crossed out at the beginning. I hope the depression has lifted a bit – everybody gets depressed at times, petkins; it is one of the afflictions of humanity and being in a hot climate always intensifies it. Living by oneself does not help either – I am sure I should be miserable in the same circumstances. We will try hard to make life pleasant for both of us in India and in England and you will find that as your worries lessen, so the depressions will lessen. Even at the very worst, our worries are not insurmountable. Someone once told me when I was little that the easiest burdens to tackle were financial ones. I did not believe her at the time but I know from experience that it is true. As long as one has

health and strength one can work and patient work will produce money.

If you could have seen my efforts in the last few days to buy a cheap parasol, you would have laughed. First I tried every shop in Liverpool, Birkenhead, Moreton, Hoylake and West Kirby. They always did think I was a little mad in Moreton, and now they are quite sure. Who ever heard of anyone buying a parasol so far north! Then I started on all the old ladies of my acquaintance – a parasol used always to be part of the equipment of an old lady. I drank gallons of tea with them and spent some interesting hours (even found one whose first husband was a Siamese) but no parasol. After that, I staggered into the office of the local paper and put a one shilling advertisement in the 'wanted' column. I now await the result – if any. Probably thousands of parasols will descend on my head! The things I do for love!

I am now completely packed up except for the clothes I am wearing and another dress which, even in this cool climate, is quite a problem. I can see that I shall have to sit in a blanket, waiting for my underwear to dry, next washing day. Ah well, it won't be the first time in my life!

You know, I am so looking forward to seeing you, no matter what storm descends on our heads. We will get some laughs out of it, never fear, and show them who will win out in the end.

On 5 April, Avadh received Helen's letters of 31 March and 1 April in which she responded lovingly to his earlier letter baring his soul about being torn between India and England. Seeing the depth of her commitment and determination, he realized that his more recent letter telling her not to come to India and that they should delay their marriage was, to say the least, hurtful. He wrote: 'I am going to give you a cable this afternoon, saying that if my last Sunday's letter is very inconvenient, you can cancel it – I am afraid, I do not know, how much we will have to face – but if we are both prepared to face it, then we might as well and hope for the best.'

Today people are warned to think twice before pressing 'send' on their emails. The same should apply to dropping letters into post boxes.

*

On 8 April, Avadh responded to Helen's determination to come to India. Despite the high emotional stakes, his tone is moderate and slightly ironic.

> Where Angels fear to tread in, Devils do and that is what you have decided to do. Not that I very much disagree with your decision, only sometimes, I shudder to think what will happen if we really get pickled. But I suppose we can hope for the best and I hope you will curse me a little less than infinite amount, if due to some unfortunate circumstances we found ourselves together in an unfortunate position. Nevertheless, for the moment, I am happy at the prospect of being able to put my arms around you at a near date. I hope you will forgive me for rattling you like this and I hope I will not have to do it again. Can you tell me whether you still love me and like me, in spite of all this. I personally think that you must be a really sweet sweetie for doing so.

On the 13th, Helen wrote to reassure him:

> Of course I love you dearly still. I do understand the various stresses and strains which make you undecided about my coming and had I not been in such an awkward fix myself, I should certainly not have sailed, but waited for you here. However being with you will in one way help – as the various difficulties come up, two brains can be pressed into service to deal with them instead of one, as at present. At the moment I'm such a long way away that all the news I get is so stale as to no longer be news about which one can do anything, but more like history!
>
> Of course, I write to you every day, you devil. Look at the dates on my letters and you will see. Even on days when I have felt like slaughtering you or even thought of suicide myself I have always written!
>
> I often chuckle to myself when I think of our life together. I'm sure we shall have some fun and enjoy it, even if we get into some on holy messes at times. We must try and write a detective novel, or at any rate a short novel, together, if I have a little leisure. As far as I can see at the moment, I am going to be pretty busy, if I take a job, keep house, and deal with my favourite devil as well, but we must try and squeeze a little time. I have a very real urge to learn to write fairly well and wittily and you can already do so, so perhaps between us we can make something of it. Anyway, we shall probably tear up literally acres of the laboratory notepaper. Pay for our own paper – how shocking – I should think not – professor's perquisite when composing novels.

Avadh never did collaborate with Helen on a novel but he was endlessly supportive of her writing and always insisted she keep for herself any money she earned from books. He also supplied his used course notes for her to type on the blank backs of the pages.

On 9 April he wrote:

My dear Chutney,

Don't be afraid of reading this letter – there is nothing in it to rattle you, even though it is a long one.

Yesterday I received two of your lovely letters. First of all I want to tell you that I love you very much and do want to marry you and live with you and etc., etc. (no emotions cloud my judgment?). And if I wrote some other things, it was only because I was very depressed and did not know how to handle the situations and circumstances and also whether I would finally make you happy, if things did not take a smooth shape.

Anyhow, don't think that I am not happy that we shall see each other within a month, the very thought of holding you in my arms again and talking to you nonsense in person makes me forget everything – such devilishness you have around your person and soul (no offence?).

I had been thinking that so long as Kashi remains with my father, I should not send a maintenance to her. But the present situation demands action (at least that is what I think) and on my own counsel, I am sending a registered letter telling her that I had fixed maintenance of [a percentage] of salary minus income tax and am sending her the money. If she accepts it – she accepts the situation and her parents can at best try to get a little more out of me – if she does not – then we shall think about it.

Late in the evening of Friday 14 April, Helen wrote:

> The reason I am so late is firstly I was late from work because everyone came to wish me goodbye and good luck, and after everyone was gone, I felt a little bit sad and walked all round the office and looked at the sample tins and fingered them and said their specifications to myself and thought how stupid it was to have only knowledge of a trade which is of no use in a house. However, after a while I thought of my new life and how, despite troubles which may come, it would be happy and interesting and I felt better, and came home.
>
> After tea, I looked at the avalanche of replies I had after advertising for a parasol. However, I got lost in Hoylake when looking for the house of one of the replies and I am only just home now. I have not yet seen what I want, but I have heaps more replies to look at tomorrow. Press on regardless! I said I would be nearly drowned in parasols, didn't I!

A few days later, she wrote: 'After battling round Hoylake and West Kirby, I managed to buy a parasol– a Japanese one – which I hope will last me through this hot season at least. I was offered one or two silk or cotton ones but the cost of £2 or £3 seemed absolutely excessive so I was glad to get a Japanese one. I nearly bought a straw hat instead – but it would hardly go with the dainty costume I shall wear in India!'

That weekend, she triumphantly told Avadh that she had managed to sell his radio for the remarkable sum of £20, which she would bring out with her to add to their funds. She added:

> I have written another article, which Avril is going to get typed for me. I shall spit on it for luck. It is on

> the work of typists. I can see that if we can afford any pocket money, all my share will go on postage for articles. If I can write small 1000 word articles on things Indian, in an interesting manner, I know I can sell in England as much as I can write. India is news at present.

On 12 and 14 April Avadh wrote in some detail about plans for Helen's arrival. She would arrive in Bombay and almost immediately she would take a Hindu name, which was apparently straightforward to do and a prerequisite for marriage. The wedding would be a little later, likely with Avadh's friend Venket as the only guest. Because May and June temperatures in Ahmedabad could reach 46° C (115° F), he proposed they go to a hill station 80 kilometres from Bombay for a couple of weeks and then go north to be married. While Avadh had to return to Ahmedabad after that, Helen could stay in Bombay and get a job. This would save money because they wouldn't have to buy as much for the flat while they waited to find out if Avadh had been awarded the fellowship back in England.

He added that, if they went to England, Helen would likely have to work until all their debts were cleared and then perhaps part time after that. He wasn't sure how expensive married life in England was but he hoped that she wouldn't ask him to stop smoking his pipe.

Helen replied on the 17th:

> It would seem sensible to stay in Bombay and at least work through the hot season; I should like to get a job before we went to the hills – arranged to start as soon as I came back from the hills. If you can fix the marriage bright and early after I land, please do.

> Love, I don't know what you think you must do to the flat to make it habitable for me – the only things I can think of are to add another bed, if yours is not wide enough. I have stacks of things in my luggage from which I can make the flat look pretty – and I don't know what you are doing your cooking on, but I gather you have something, and probably I can manage on it. I think we have two chairs, haven't we – that would be two beds and two chairs more than our family had when we started in Liverpool.

Avadh was still slightly nervous at the prospect of entering into a second marriage when his first had failed, and he returned to a topic he had raised several months earlier:

> You ask me to write to my father, that I have to marry you for your sake. (1) I am not marrying you for your sake but for my sake. (2) My father or brother will only move (if they move at all) for my sake – do not take it ill – but in general people are prejudiced here against marrying an English girl. You remember I told you once. This prejudice is because in the days of British rule in India, certain English women married Indians and after a few years got a damagingly high maintenance from the courts. Otherwise even in the past, some English ladies who married Indians remained admirably devoted to their husbands but people here, who are still unaccustomed to go to courts for separation or divorce, look and remember only the facts which glare in their eyes. I have not written this to hurt your feelings; I love you and trust you but my people will change their opinion only after they have seen you (of that I am sure) and when I have been with you a good long time and happy with you.

> I would never ask you to live with me if you felt miserably unhappy with me. In one of my letters, the letter of 1st January – which I had written on the train while going to Poona, I had asked you to promise me that you will not go to court under such contingency but that we shall separate by mutual consent. [That page of the letter is missing.] Probably no one talks about a prospect of failure of marriage with his own sweetheart, and yet I have done so, once again, because I remember you saying once to me in Liverpool, that nobody does ever talk about such a thing.

On a lighter note, the next day he complained that she has sent him inconsistent measurements for the clothes he was having made for her. 'Now please be a little less fickle in your physical changes, otherwise your clothes will have to be changed so often, that I shall go bankrupt, or else you will have to be dressed like Huckleberry Finn.'

Helen reacted strongly but with understanding to Avadh's request for assurance that she would never sue him.

> Today I received sections 2 and 3 of your letter of April 14th, of which I had the first bit yesterday. It was a nice letter and I shall now proceed to chop off your head!
>
> I am sure that several times before I must have told you that decently bred old families like mine never go to court, except to defend themselves, or if driven to it by utter despair. The only thing I can think of that would ever lead me to take court action would be if you left me with hungry children to feed. If it was only I who was left and I could work at all, I should not ask for myself. Since I know perfectly well that you would never let children starve while

you had a ha'penny in your pocket, you are perfectly safe.

If all I had wanted from you was money, I could have fixed that long ago! All I want is a loving and gentle husband whom I can trust – and I think I have found that. When you talk about Indians who have married English ladies and have been double-crossed, I can tell you in a flash what has happened. To begin with, until after this war, Indians visiting this country had very little opportunity indeed to meet nicely brought up English girls. The only women they met were the daughters of their landladies (who were usually lower working class women) or they met prostitutes or at the best casual street women and these women fastened themselves to them like leeches with the sole idea of making as much money out of them as possible. With the commencement of the British Council and many similar organizations during the war, the position has changed considerably, and, as you know, a good many girls of excellent social standing are now able to meet Asiatic people quite freely. I can say quite frankly that before the war no one except a European would have had the slightest chance of meeting anyone like myself – and even Europeans did not stand much chance.

I can understand how you feel, my dear, and have, therefore, answered you patiently, but frankly my pride is stung that you should think that I would stoop to such a contemptible trick.

On the clothing question, she answered:

I am undoubtedly quite crazy with regard to my measurements. Probably I did one lot with clothes and shoes

> on and the other lot with them off. Here are my findings:
>
> Chest 32 inches;
>
> Waist 25 inches (perhaps you had better make it 25½ inches to allow for an undergarment);
>
> Waist to ankle 42½ inches (this leaves only about 1 inch from the floor when I have flat-heeled shoes on).
>
> If there is any doubt about it, have everything made a little larger – an hour's sewing on my part could alter, say, the waist and length, if necessary.

On Saturday 15 April, Avadh wrote a letter expecting it to be the last Helen would receive before she left home. It pledges his enduring love once more and assures her that they will make decisions about their future together. On the 17th, he wrote a similar letter to be delivered to Cabin 8 (Promenade Deck) of the *Jal-Azad* at the Royal Albert Dock in London.

Helen received his letter of the 15th just four days later and was delighted:

> It really was the most beautiful letter that ever a wife-to-be could hope to receive. It touched my heartstrings and I know that I shall never regret being married to you. I love you, my dearest, my darling, and my sad heart has been made very happy by you. I am really looking forward to coming to you as I have never looked forward to anything in my life. I feel we are real partners as well as lovers.
>
> Now I shall tell you something which I had intended to keep secret until I saw you at Bombay, but it might rest your mind a little. When I land in Bombay, after paying customs etc., I should have with me about £60

[roughly the equivalent of £1,500 today] made up as follows: – £20 wireless, £13.10.0 gifts (about which I had forgotten!) And about £25 miscellaneous savings which I have made over and above the various expenses for which I have had to save such as £20 for my passage. These odd savings had been made up of sixpences saved in a box and all sorts of small oddments like a 5/- occasionally paid into my banking account. This means that I shall arrive in Bombay with the best part of my return passage in my hand (barring being robbed or something dreadful occurring). I did not know I was so rich until I scraped together every *pie* [1/192 of a rupee] I possessed on Monday last, ready to put it into travellers' cheques.

It is now 11:30 PM and my eyes are drooping, so that I can hardly write and I must, therefore kiss you good night. Sleep well, my heart, we shall soon be walking up the avenue together. Be of good courage and don't worry.

Ever your own loving,
Chutney

Chapter Fourteen

> *I am wishing all the time that you were with me because you would like the peace aboard ship – and, of course, because I am longing to be with you.*

At last, on Friday 21 April 1950, Helen said her goodbyes to her family and caught a train to London to start her long voyage to India. She must have been nervous – anyone would have been – but at the same time mightily relieved that no more spanners had been thrown in the works. She had no idea what reception to expect in India, given that Avadh's first wife was still staying in the family compound near Delhi, but at least she knew that Avadh would be there waiting for her in Bombay. That evening she wrote to him:

> My dearest Loving one,
>
> This is written in a funny little hotel bedroom in London, resting the paper precariously on my suitcase. This evening Tony will come and have dinner with me, but, in the meantime, I feel I must write to you because at this minute I feel like the wise men in the Bible who

had only a star shining in the east to guide them through the darkness. They knew that what they would find at the end of the journey would be worthwhile, but they were mortally afraid of the Desert before them. You are my star – in fact, you are now my life, you scallywag. I have just read again your dear last letter to me and it gives me new courage to help me on my way. I just love you and love you and I couldn't live without you and I am glad I'm coming to you. Damn the heat and all the other woes. What are they, anyway, but things that can be got over?

I do not know exactly when or where I shall dock in Bombay, but now that you know that I shall sail tomorrow, 22nd, you will be able to check my arrival with Scindia. There is a dock strike here and before I post this I shall just check that it will not delay the sailing. I shall be looking for you so hard when we reach Bombay that the porters will steal all my oddments – and I can't even kiss you when I see you – wot a life!

Leaving England and my family is a very big wrench, but I was in such a mess I had little option. The thought of being with you, however, more than compensates for these things and I can hardly believe I am so near to seeing you.

Good hunting, petkins – that is another way of saying good luck in all your endeavours. We are not going to sink – we are going to swim strongly together. As Mr Churchill used to say 'We shall not falter nor fail'.

The following day she wrote to him from on board the *Jal-Azad*:

How I wish you were with me to share the comforts of this journey – that would be paradise indeed. I have a two-berth cabin to myself, with everything in it to please a woman's heart – except you. In fact, I have so much luxury that I am ashamed and feel I ought to be travelling second-class – but I could not get such a passage.

The ship is well out in the English Channel now but the sea is not rough. I have a 'boy' to look after my cabin and he is nicely trained. He walked all round the ship looking for me to give your letter to me, rather than just leave it in the Cabin. There are some very kind Indian ladies aboard, including an Indian Jewess (I did not know such a thing existed!).

People say that this ship is not as good as P&O steamers, but really it is most comfortable and the food is very well cooked. There is everything to make life pleasant. My poor, tired body and mind will both get a good rest and, I hope, if we go up to the hills together, you will get a rest too. I do so wish you were with me.

Now my head is nodding and I must go to bed. Goodnight Beloved Star.

Each day at sea, she added to the letter. On the 23rd she wrote:

I am told that this ship is unlikely to reach India before 12th May at the earliest. If we stop at Naples it is likely to be a day or two later, but if I can get more definite news I shall send you a cable.

I find I am very good at doing nothing at present – I have not been seasick, but I have felt not very well inside, but it will pass and I shall feel fine after a day or two. The sea has been miraculously calm up to now

– it must know that I must be delivered to you in good order.

The food is very good and I am sure I shall gain a pound or two, so that if I lose it in the Indian heat it will not matter. I do hope you are not nearly killing yourself trying to get everything ready before I come – you are far more important to me than anything else!

On the 24th:

When I got onto this boat I was weary worn, but two days of complete rest have worked wonders already and I am beginning to look quite presentable again. I do not think I have had such a complete rest before. Even on holiday I have always walked dozens of miles each week, but here five times round the deck is about the limit. I have not been seasick, but some of the more delicate ladies have been very sick – you are marrying a tough little alley-cat!

When people have asked my reason for coming to India I have just said 'to be married', but have not enlarged on it. I have had to declare on the outside of my trunks, which have been seen by the officers, our small wedding presents, so the purpose of my trip was very apparent.

In a letter written on the 25th and 26th, she wrote:

Today I have sent you a cable telling you that I shall be arriving about the 12th. I thought you might like to make your leave start a little later in view of this. I won the money for the cable (shameful hussy!) by hazarding one shilling on Housie-Housie [bingo] games! What a woman!

> There are all kinds, classes and castes of Indian ladies on this boat and I can honestly say that we are all getting along in a most friendly spirit – I am quite surprised at it.

And then on the 27th:

> Last night as I lay in bed I was thinking deeply of you and somehow I had a very strong feeling that, in coming to marry you, I was doing right. Sometimes one does not know where a path will lead one and yet instinctively one knows it is the right path. Perhaps between us we shall breed another great Prime Minister for India – God has his own ways of arranging matters so that his purposes may be carried out, and he has a habit of making the right mixture to produce the men he wants when he wants them. I do not suppose that Mahatma Gandhi's mother knew that in her arms lay the inspiration of millions, when first the child was put into her arms.
>
> At the moment, however, this little woman is concentrating on such deep intricacies as how to make a hot house cool and pleasant for her best beloved and on what he would like for breakfast. These deep matters of state are the subject of much cogitation – of course, that is supposing she is not banished to durance vile in Bombay.

Friday the 28th:

> Yesterday I had to stop writing suddenly because I had to go on deck and stay there – I felt so sick. I stayed out some six hours in the dark, but it saved me being sick. The sea was roaring past and the ship kept

pitching. Today it is better. Up to now I have taken each day at least one Indian dish – but feeling so sick yesterday evening and today, I could not. In fact, I could not eat anything much.

I am taking life very quietly and not doing much at all. The other first-class passengers get very drunk and noisy, which stops my sleep, but I shall go to bed early tonight and be asleep before they start.

The nearer I get to you the more I miss you but it is only about a fortnight now. I seem to have been waiting five years instead of five months.

29 April:

This is a funny disjointed letter, but that is inevitable because it is really a series of letters. It will serve, however, to show that each day I thought of you and that my love for you is very much alive, that, of all things in life, my dear brown man is most precious to me. I do hope there is news for me at Port Said – it is surprising how apprehensive one becomes when one is cut off from news particularly at this time when you are trying to do so much.

Very many students are coming home in this ship and it is touching how much they want to do something for India. I am afraid the disillusionment for many will be bitter, but such a constant flow of enthusiasm must act like a leaven in the solid weight which is India, raising it no little.

30 April:

Last night I was invited to 2nd Class to have a dance and I went and danced merrily with the students, which was a great relief after sitting every evening watching the 1st Class get tight. 2nd Class is a trifle less comfortable but infinitely more fun. You would have liked last evening. There was a general air of merriment which made one feel most cheerful. The fact that half the students haven't a clue about dancing didn't matter at all.

I expect that today you are stretched out on your bed reading detective novels. I expect I shall need a shovel to dig my way through to the flat, it being buried in detective novels!

Now I am learning Gujarati, I know how you can make the servant understand. Cheat, Rogue! The two languages are so similar that anyone having a good knowledge of Hindi could make himself understood in Gujarati. Scallywag!

1 May:

I am getting so excited at the thought of really being with you that my legs feel quite weak at times. I am so afraid and yet at the same time so happy.

It is not yet even uncomfortably warm in the ship, but I suppose tomorrow will be quite hot and the next day very hot, so I shall know when going through the Red Sea how hot 'very hot' is.

Today I swam in the little swimming pool which they have erected. It was very cold but I was most glad to have some exercise. The doctors on the ship all say we must take a walk or a swim every day no matter how hot, both on the ship and in India.

When the *Jal-Azad* docked at Port Said (the northern terminus of the Suez Canal on 2 May, there were three letters waiting for Helen, which Avadh had written on 22, 25 and 27 April. In them he apologized profusely and begged forgiveness for suggesting that Helen might ever sue him, then told her the good news that Kashi had accepted the sum he had offered to pay her in maintenance. This led to an amicable dissolution of the marriage. While Avadh's Doctor Brother had managed the negotiations, Kailash, the lawyer, took over the final legal arrangements for which my parents were eternally grateful.

Helen's name would change to a Hindu one when she converted to the religion before her marriage, and she had invited Avadh to choose one for her, but he wrote: 'Whatever your name changes to, somehow I love your present name and I think you will allow me to call you by that name. Otherwise we shall think of a suitable and lovely name for you – but no name can be lovelier than the present.'

With great excitement, Helen replied:

> My darling Husband to be,
>
> Last night at Port Said I had your letters and they brought with them such a breath of love and affection that I was almost overwhelmed and hardly knew how to put into words the love I feel for you.
>
> I am relieved Kashi has accepted the money – it shows at least that she is in a more reasonable frame of mind. I do not want her to be bereft of money or affection and if she has a little from us, she will not be unwelcome in her parents' house or feel quite helpless.
>
> Dearest I know I have chosen the sweetest and best of men for my husband and I have no doubts and no regrets about it. God knows what storms may face us, but, in them, I would rather have you by my side than anyone else. I have seen much of men and women in my chequered career and the number I would trust are

indeed few, but even if I did not love you, I would trust you; since I both love and trust you I am really happy.

Should anything unforeseen happen and you were not at Bombay to meet me, e.g. train is late or something, I will leave my address with Scindia by telephoning them.

All the Indian ladies are complaining that today is very hot, but it cannot be more than 90° [32°C] as the ship makes a little draught. It is hot enough to make my hands and back perspire, but it is good to be warm. Time enough to moan when it is intolerable.

4 May:

I went ashore at Port Said, but could not wander as the party I was with was bent on shopping. They bought bags of nylons and so forth, but the only thing I wanted was a cigar case for you – which request simply flattened Port Said, it being about the only thing on earth they had not got! So I went with 15/- and came back with 15/-.

The river, however, looked beautiful, lit with the light of many vessels and with stars and a full moon glittering above. *Jal-Azad* looked like a bejewelled queen surrounded by scurrying ladies in waiting. She was reloaded with oil, water and food. Before going ashore, a sort of Army Captain arrived like an invading German general, scrutinized our passports, stamped them and demanded if there were any Jews aboard, to which the Purser said airily and disgustedly 'no' as if Jews were something with which he never did business – there must be at least six aboard! They took our passports from us while we were ashore and these

> were guarded by a couple of bored-looking soldiers – this was to make sure we came back – they seemed frightened of infiltration of spies or refugees – although I know in England we take similar precautions.

Only two years earlier, the State of Israel had been established in what had been British Palestine and war broke out between Arabs and Jews of the region. Following the ten-month hostilities, around 700,000 Palestinians were expelled from the territory now occupied by Israel and the atmosphere was still tense when Helen passed through the Suez Canal in May 1950.

On 5 May, Helen wrote of some advice she had had from the Indian Jewess she had met, whom she discovered was to be employed at the hospital in Ahmedabad, where her employer would be Professor Cosmic Rays:

> Dr Solomon was telling me that in Ahmedabad it is essential that one should sleep under nets and take some Paludrine each week as the mosquitoes are malarial. Perhaps you already do so – it is more important that you should not be ill, than that I should not, as you are the breadwinner.

6 May:

> I was determined that there was going to be no love in this letter, since I can express it in person, but I have literally nothing to write about so I suppose I must say I love you and I love you, although I am almost too hot to say anything. Your favourite devil looks at the moment as if she had just popped up from hell! She is sweating like a Chief Stoker!
>
> The temperature of the sea itself is 90° [32°C] – the

air must be about another 15° [9°C] up. Not a breath of wind stirred in my cabin at the beginning of the day but this evening a breeze sprang up and life was again liveable.

7 May:

Next Sunday will be our first full day together – it seems so long since we were together – and sometimes I wonder how I have survived and I think often very deeply of the struggle you have had and I do appreciate it. No man could have done more for the girl he loved and she loves him all the more for it.

8 May:

I was very tired yesterday as I danced too long on Saturday evening, but it was only healthy fatigue. I am very well indeed now and I hope to remain well in India. I do not want to ever be so exhausted again as I was in England. In India at least I shall have time to eat.

I am getting used to being damp with perspiration – getting washed and dressed, however, is quite a test! One must shut the cabin door and draw heavy curtains across the porthole as otherwise one is too public. Without a fan the temperatures seems to rocket up and I am usually running with perspiration by the time I am dressed. I do manage, however.

9 May:

What shall I tell you today – make you suffer from swelled head by saying that I am haunted by thoughts of you, that all I can think of is you, that I simply cannot live without you, all of which are true, or shall I tell you of things about what I eat, drink or do, which will also be true. Somehow I feel you would prefer the former, and I shall leave it written and let you get swelled head!

10 May:

Today I have been on a tour of the ship with the chief engineer. I have sweltered in the engine room, sweated in the laundry and merely perspired out what juice was left in me in the kitchens. The engine room was 110° [43°C] without a breath of air moving or rather gusts of heat ascending every minute or so. The laundry was small but I examined their work and it was excellent, although they did not work very fast! In the kitchens, they have a butcher, baker, vegetable cooks and goodness only knows how many general factotums. They have a potato peeler, refrigerator, cold store and automatic mixer.

11 May:

The more I solemnly write this letter the more it amuses me now I am quite certain I am most in love with you – I am either that or quite mad – otherwise I am sure I should never do such a crazy thing! I must have held multitudes of conversations on this boat with English, Indians, French, and Germans and the more I learn of them the more I think what a lucky woman I am to have you.

12 May:

Someone once wrote that it is sweet to look on the face of the Beloved and tomorrow will be filled with sweetness, for I shall be doing just that. It is the beginning of a great adventure and we do not know quite where it will lead us, but at this moment a Psalm comes to my mind which was sung by a king in the wilderness and it is what I believe – not literally but in the spirit of it: The Lord is my Shepherd; I shall not want. He maketh me down to lie in pastures green; he leadeth me the still waters by. In him shall I trust.

So soon to kiss your dear face.

Your,

Chutney.

PART III

Chapter Fifteen

Your flesh is my flesh, your mind my mind, and your spirit my spirit. We are each other.

As the *Jal-Azad* approached Bombay, Helen would have seen an impressive vista. On the water's edge was the famous Gateway to India, the twenty-six-metre-tall white basalt arch built to commemorate the visit of George V and Queen Mary in 1911. Just to the left of that was the elaborate domed Taj Mahal Palace Hotel, and stretching away around the bay was Marine Drive, lined with glamorous Art Deco buildings. Those sights were an impressive introduction to the grandeur of India, but docked them the culture shock began.

For almost any Westerner, arriving in India for the first time is jarring to the senses. The teeming masses of people seem to be in constant, confusing motion. With many men dressed in gleaming white and women brightly clothed in a riot of colour, under the sub-tropical sun the effect can be literally dazzling. Then there is the noise of people talking rapidly and loudly, voices often cutting across multiple other conversations. And finally the air is hot, humid and fragrant with pleasant, and some not-so-pleasant, smells of life lived far more in the open than we are used to.

As the *Jal-Azad* moved closer to the dock, Helen's excitement about her imminent reunion with Avadh must have been almost overwhelming. In a photograph, we can see her standing still on the deck looking out at the chaotic scene. She hasn't picked Avadh out of the crowd yet, perhaps because his face is hidden behind the camera. As she descended the gangplank, there could have been no doubt in her mind that she had entered a new world.

Avadh had warned her that it was not customary to kiss in public, and I don't know whether the custom was observed on this occasion. In *Thursday's Child*, my mother wrote of Peggie's reunion with Ajit when her ship docked in Bombay: 'Ajit had bounded up the gangway as soon as he was permitted to do so, caught my hands and looked into my face, while porters and passengers fought around us. Words did not come easily to either of us, but we both knew a wave of feeling. I knew I had come home.'

Avadh's Doctor Brother accompanied him to meet Helen; months later he confessed that his job had been to ensure she was well-bred and would be acceptable to the family before they gave the match any further blessing. She apparently passed with flying colours.

The couple stayed in Bombay for several days after her arrival. Avadh took Helen to an Arya Samaj temple and when the monks realized that she had read a lot about Hinduism – in fact, she was more knowledgeable than many people born into the faith – they welcomed her and gave her further instruction. Knowing that she wished to be married in the faith and accepted by her parents-in-law, they gave her the Indian name Jamunadevi, which means 'Daughter of the Jamuna River', the sacred river that flows just behind the Taj Mahal.

Arya Samaj's monotheistic approach, together with a dedication to the education and empowerment of women, within a Hindu context, fitted well with Avadh's modern views. For Helen, brought up in the Church of England, it provided an accessible entry point into Hinduism. According to her Certificate of Conversion, she 'applied on 14-5-1950 for conversion into Vedic Religion wholeheartedly after full understanding and vowed to act accordingly hence she was admitted into Vedic [Hindu] Religion after due Religious conversion ceremony.'

Helen and Avadh travelled to Ahmedabad to drop off her luggage and then on to Ajmer in Rajasthan, closer to Delhi, where Avadh, with his family's help, had arranged the wedding. There, at the Arya Samaj temple, Helen and Avadh were married on 24 May 1950.

The Arya Samaj wedding ceremony is less elaborate than most Hindu weddings, lasting only an hour or so, and Helen and Avadh's was very small. The ceremony was presided over by a Brahmin friend of Avadh's father. Both Helen and Avadh were dressed in off-white silk salwar kameez – a long shirt or tunic combined with pyjama-like pants that taper from the waist to ankles – and garlanded with flowers.

Three times Helen made a ritual offering of water to Avadh: first to pour on his feet, then his body and finally to drink. She offered him yoghurt, ghee and honey, which he sprinkled in all directions and then ate. After that, taking Helen's hand in his, Avadh chanted mantras promising to look after her and provide for her always.

Fire, the purest of all elements, is central to the wedding ceremony as it is said to strengthen the vows of the couple. In the 49° C (120° F) heat, they circled the fire four times, then were bound together ceremonially with a sash tied with three knots. They took seven steps together around the fire, binding themselves in spirit, and then made a final circling. After blessings by the Brahmin, they placed their hands on their hearts and chanted mantras pledging their love and asking for the Almighty's blessing.

This was the moment Helen had been awaiting for such a long time. She hadn't made it to the altar with either Harry or Eddie but, at last, she was marrying a man she loved deeply and passionately, to whom she was happy to devote her life. In *Thursday's Child*, she writes: 'With a flow of tender understanding between us we were married in front of the Creator.' Perhaps she was speaking for herself.

I'm sure there was a tinge of regret that none of her family could be there. Sadly, none of Avadh's family could attend either. Back at the family home in Delhi, his father had been taken ill and the doctors said he was dying. According to Hindu tradition, if Avadh's father died, there could be no wedding for a year so there was no time to lose. Avadh must have been worried about his father, but nothing could mar the perfect day when Helen at last became his wife.

Without taking a honeymoon, they headed back to their new home in Ahmedabad. Helen described what happened next in a letter to a friend, written in the 1990s:

> After a few days, my eldest brother-in-law called us to Delhi, and I stayed in the old Imperial hotel, so that Avadh could be present at his father's death. Since the communal family included aged and crosspatch uncles who did not approve of Avadh's marriage, I did not attend either the death or the cremation.
>
> I never saw my father-in-law, but he was tremendously good to me in organizing our wedding from his deathbed and changing his will, so that I inherited the appropriate small gifts he left to all his daughters-in-law. I still have

> the four bracelets I had made out of the lump of gold he left me, and a number of gold British sovereigns which I hope to pass on to my grandchildren in his memory. It was not a very happy start to a marriage but we sustained each other.

There is no surviving description of my grandfather but in *Thursday's Child* there is a passage about the family patriarch, Ram Singh, that is broadly consistent with references in Avadh's letters to his own father.

> [He] was noted for his toleration of the unorthodox behaviour of others, and, in fact, his own household was by no means orthodox. Many Western innovations had crept in. He had, however, insisted upon the observance of certain customs. No meat or eggs ever entered his house, although he had been discreetly deaf when busybodies told him that his sons ate both of these in restaurants. Prayers were said, fasts and festivals were kept, food was prepared in accordance with caste rules, and his charity was unfailing. He accepted his sons' Western mode of dress, since it had long been adopted by civil servants, and he himself wore it on official occasions; but when he was at home he wore the village-woven shirts and dhotis of his own people. When his father, Ajit's grandfather, died, Ram Singh abolished purdah throughout the family, much to his mother's disgust. He expected, however, that his womenfolk would not go out alone and would behave with modesty.
>
> Ram Singh ruled with justice what was still really a communal family, banded together for safety in troubled times, and for the protection of their weak and helpless ones. He considered every action and

> every question raised from the viewpoint of what was best for the family as a whole, and this frequently meant the sublimation of the desires of one member for the good of the many.

The sovereigns Avadh's father left to Helen in his will sit in a frame on the corner of my desk as I write this, a lasting connection to my tolerant grandfather and to that hot wedding day in Ajmer. They will indeed pass to Helen's grandchildren.

While Avadh was in Delhi attending to his father, Helen wrote to him from the Imperial Hotel with all the ardour of a newlywed: 'Ten days seems like eternity without you. How on earth did I ever wait five months before!! A month of marriage has taught me that I cannot do without you. Your flesh is my flesh, your mind my mind, and your spirit my spirit. We are each other.'

Chapter Sixteen

I had a new name, a new religion, a new language, a new diet and a totally new way of doing everything, domestic or social. I wore Indian clothes and learned Indian manners, to the best of my ability.

When Helen arrived in Ahmedabad in 1950 it had a population of about three-quarters of a million. This was roughly the same size as Liverpool or Manchester at the time, but while these English cities were declining in population, Ahmedabad had almost trebled in size since 1920. Its diverse mixture of Hindus, Muslims, Parsis and Jains contributed to a complex society, one that greatly fascinated my mother. She wrote in *The Moneylenders of Shahpur* about the intricacies of inter-caste marriage, and about a university teacher who was vilified by the local Jains for killing a fish for his biological research. Jains do not permit killing of any animals. In fact, Jain monks sweep the floor in front of them with a long feather to brush aside any insects so they do not accidentally step on them.

Ahmedabad is located in the western state of Gujarat, about eighty kilometres inland from the Arabian Sea.

Historically, it had been a strong commercial, financial and industrial centre, specializing in the trade of gold, silk and cotton. In 1950 it had a significant and progressive business establishment.

The first major cotton mill was established in 1861 and the industry grew rapidly. Because the mills produced a coarse product that was well suited to the domestic market, Ahmedabad's industry withstood the onslaught of cotton imports from Great Britain relatively well. By the 1940s, the textile industry was booming and the city was nicknamed the 'Manchester of India'. The 1940s also brought the establishment of the Physical Research Laboratory, several other educational institutions and finally, in 1949, Gujarat University.

Ahmedabad was particularly active in the Indian independence movement. Mahatma Gandhi had established two ashrams (a type of monastery) in the area in 1915 and 1917, and these later became centres of independence activism. Significant protests and strikes by textile workers against various aspects of English rule occurred from 1919 on. Ahmedabad was also the scene of much violence in the Hindu/Muslim riots that followed Partition in 1947, so the vibrant city in which Helen arrived in 1950 had had a turbulent recent past.

If someone were looking for the 'real' India in 1950, Ahmedabad must have been a good place to start because the influence of the British colonizers had been less there than elsewhere on the subcontinent. The English as a race were generally viewed with suspicion outside the upper echelons of big business. However, despite its good rail and road links, Ahmedabad was sufficiently isolated that Helen was seen more as a curiosity than as a representative of the former oppressor.

In *Thursday's Child*, Peggie describes her arrival in the fictional city of Shahpur, which is based on Ahmedabad:

> Shahpur station is big, but when our train drew into the platform at the end of a hot May day it was crammed to capacity with a shouting, milling crowd and with immense piles of luggage, amongst which strode the railway police with their rifles slung over their shoulders. A thin, red-shirted, red-turbaned porter piled onto his head our tin trunk, two pigskin trunks and a bedding roll, took a suitcase in each hand, and then motioned us to lead the way to the ticket barrier.

Peggie then embarks on a long, harrowing ride in a horse-drawn tonga [a light carriage]. While she mentions car horns in the centre of the city, motor vehicles would have been few and far between. Thirty years later, I looked out of a hotel window in the centre of Kanpur, another big industrial city, watching the endless oxen, bullocks, goats, pedestrians and cycle rickshaws passing by, and counted several minutes between each motorized vehicle, so I am sure there were even fewer in 1950. Helen and Avadh's eight- to nine-kilometre trip to their flat on the outskirts of the city could easily have taken a couple of hours by tonga because of the narrow, rutted streets crowded with people, camels and all manner of commerce.

In May, the temperature was probably over 43°C (110°F) and unlikely to drop below 27°C (80°F) at night-time. How did my mother cope with the heat? She describes English characters in her Indian novels whose pale skin is flushed scarlet with the effects of the climate. She said that the local women 'always made a joke of me because I used to go tomato red in the heat, which was a phenomenon they could not understand'.

Helen and Avadh had been promised a bungalow by the Physical Research Laboratory but it had not yet been built so they lived in a flat on the edge of the desert outside the city. Helen wrote:

> Our district was called 'The Garden of Gujarat' but it often reminds me of those beautiful abstract gardens that the Japanese sometimes construct – out of sand and stones!
>
> Hidden in the nothingness of it, however, were many villages including a Criminal Tribe Village [one in which a caste of criminals resided] (which very obligingly never robbed our little community; they preferred to raid the city suburbs.)
>
> Now it is all built over. But when I lived there, the land around the house was grazed by buffalo, racing camels, and goats. There were also lots of semi-wild dogs, the same colour as the sand, and it was strange to see them, if scared, suddenly rise out of the hollows they dug to sleep in and hurry away. In a tree at the back, a huge collection of baboons lived, and they used to put their long arms through the bars of the kitchen window, to try to steal anything edible.
>
> I had to learn never to open the door to strangers, because the times, just after the partition of India into India and Pakistan, were very troubled. Sometimes I would see a local police constable on his bike struggling through the sand to a nearby village, to sort out some kind of problem. Bullock carts strained through the sand, carrying goods to market – sometimes, they were pulled by black buffalo, with the most beautiful eyes and eyelashes I have ever seen.

The bungalow that Helen and Avadh had been promised was never built. She explained:

> The material for the bungalow had already been delivered and was piled nearby. However, an argument broke out between two different factions of the education world as to who should be responsible for building it. As the fight went on, the local villagers found the pile of building material irresistible and it slowly shrank to almost nothing. The battle was still being waged when we left, still bungalowless. I do not know who won or what they did about the missing building materials!

Language – or, more precisely, languages – was a major challenge. Avadh spoke Hindi and those in the university community conversed in both English and Hindi, the national languages. In Helen and Avadh's block, there were sixteen flats and almost as many different languages from every corner of the country. And the local language was Gujarati, which was considerably different from Hindi. Avadh struggled to learn the minimal phrases he needed to communicate with the servant he employed, although the written language was sufficiently similar to Hindi that he could read it. But Helen was torn between Hindi, which she was still trying to teach herself, and Gujarati, which looked to her like a hopeless mess of squiggles. 'I was in a strange country with no language, except a few words of Hindi, no knowledge of the customs, not able to read, and yet expected to be a good Indian wife,' she wrote in a speech in later life. It was a struggle, but she managed to adapt remarkably well.

Avadh's friend Venket also brought a new wife, Bharati, to Ahmedabad. She was a scientist and came from Pondicherry, the French part of old India. Like Helen, she spoke no Gujarati and since neither of the men spoke much, they struggled to shop in the bazaars.

> Just to walk the three miles to the nearest bus stop, get to town each day to buy food in 110 degrees of heat [43°C] was an appalling effort. Then which bus? How to ask for what I wanted? How to manage a strange currency, a strange set of weights and measures in a country where everything is bargained for?
>
> Many of the men in our little settlement spoke English but none of their wives did. Only a single lady professor [in a neighbouring flat, whom Avadh had mentioned in his letters], who also spoke a little English could help me out. She had no time to teach me, but she did have a little English-Hindi grammar book and I got an English-Gujarati one from London, and I started in, from scratch, to teach myself to read again.
>
> I taught myself the numbers and the currency first. Then I would stand behind a Gujarati housewife as she bought things and watch what she paid. And I would pay no more. After a couple of months, I could read prices and the housekeeping began to balance!

Helen learned to shop in the bazaar but she was aware that as an Englishwoman she would always struggle not to be overcharged. In *Thursday's Child* she recounts an anecdote about a fruit seller who complained bitterly that Ajit had driven too hard a bargain for someone with an English wife – implying that he must be well-off to afford one.

It was such a long, hot trip to the bazaar that it made sense for their servant to do the shopping most of the time. Helen had grown up with servants until the age of ten, so she knew to treat them with a balance of fairness and firmness.

> Shopping [took] a long time because there was no fixed price for anything, and a good servant charged only a small percentage on each shopping list. For example, if I gave my servant two rupees, about six percent would go into his own pocket, unless he managed to drive a very hard bargain and make it more in that way.
>
> Avadh was surprised that the two of us could live on the same amount of money that he had lived on, when he was alone with a servant. Of course, his servant cheated him.
>
> My servant was paid about £2 per month, plus three or four sets of shorts, shirts and undervests per year. He had a half day a week off – an innovation which was too much for my neighbours altogether, and occasionally he would get a week off to go to a marriage or back to his village. We also took a paternal interest in his health and family – these are all usual things with good employers. Heaven help a servant with a bad employer!

Helen and Avadh's servant was named (or nicknamed) Buchoo. As a youngster, that name was more familiar to me than the names of most of my cousins. He made my parents', and especially my mother's, lives in India much more manageable. Despite both Helen and Avadh's misgivings about servants, he proved trustworthy, hard-working and happy to have an English mistress. My mother said that when they were leaving India, Buchoo pleaded with them to take him along. I sometimes wonder what happened to him. I don't think my parents knew.

All Helen's practice cooking Indian food back in Liverpool was of little use to her when faced with the real ingredients and cooking methods of Ahmedabad.

> We received our inadequate rations as raw grain, rice and barley, sometimes wheat or millet. These had to be spread on a tray and stones and insects removed. Then they were washed and dried in the sun, after which we took them to the miller to be ground.
>
> Bread [rotis, which are a whole-wheat flatbread] was made fresh for every meal – as was every other dish. We had no refrigeration and food went bad in a very few hours. Anything left from a meal was taken outside, where beggars and holy men would wait, with their little brass bowls to receive it.

While the servant made some of the food, Helen learned to cook North Indian vegetarian staples such as pulao rice and vegetable curries, as well as party items such as puris (deep-fried bread, made for special occasions), snacks such as samosas (filled pastries), and sweets such as burfi (which is milk-based) and halwa (fried semolina with raisins and cashew nuts). She was not shy about asking Indian women for their recipes and worked hard at her cooking while in India. Her efforts were considerably more successful than her early attempts back in England and, when we lived in Canada later, she was quite capable of producing a full-fledged Indian meal for a visiting professor. Once a month or so she would cook an Indian meal just for my father and me. But it was the samosas, and sweets like burfi and halwa that I really looked forward to.

Our children were introduced to Indian food early and enjoy it too. I try my hand at Indian cooking from time to time but, despite a lesson from Vijay's wife and her daughter-in-law on my last trip there, rotis are beyond me.

Conditions in Helen's kitchen in Ahmedabad were fairly primitive, but nothing she could not handle after cooking over an open fire in Liverpool during the Depression.

> I cooked on a tiny stove, about 12 inches wide and 12 inches deep, filled with charcoal. It was set on the floor and I sat in front of it cross-legged. I felt I had hit the height of modern technology when we could afford to buy a tiny Primus stove which ran on paraffin; it boiled a pan of water in almost no time!
>
> The well gave water for one hour in the morning and one in the evening, so the first job was to fill big pots with water to last the day. I had a nice serving boy [Buchoo], who cleaned the house for me and did any other job I wanted done. He wore a loincloth and that was all.

In 1995, amid concerns about the impact of water utility privatization in the UK, Helen wrote to her sister Avril about the water shortage in India:

> I became very used to having little water in India. The tap was turned on for an hour every morning, and you had to draw enough from a trickling tap to last the day. This went on, even when our little settlement had its own well. I used to have about six pails of water for the three of us [including the servant] for absolutely everything [including bathing]. We had a lavatory that flushed and keeping it from getting blocked was a real headache. We used every ounce of water several times, and the residue went down the loo, needless to say.
>
> I felt I was lucky to have a loo that flushed, but after eighteen months, I began to think that the old-fashioned arrival of the untouchable [former term for someone outside the caste system, many of whom performed tasks considered unclean] who removed and cleaned the chamber pots had a lot of merit. He stank

and his cart stank, as did the little privy room – but at least it worked. He had a special back door straight into the lavatory room, because, as an untouchable, he would pollute the house if he walked through it – and of course, there was also the understandable danger that he carried germs which, through the centuries, he was immune to, and we were not. He would come in and clean the floor and the loo and I would pay him. And after he had gone, I would clean it all over again.

I washed my clothes in the traditional way, using a bucket of hot water in which to wet the garments. Then I would put them on the floor and rub salt into them. Then I would stand up and swing them round and round to beat them on the stone floor to get the dirt out. They were rinsed in cold water, hand wrung and put out on the verandah to dry. In summer, a double, heavy cotton sheet would dry in about five or 10 minutes. Later on, a washerman came out and took the clothes away to wash them in the River. They came back reasonably clean and ironed.

The washerman would also, on request, come to the house and press one's better saris right there. Since the minimum length of a sari is five yards, this is no mean amount of work taken off one's hands.

On a practical level, Helen learned to cook, keep house and manage life in India. She did her best to become a good Indian faculty wife. There were no doubt annoying frustrations – such as the standard of cleanliness in toilets, or the inefficiency of Indian bureaucracy – but for Helen these were just challenges to be overcome or accepted. However, there were some exceptional circumstances to contend with when Helen first arrived:

> In 1949, Ahmedabad had had an epidemic [of cholera], which had begun on the college campus. This year, the city was ready to combat it. Avadh and I stood in the longest queue I have ever seen, while two health workers filled syringes with the necessary shots and shoved the needles into the populace's proffered arms. They used the same needles again and again, washing them, rather ineffectually, in disinfectant between shots. One shudders to think what the result might be in this day of the much greater threat of AIDS from the needle itself. However, the cholera did not spread too much, so the Health authorities' efforts obviously worked.

Helen escaped the cholera but she soon became very ill with other diseases: 'My greatest single problem was ill health, because I had no natural defence against local germs. We did have a new well – polluted water is a great health problem in India. I contracted amoebic dysentery, pneumonia, influenza, etc, and became very anaemic.' She battled dysentery for several months, during which her weight dropped below seven stone and she struggled to regain her energy.

While she was trying to build up her strength, Helen was often on her own.

> My husband was the first theoretical physicist to be appointed to the new University of Gujarat, and he was, in consequence, a very busy man. I must say that I often had a quiet cry, as I tried, alone, to deal with circumstances which I had never met before, like two huge goats which walked in through the front door – and refused to go out! A shepherd kindly got them out for me, eventually.

The practicalities of her new life in India could easily have overwhelmed Helen but she was used to having little, overcoming hardship and being resourceful. She persevered and the reward was the people she encountered, the friendships she forged and the ever-deepening bond with her husband.

For the first year in India she did not meet Avadh's mother because of the Hindu period of mourning. Perhaps she still felt nervous at the thought of a visit from her new mother-in-law but at least by the time it took place she'd had some time to learn Indian customs.

> My mother-in-law, kind and willing, could not come to me, because my father-in-law died within a few weeks of our marriage. She was, by strong custom, confined to the family home or garden for one year of mourning. By the time she was free to visit, I had learned, at least, to cook, speak some mixed Gujarati and Hindi and put on a sari the right way round! We got on very well indeed, thank heavens.
>
> Her attitude about religion amused me greatly. She said one day, 'Religion is for men – women don't have time.' I asked her about her beliefs and she said, 'I believe what is, Is.' Which if you meditate upon it, is quite profound – for a little village lady who could not read or write.

Helen knew that Kashi had remained at the Bhatia family home in Bulandshahr, and was raising Vijay between there and his maternal grandparents' home in Kashmir. Avadh sent money every month for her and Vijay and relations between them became amicable. Not long after Avadh died and immediately after my son, Stephen, was born in 1985, Kashi wrote a most gracious letter to Helen. She said:

Robert Bhatia

'Avadh was a great learned person and you are a great writer, both were a perfect match, and were made for each other. My dear Avadh be always famous and be in the heart of everyone till sun and moon shines.'

Chapter Seventeen

> *A great, devout and wonderfully tolerant band of wonderful women – I was proud to know them.*

None of the letters my mother wrote from India has survived, but in later life she gave several speeches about the time she spent there. Somewhat surprisingly, one of the most extensive was a speech in 1978 to high-school students in the small city of Grande Prairie, Alberta, 460 kilometers north-west of Edmonton. This and a couple of other talks she gave offer very colourful descriptions of Indian society in the period so I have quoted from them at length in this chapter.

> Indians are a very, very tolerant people, and they had great experience of English people, because the English ruled them for 200 years. They were invariably very kind to me, rich and poor alike. And they forgave me the inevitable social blunders that I made.
>
> But I learned, and my moral values are based on Indian attitudes. Everybody loves money, but the Indians do not put it first in importance. First come

religious beliefs and, second, devotion to family, then hospitality.

Life was always interesting in India, because one interacted closely with people, with neighbours, those that serve you and those that you had to respect and serve. To my door came beggars, the umbrella man, the sweeper who cleaned the lavatory and took away the garbage; the milkman with his cow, the vegetable vendor, the cloth merchant, strolling players; [distant] relations arrived to camp out on the veranda; people from all over India who had come to work at the University – the latter caused me quite a lot of problems, because each one seemed to speak a different language!

The local people, Gujaratis, are famous for their beauty and, in those days wore most attractive costumes. The women wore red skirts and blouses with a veil. The men wore raspberry red turbans, tight, short, frilled jackets and dhotis – a dhoti is a long loincloth. When they were going to town, both sexes wore heavy leather shoes with pointed, turned up toes, trimmed with brass; otherwise, they went barefoot. The middle classes wore plain white and were Jains by religion.

As I learned Hindi and Gujarati, and came to understand the manners and customs, I was very happy there.

Helen's position as an outsider, combined with her fascination for the people around her, enabled her to interact with ordinary locals in a unique way.

Because I had no caste, I was very willing to give water to any passersby, most of whom were very low caste or actually untouchables. I did not feel that they

> would pollute me or my water jugs, which is what my higher-caste neighbours would feel if they gave water to the travellers.
>
> The result was that I had more loving friends in that isolated spot than I have ever had since. It was wonderful. Lots of jokes at the expense of the high-caste members of the university staff! And lots of little gifts of fresh vegetables from the travellers' farms. I learned to really love camels, which are so badly treated but seemed quite gentle once they got to know me.

In a speech to an Edmonton audience about women in India, Helen paid tribute to the village women she met, who made a very strong impression on her.

> When the rains were good, the farmers managed to raise good crops of millet, wheat and vegetables to feed themselves and the huge mill town of Ahmedabad. They were often helped in the fields by their women folk.
>
> I think that the women of that district were the most beautiful I have ever seen. They looked as if they had stepped out of some ancient Persian painting. I used to look forward to their passing my home on their way to market with milk, vegetables, and kitchen tools. They would sometimes stop and talk to me.
>
> They wear a very full, dark red skirt – the more material in it, the better off the family – and with it a backless, multi-coloured blouse with sleeves, which is tied by a thread around neck and waist. On their heads they wore a veil of thin red cloth and their holiday veils were usually exquisitely embroidered with mirror embroidery, which I have not seen anywhere else. Tiny pieces of mirror are held by embroidery in

> a large pattern and they look very attractive indeed dancing in the sunlight.
>
> To enable them to carry their brass jars of milk etc. safely, they plaited a little crown out of rope, which they put on their heads. Into this the rounded bottom of the largest jar was fitted, on top of that a smaller one and again on top of that a smaller one still – and on the very top were put her shoes, to preserve them until she got to town. The shoes were heavy leather embossed with brass rings and turned up at the toes.
>
> To lift this heavy load on to her head without spilling any of the milk or grain was an art, and I always found it incredible that such delicate, princess-like women could do it. They had, however, small rippling muscles, perfectly coordinated and even when with a small child still seemed to be able to do it effortlessly.
>
> They always sang as they walked along, perhaps six of them together and they laughed and joked without an atom of shyness, though they were very modest.
>
> The time of harvest was a wonderful time of little parties and of weddings. I was amused one night to see the men and women harvesting together, cutting the millet with sickles under the light of arc lamps. While we were there, there had been no proper harvests for three years and every single ear of grain was precious. And still the women sang as they worked. Even the oldest crone who came to beg a few annas [1/16 of a rupee] from me each week seemed to be able to make some wisecrack or quote some piece of country wisdom to show that things might be worse.

The village women were curious why the women in the university accommodation had so few babies while they themselves constantly had new arrivals. Since the methods used by the university women were far too expensive for villagers, Helen explained in her rudimentary Gujarati the art of timing and the importance of traditional ways of limiting a family – such as going to stay with their mothers during the part of the month when they were likely to become pregnant.

It seems obvious to me that my mother's language skills developed to be much more proficient than she admits, because to understand humour and folk sayings in another language takes considerable fluency. I think her natural friendliness was also an asset: she was determined to make friends in this new and, in many ways strange, land.

> I talked with village women, holy men, priests, shepherds, camel drivers, shopkeepers, beggars. I was called the Memsahib with the book, because I had always to carry a dictionary. I had no one to teach me Gujarati: my husband's language was Hindi. India is a very talkative country. My mind expanded.
>
> Just as thousands of other visitors and invaders have been, I was absorbed into the Indian mosaic. When I walk down an English street, and see the tired, sad faces approaching me, I think of the Red Gate in Ahmedabad or the Colaba in Bombay and people surging by me, laughing, talking, arguing, quarrelling – alive.

As well as village people and travellers, Helen made friends with Avadh's university colleagues. In the late 1990s, she wrote about some of her memories for the fiftieth anniversary commemoration of the establishment of the Physics Research Laboratory where Avadh worked.

> Professor Bhatia was encouraged to come to Ahmedabad by his friend, Dr Vikram Sarabhai, himself a Cosmic

> Ray specialist. Dr Sarabhai was the son of a great Ahmedabad family with huge business interests, so his life was, of a necessity, split between science and commerce. He and his family were extremely kind to us while we were in Ahmedabad.

Before Helen came, Avadh had felt snubbed when he was not invited by Dr Sarabhai to attend a function with a visiting professor, but after Helen arrived, they were invited by the Sarabhais a number of times. Coincidentally, in the 1990s, while on a tour of India, Helen found herself in the Sarabhai family mansion, which had by then been converted into a textile museum. It brought back fond memories of playing pat-a-cake with Professor Sarabhai's little boy.

> When we arrived, the Laboratory was in the charge of Dr Ramanathan, a wonderfully gentle soul. He and his wife showered kindnesses upon us which were particularly appreciated by the Professor's English, casteless wife [Helen], who did understand the problems she presented to such households [as a foreigner, lacking a proper caste, and therefore a proper place in the social order]. Later on, we were joined by Dr Venketesen [Venket] and his new wife, Bharati, both of whom worked in Cosmic Rays. They had to stay in a barracks of a students' residence, because, as with us, permanent accommodation had not yet been built.

There was similar confusion and disorganization surrounding the facilities at the laboratory, which was on the outskirts of Ahmedabad, with no local bazaar to serve it, but Helen soon discovered who to ask if there was a problem.

> One of the most useful people in the laboratory was not a scientist. He was an elderly Brahmin who lived in the woodshed. His name was Jokha Pandey. He was the Commissionaire in charge of the watchmen, and he was the person who was consulted by the entire staff on how to get ration books, seats in trains, get paraffin for pressure stoves, move furniture, etc. He knew everything about the city and everybody in it. When he was off duty, he would recite the scriptures to anyone who invited him. He was so capable that I doubt whether the staff could have survived without him. We certainly could not have done. Dr Bhatia was from United Provinces, and he did not know much about local Gujarati affairs, and, for myself, as a foreigner floundering in a totally alien environment, he was wise grandfather, friend and mentor, who saved me from many a social faux pas.

In 1950 Helen attended the ceremony at which the foundation stone of the permanent laboratory was laid by Sardar Patel, a very prominent leader in the Anti-British movement, who after independence became Deputy Prime Minister. He died of heart failure in December 1950. She wrote:

> I think it was Sardar Patel who came to lay it. Later, I heard him give a public address. I could not, at that time, understand all he said because he spoke in Gujarati, but I remember being enormously impressed at how this tiny crumpled autumn leaf of a man could hold an audience so brilliantly. Within a year, I was, with a million others, in Bombay to weep at his funeral. Truly, Gujarat has produced some amazing men and women.

My father was already fairly well known for his work in theoretical nuclear physics and in solid state physics when he arrived at the laboratory at the age of twenty-eight. He loved his subject, although he was unhappy about the military applications of nuclear physics. For this reason, he steered his research towards other fields such as the properties of matter, in particular liquid metals, in which he became very well known. It was a struggle for him to set up a research and teaching department, with adequate facilities for students. When he left Ahmedabad in 1952, he was still fighting for the funds to subscribe to appropriate journals of physics to help the staff keep up with modern developments.

*

In coming to India, my mother committed herself emotionally and intellectually to Avadh but also to India and whatever it brought. Her experience there became fundamental to her being.

On an intimate level she found deep, true and lasting love with an Indian man. While Avadh worried, in some of his letters, about the challenges of a relationship spanning a cultural divide, Helen's approach was to fling herself wholeheartedly into Indian life and to become as Indian as she possibly could.

Her adoption of Hinduism was genuine. While Helen was not outwardly religious or spiritual, she did seek solace, acceptance and understanding in Hindu philosophy for the rest of her life. At the same time, she did not lose her appreciation for the beauty and goodness of the Church of England.

When I was growing up, she often described to me the near-desert scenes outside the Ahmedabad flat and the many different types of people she met. Her experience as a social worker, as well as her personal experience of poverty, gave her an empathy with the rural and urban poor in India. She had been brought up in villages and small towns, so could appreciate and begin to understand the rural lifestyles around her. In particular, her admiration for the village women was always evident.

At the same time, her early exposure to the upper-middle-class circle of her parents' friends, together with her experience in business, would have amply prepared her for socializing with Dr Sarabhai and his wealthy family.

Despite the language barrier, she had a strong and deep respect for everyone she met in India, especially the ordinary people she encountered in her day-to-day life.

She was less shocked by the physical manifestations of poverty in India than most Westerners because she had seen, and experienced, many of them herself in the slums of Liverpool. In some ways, my mother was also very accepting of the broader social context of India and its inequalities and injustices. Perhaps having watched her own society being torn apart by Depression and then war, she felt she had no right, or need, to criticize another.

Her plunge into poverty as a girl and her slow re-emergence as a young woman were fundamental to the arc of her life story but her years in India were equally important in shaping her future intellectual, spiritual and day-to-day life. It is not surprising that when she turned to writing she produced two novels set in India. As she told her young audience in Grande Prairie, 'My books, *The Moneylenders of Shahpur* and *Thursday's Child,* both contain descriptions of the countryside and the local customs. I used the background in the books, but I made up the stories – they are not my life.'

My mother was frequently asked if *Thursday's Child* was autobiographical. After all, it is a novel about a young Liverpool woman marrying an Indian man and going to live in India, written by a woman from Liverpool who went to India, married an Indian man and lived there for two years. There are clear differences between Peggie and Helen's stories but many similarities, as well.

As I delved into the details of this period of my parents' lives, and reread *Thursday's Child*, I enjoyed observing how my mother had used the broadest outline of her own dramatic experience to create a gentle love story with just a little of her own drama. It is very much a novel, but it is very much Helen's novel too.

Like many good stories, *The Moneylenders of Shahpur* is based on universal themes and human characteristics placed in a distinctive setting and context. It draws very directly on the university community at the edge of 'Shahpur', describing the village life and the physical environment that Helen experienced in Ahmedabad. Most interestingly, it draws on the particular diversity of Ahmedabad, with its sizeable and influential Jain community. The novel is clearly rooted in Helen's experience, and has some very witty observations on village life, but is not directly connected to her personal life.

Avadh had always intended his tenure in Ahmedabad to be limited, just a rung on the career ladder. At one point, he applied for a position in Delhi. Ultimately it was the draw of physics in the West that would tempt him, and wrench Helen away from her Indian home which, in just two years, she had grown to love very deeply.

Chapter Eighteen

I shut myself up in my minute flat with my husband's old typewriter, and on the back of some of his old lecture notes, I drafted Thursday's Child, *to assuage the homesickness for India.*

In 1951, Avadh received an invitation to move to the University of Edinburgh to work with Professor Max Born, a Jewish German refugee and a brilliant physicist. Then nearly seventy years of age, Max Born had been a pioneer of quantum mechanics; the important breakthroughs he made during the 1920s would be rewarded with a Nobel Prize in Physics in 1954. Born in Germany, he had moved to the UK in 1933 and had worked at the University of Edinburgh from 1936 onwards, attracting a number of brilliant young physicists to his department. It was a great honour for Avadh to be invited to join them. His old mentor Professor Fröhlich's high opinion of Avadh had played a part, but by this stage he also had a growing body of research in his own right.

When Avadh told Helen about the offer, she was torn. She had immersed herself in India and had grown to love its colour and vibrancy as well as the fascinating people she met. She had respected her husband's desire to help contribute to scientific research in the country of his birth, and had been prepared for them to spend the rest of their lives there. While there would be some advantages to returning to Britain – not least that she would presumably not get ill so often – she had definite misgivings about the move. In the end, though, she wanted what was best for Avadh's career and moving to Edinburgh was a great step forwards for him.

Helen and Avadh found a flat on Torphichen Street, just a stone's throw from majestic Edinburgh Castle. It was also only a few minutes' walk from Princes Street, which became her favourite high street anywhere. However, she had not expected to find the culture to which she was transported so radically different from that of her English upbringing. In 1992, she described this in a lecture.

> Now Edinburgh, as you know, is the capital of Scotland; it is far from being English, despite our best unkind efforts in the past. My husband had the continuity of his physics and the company of a number of very brilliant young physicists drawn from many parts of the world, and he slid into his new life like a duck into water.
>
> The culture shock was for me so great that I felt more like a hen in deep water than a duck, as I reversed gears to become again an English woman – with an Indian name – in a Scottish city, which rightly did not like Sassenachs [English people] too much. I was shaky from much illness and very underweight.
>
> I had so sunk myself into Indian society and got so used to the quiet life in the semi-desert that I had a very hard battle to go into reverse. I remember teetering

> on the edge of Princes Street, too afraid to cross the road because of the traffic. After all, when you have been used to bullocks and camels, a stream of cars is quite terrifying. Finally, the police constable directing traffic came over to me and, when I explained, he helped me across. After that, I was less afraid.

Avadh started work in Max Born's department, but was soon to find that working with a physics genius had its price. The following anecdote about Born's propensity to make computational errors is told in a book by a future colleague of Avadh's called Anton Capri:

> In the 1940s [*sic*, actually early 1950s] when Bhatia and R. B. Dingle were post-doctoral fellows with Born, he gave them one of his manuscripts to review. These two young physicists checked his work and found several silly mistakes. The next day when Born asked them about the work they pointed out that they had found some mistakes. Much to their surprise, Born became quite angry and even threw chalk at them while declaring that they were not competent to understand his work. Naturally they were visibly distraught and doubted whether they had the necessary ability to do physics. The next day Born returned, apologized, and told them that they were right. Both young physicists went on to have brilliant careers.

The fellowship awarded to Avadh did not pay enough for them both to live on, so Helen decided to look for a job of her own in Edinburgh.

> Packaging there was none, so I became the secretary of a Scottish chemical engineer. I did not enjoy the

> people or the job, even when he raised my salary. But Edinburgh is a fine 18th-century city, and I enjoyed walking around it and comparing it with Liverpool's 19th-century buildings. And I have retained this interest in habitat ever since.
>
> I worked for Imperial Chemicals there and learned a lot about the inner machinations of very big business. Of course, oil companies had taught me a lot and so had the packaging industry – but huge international cartels in the chemical industry taught me who really ruled the world.

Post-doctoral fellow appointments are limited in duration and Avadh's was no exception. Helen was just having their trunks repaired for a return to India in 1953 when the Canadian National Research Council sent a representative to Edinburgh and asked Avadh if he would consider working in Ottawa. Once again, it looked like a very good opportunity for Avadh to build his research career, and he accepted.

On the sea voyage to Canada, Helen was very ill with flu. Her health was already fragile from all the diseases she had caught in India, so when they arrived in Ottawa, Avadh did not want her to work. However, she found little to occupy her without a job since the city was almost impossibly tiny and unsophisticated for a national capital: 'Ottawa in those days was not the emporium of culture it is today. It still had wooden sidewalks; and diplomats were sent there to recover from nervous breakdowns they suffered while serving in Moscow and Washington. The life for educated women was so empty and vapid that I could not face it.'

To occupy her time, she turned to the pursuit she had often talked about over the years but never got around to: writing. Her only previous experience was the two short magazine articles she had written back in Liverpool, but sitting at home in a strange country, she said she created characters for her first book 'from a desperate need to have someone to talk to, someone to tell about her gnawing homesickness and her fear of this enormous new country'.

Alien There Is None (later published as *Thursday's Child*) quickly took shape during 1953 and 1954. In the first draft Helen had to write all the letter 'e's in by hand because that typewriter key had broken but she invested some money to retype a clean final version: 'I had the letter E replaced on the typewriter, at what seemed great expense in those days, and I splurged on a quire of decent typing paper. I plodded through a neat copy.'

Meanwhile, disillusioned with a research post in Ottawa that was not all that had been promised Avadh began to search for another position within a year of their arrival.

> We had an offer from the University of Alberta. Now was the moment of decision. I was pregnant. What was our baby to be? An Indian – because there was a job waiting for my husband in India. An Englishman – Avadh could have a job in England if he wanted it. Or a Canadian in the tiny prairie town of Edmonton, just beginning to expand in the oil boom.

Avadh was also offered a position with the Ford Motor Company near Detroit but wisely chose to steer clear of the corporate world, which would not have suited him. After much soul-searching, my parents chose Edmonton because it offered Avadh a secure position as a professor. In the summer of 1955 my mother packed their trunks once more and they set off by rail for the three-day train journey west from Ottawa to Edmonton. By this time she was eight months pregnant.

Mum often described to me her impressions of this journey, on which the rugged forests of Northern Ontario seemed to go on forever. The only people she saw from the window were Canadian Natives dressed in traditional garb, waving to the train as it lumbered by. 'I have never been so frightened of what was to become of me as I was on that journey,' she told me. She felt a glimmer of hope when the train pulled in to the large limestone station in Winnipeg: perhaps they were going to reach civilization after all? But Edmonton was still a day's travel away and when they arrived, she was doubtless near despair.

My parents moved into a rented house on the university campus. Fortunately it was just 200 metres from the biggest and best hospital in the province of Alberta, where I was born on a snowy late September day a few weeks after their arrival. I could just as easily have been born in three other countries but, as the dice rolled, I was to be an Edmontonian and Canadian.

*

In 1955, Edmonton, the capital city of the province of Alberta, was not exactly a 'tiny prairie town' but a modest-sized city of about 225,000 people. It had grown rapidly during the twentieth century from what was originally a small settlement outside a fort built for fur trading in 1795. The city had long been a centre for meat processing and a gateway to northern Canada but, since 1947, it had boomed because of the discovery of oil nearby. Since almost nothing was more than fifty years old it had a newness that was either refreshing, or raw and unwelcoming, depending on your point of view.

To his eternal credit, Alexander Rutherford, the first premier of the province of Alberta, had in 1906 established a university just across the beautiful wooded parkland of the North Saskatchewan River valley from the brand-new Legislature. By the mid 1950s, the university was growing rapidly and the space race between the United States and the Soviet Union added impetus to the need for scientists, especially physicists.

Despite his self-doubts and physical frailty, for my father, the university was a peaceful place where he could teach and think and generate research. The inevitable academic politics were relatively tame compared to those in India, the intellectual freedom was enviable and the salary was a living wage, just. My father's early academic colleagues there had unusually deep Canadian roots in Nova Scotia, Ontario and Montreal, in some cases dating back to the eighteenth century in a country that was otherwise full of recent immigrants. While East Indians were almost non-existent on campus – or anywhere else in Alberta (or most of Canada) – for the most part, academic respect and commonality trumped any inclinations toward discrimination. My father got on with his work, protected from the outside world by the university and by my mother.

Mum had her hands full caring for a colicky newborn through the depths of winter in a place where temperatures fell to -30°C (22°F) and snow was piled high through a long winter. Her isolation as a new mother was compounded by the loneliness of being a recent immigrant. She missed the boisterous and busy streets of Liverpool, the vibrant and colourful outdoor life of India and, in retrospect, the refinement of Edinburgh. Casual social contact was both rare and difficult in a cold climate and a more reserved and private society.

English immigrants were in an odd position in Alberta. The English were the source of the dominant culture in Ontario, Canada's Maritime Provinces and on the west coast of British Columbia, but on the prairies they had a tendency to be curiously marginalized, especially if they were perceived as being 'upper class'.

Canadian government policy had explicitly favoured 'stalwart peasant' immigrants from Germany and Eastern Europe, who would develop the agricultural economy of the prairies, over British immigrants who would be more likely to congregate in cities. I remember my mother returning from a department store in tears because a clerk had made fun of her accent and use of Anglicisms.

My mother was not alone in this. She spoke in reverential tones about a book written by a University of Alberta professor entitled *No Englishman Need Apply*. It was clear she was relieved that someone had addressed this normally taboo subject. A summary in a more recent book entitled *Invisible Immigrants*, by Marilyn Barber and Murray Watson, explains the phenomenon further:

> Postwar English immigrants believed they were moving to a familiar British country. Instead, like other immigrants, they found they had to deal with separation from home and family while adapting to a new country, a new landscape, and a new culture. Although English immigrants did not appear visibly different from their new neighbours, as soon as they spoke they were immediately identified as 'foreign'.

For my mother, her capacity to adapt may simply have been exhausted by that point.

> Western Canada was a far more difficult place to get used to than any other place I had ever faced. Absolutely nothing that we believed in or cared for fitted in. We had simply seen and experienced so much that when we opened our mouths, we found we could not explain

> what was obvious to us, to our colleagues and neighbours. Of course, nowadays, Albertan city dwellers are about as sophisticated as anyone would find anywhere. But we were the first of a flood of people from East and West, who brought our expertise and added it to a basically rural experience.

I was oblivious to the significance of this at the time but it perpetuated a key theme of Mum's life story: that of the outsider, stuck behind invisible boundaries. As she described in *Twopence to Cross the Mersey*, she had been an upper-middle-class girl thrown into the slums of Liverpool. Once she married my father, she was an Englishwoman in India, shortly after its hard-won independence from Britain. For almost two years she was a Sassenach in Edinburgh and now she was an immigrant in Canada. Later in life she was very aware that she was an English writer whose readers were primarily English but, since 1952, she had only lived in the United Kingdom for two years.

No wonder she often felt lonely.

Chapter Nineteen

Wherever we went, our child went with us. He spent a lot of time sitting on my lap to see what I did and how I did it. I'm very close to Robert. I'm so glad I had him.

After two years living on the university campus, we moved into a small bungalow with a mustard-yellow stucco exterior. The street was lined on both sides with beautiful elm trees, which gave it an old-world charm. The house itself had been built during the Depression and, while it was very basic, it had a few flourishes of craftsmanship in some of the carpentry and metal work. Textured brass door handles, French doors with multiple panes of glass, stylish hot-water radiators, and a built-in wooden desk suggested that those builders had worked on more grandiose projects in wealthier times.

'The front garden was so overgrown when we first saw it that we didn't think there was a house there. But when we saw it, we leapt at it,' my mother told me. She loved that house until the neighbourhood succumbed to high-rise developers in the mid 1960s, and we moved on.

After I got through the colicky baby years, as a toddler I frequently woke at night with cramps in my legs. One of my earliest memories, from when I must have been about three, is of my mother carrying me into the kitchen in the dead of night. She sat me on the kitchen counter for a moment, probably planning to heat some towels to wrap around my legs, then all of a sudden she collapsed in a faint. I was terrified to see her lying on the floor but Mum was used to pushing herself through extreme fatigue so she recovered quickly and got up to retrieve me before I came to any harm.

She always worried that I would waken Dad at night. He could not be disturbed because he desperately needed his sleep. Although he was productive in his research, and was taking to teaching well, he pushed himself hard in an effort to earn the respect of his colleagues and the university administration in this foreign land. He also suffered from frail health as a result of a tropical disease he'd had in his youth (likely typhoid) and an ulcer that would plague him for years before it was diagnosed and treated effectively.

Mum had no time for further writing in these years but she began to send *Alien There Is None* to potential publishers. Her story of an Englishwoman who marries an Indian man and moves to India had a similar experience to many other first novels: it collected a growing pile of rejection slips. This was frustrating in itself but the process was exacerbated by the distance from Edmonton to London, which meant it took a long time to get a response and the cost of the postage was high. Helen sought help from a friend of a friend in the book business who read the manuscript and sent back a critique, at the same time suggesting some publishers she might try next. In October 1957 Helen wrote to her:

Thank you very much for your letter and your most helpful criticisms of my book. It was very good of you to take so much trouble over the work of a perfect stranger at a time when you must have been proper 'arassed'.

I have no hope at present of having time to do any more work on the book, so I think the best I can do is to let it travel to one of the publishers you mention and see what happens to it. I am enclosing a covering letter to Hodder and Stoughton, and hoped to trespass on your kindness further by asking you to send it to them.

One of the minor difficulties of life here is the lack of international postal coupons – the only post office which sells them is five miles away and is usually out of stock – so I am sending another dollar bill and trust that you may be able to enclose with the parcel to H and S about six shillings worth of English stamps. I hope this will not cause you a lot of trouble.

I feel that your criticism of the first half of the book is justified and I certainly could cut it considerably and still retain that 'flavour' of Peggie's English life in it, by omitting Angela's adventures and telescoping Peggie's earlier history.

I am rather attached to Khan and think I would leave him safely down the well [he committed suicide], as it is a very ordinary example of how the not inconsiderable amount of straying done by Indian wives is dealt with, and is the pivot on which the second thoughts of Father Singh regarding Peggie and Ajit revolve. Life in India is so frequently melodramatic by European standards that one of my greatest problems when writing about it was to find incidents which would sound plausible to European ears!

> I learned so much while writing this book and I wish very much that I could do some more work on it, but I have a husband in permanently poor health and a boy of two to cope with – and two-year-olds just do not understand about the need for quiet for invalids! The little lad also does not understand that most little boys go to sleep at night and take naps in the day time. I do hope your baby sleeps well and is thriving happily.
>
> I agree with you about agents and have always marketed my own work.
>
> With very many thanks for all your help I hope I may have the pleasure of meeting you one day.

Over forty years later, Helen claimed that the highlight of her entire writing career was getting the phone call from Hodder & Stoughton to say they had accepted *Alien There Is None*. A written offer followed and on 21 February 1958, Helen responded to Paul Hodder-Willams, Esq., with a hint of the shrewd business sense she had developed while working for the Metal Box Company in Liverpool.

> Thank you for your letter dated February 10, for your offer, and for your kind remarks regarding *Alien There is None*.
>
> I hope very much that our business association may be a long and pleasant one, and profitable to both of us.
>
> Before I sign the memorandum of agreement, I should be grateful if you would clarify a few points for me.
>
> I am sorry to question what is probably your standard memorandum of agreement and I feel sure that your firm would treat me fairly if anything unto-

> ward occurred so that publication was indefinitely delayed, but it would seem inadvisable on my part to sign a memorandum of agreement whereby a manuscript could languish on someone's desk for years without being published and without my being able to regain possession of it.

Despite the trepidation she must have felt at questioning anything that might get in the way of the triumph of being published, Helen was careful to protect herself. Her shrewdness in such matters would serve her well for decades.

My mother spent most of her £100 advance at the Hudson's Bay Company (which had been founded in 1670 as a fur-trading company but was now a chain of department stores), where she bought a lovely set of Queen Anne china with a delicate snowdrop pattern. It was probably the only truly luxurious purchase she made in the first forty years of her life. The appearance of that china always signified a very special occasion. I knew its significance and, while some pieces got broken or faded over the years, I used it in December 2015 to serve tea, sausage rolls and shortbread to friends with enough of an English connection to appreciate it.

The first copies of the book were sent to Mum in March 1959, an event that she greeted with excitement almost as great as the day when she got the phone call to tell her she was to be a published author. Although her novel was coming out in Britain, copies would also be sold in Canada – thus the interest of the *Edmonton Journal,* who sent a photographer to take the picture described in the Prologue to this book.

Shortly after this, my mother's efforts shifted to the task of getting us all across to England, since my father was to spend the summer of 1959 at the University of Liverpool.

He was flying to India first to visit his family and then to England, which was no inconsiderable journey. My mother and I, along with several large steamer trunks and suitcases, would make the three-day train journey to Montreal and then the seven-day voyage to Liverpool. She organized everything.

There was snow on the front steps on the cold May morning when the taxi arrived to take us to the railway station. I remember being awestruck by that train journey. We had the luxury of a private 'bedroom' with its own bathroom and a bed that magically appeared from the ceiling while we were eating dinner in the dining car. The heartland of Canada unfolded before my eyes as my mother read to me or played games like Snap and Happy Family. For me this excitement was only surpassed when we embarked from Montreal on Cunard's *Carinthia* for the crossing to Liverpool.

It's only now I appreciate what a tremendous relief that trip must have been for Mum. After almost six lonely years in Canada, she was going home.

*

I was not yet four years old, but my mother's enthusiasm for England and the novelty of our experiences there had a marked effect on me. The country had largely recovered from the war and for a child in 1959 it was charming. Rationing had ended five years earlier, unemployment was very low and the lush green countryside had yet to be crisscrossed by motorways. We stayed in a flat in Birkenhead, across the Mersey from Liverpool and just along from the Wirral peninsula. Digging in the sand at the seaside with both Mummy and Daddy, riding on a donkey along the shore, taking the train or double-decker bus and exploring the villages of the Wirral was magical. I remember meeting my grandparents and thinking them quite ordinary little people, long before I read about them in my mother's memoirs. I also met Mum's sister Fiona and her brother Brian, but I still had no real idea of the desperately hard childhood they'd all endured.

Years later, when my wife and I read Shirley Hughes's *Dogger* and her various *Alfie* books to our children, I'd often get a lump in my throat because it seemed as if she was describing those times. When researching for this paragraph, I was stunned to discover that she was born and brought up in West Kirby, precisely where I had been to the seaside and where we would live a few years later, from 1963 to '64.

I also remember the empty spaces between buildings in the centre of Liverpool, caused by wartime bombing, but they had little real meaning to me. Looking back, it was only fourteen years since the end of the war. The memories would have been very fresh and painful for my mother but it was still her home. At the time, I think she hoped that my father would return permanently to the university where he had earned his PhD, so we could live in a society she felt part of – but it was not to be.

Once or twice while we were there, my mother disappeared to do interviews about her book, which she had brought to the attention of the BBC and, I presume, the *Liverpool Echo*. This did not strike me as particularly unusual, or very interesting.

The magical summer of 1959 was a wonderful introduction to the English side of my heritage. When my mother spoke about England and Liverpool now I had real, if selective, pictures in my mind.

*

At the end of August, my mother and I boarded Cunard's *Sylvania* for the voyage to Montreal and then the *Super*

Continental back to Edmonton. I went to playschool for two years and then to school. Mum told me later that someone at the local school had warned that she and Dad should not attempt to teach me Hindi as it might confuse me when I started to learn to read. It's a shame I missed out on that opportunity, but otherwise I received a very good education.

Mum used to invite other university wives to the house and the women made polite conversation in the sitting room while I played with their children outdoors. She was always welcoming to any school friends I wanted to play with and the children whose parents were out at work tended to gravitate to our house. Later, I found out that my mother had read a book about how to teach children to play. She certainly spent a lot of time with me, playing snakes and ladders, reading Enid Blyton or *Treasure Island* to me, even letting me pitch to her in the back garden while she held a plastic baseball bat. Gradually I became more independent, but I always remained very close to my mother.

Somewhat like the caricature of the 1950s housewife that is so widespread today, Mum ensured that the house was a calm oasis for my father. Her efforts to make our home attractive and comfortable probably reflected a little of the ideal of her grandmother's house as well as a reaction to the turmoil and disorder she had endured in her family's homes. Max Born's wife had told Helen that physicists' wives had to be very practical and despite my father's occasional pleadings to 'get a man in', Helen did as many household tasks and repairs as she possibly could herself.

My father worked long hours while my mother did everything else. She always dealt with any practical matters, such as cooking meals, tending the house and caring for me. It was only once I was at school that she was able to snatch a few hours to start writing again. Her typewriter was perched on the dining-room table in our bungalow, and then on a small desk in the dining room of the house we moved to in 1968.

By 1960, Mum had grown very tired and a wise doctor suggested that my father spend Saturday afternoons with me in order to give her a break. He did, and it was wonderful. He took me shopping, we went for walks to his office, and he gamely played catch with a baseball, learned to bowl with me and later to play golf. It made our relationship closer and was good for both of us.

My father's health remained fragile, though. During the early 1960s, he gained a lot of weight due to the treatments prescribed for his ulcer, in an era when there was little understanding of ulcers. He then developed glaucoma and did not go to an eye doctor until it was almost too late. Only a new type of experimental surgery saved his sight.

Dad was due to spend a sabbatical year in Liverpool but it had to be delayed by a year because of the surgery. It was the late summer of 1963 when we set off. Once again, steamer trunks were packed and my mother and I embarked on the ten-day train and sea voyage, while my dad flew directly to England. Before we left, Mum bought a beautiful feathered hat. She had a firm belief that its charm would ease her way through British Customs with her collection of a dozen trunks and suitcases. I must say it seemed to work.

This time we lived in West Kirby, the next village along from Hoylake where my mother was born. I attended the local primary school and found I was well ahead of the other children my age, except when it came to adding pounds, shillings and pence – and even that was not insurmountable. My father was out teaching and doing research at the University of Liverpool all day, so my mother had a bit more time for her writing. *The Moneylenders of Shahpur* was finished in May 1964, although it would not find a publisher until 1987.

During that year in England I remember visiting my grandparents several times and meeting most of my aunts and uncles and a number of my cousins. At Christmas 1963 my grandparents came to our house, along with my auntie Fiona and her family, for a nice Christmas dinner and playtime with the latest toy cars.

My grandfather was ailing and he passed away that spring of 1964 at the age of seventy. I remember Mum going to see him in hospital the evening he died. Later that week my uncles and aunts gathered for the funeral. Mum attended while I stayed at home with my father during the service and then joined her at the little reception afterwards. In her private way, she grieved the loss of her father but I imagine she was also grieving for the family life that might have been had he and his wife not been such damaged individuals. At the time of his death Mum had had very little contact with him for many years, but she always kept a photograph of him on her bedroom wall.

*

When we returned to Canada in summer 1964, my mother wrote *The Latchkey Kid*, by far her most controversial novel. Inspired by a string of youth suicides that had been reported in the press, it was a satirical commentary on women who were too busy trying to achieve social prominence to attend to their families. Mum intended the book to be funny but it attracted a lot of criticism. She was a relative newcomer to Canada, a 'refined' English immigrant, and she was talking about an uncomfortable truth that Canadians were touchy about. Her strident defence of the book's satirical perspective and subsequent discussions about the interplay between fact and fiction left a strong impression on me. *The Latchkey Kid* did modestly well in Canada and was republished later in the United Kingdom but it discouraged her from writing novels with contemporary Canadian settings.

My father's career was flourishing and the Theoretical Physics Institute was established at the University of Alberta to develop research contacts at other universities, both in Canada and overseas. A flow of visiting professors came from all over the world. The custom at the time was that they were entertained in the home. As a result, my mother and I became quite expert at evening 'coffee parties'. We served sherry or whisky and soda as well as coffee, and finger foods such as the classic cocktail stick with a chunk of Cheddar cheese, a piece of pineapple and a maraschino cherry. I often helped to hand round the food and once earned a new sort of admiration from my mother when I helped her to arrange a coffee party at just three hours' notice.

As well as physics, my father was knowledgeable about English and Indian history and culture and was very well-informed on world events and politics. My mother read widely, both fiction and non-fiction, and did endless research for her novels. As a result, my parents spent a lot of time 'putting the world to rights' in the privacy of their own home. They discussed history, politics and the issues of the day in depth. My father was always supportive of my mother's writing career and, even more importantly, he was a constant source of intellectual stimulation and clearly appreciated her intelligence.

While Edmonton was still a small city and Helen did not develop many close friendships, she was not entirely isolated. There was a small writing community and a local chapter of the Canadian Authors Association, whose meetings she attended regularly. There was no dedicated independent bookstore in the city until 1956 – and then it was the first one between Toronto and Vancouver – but its ambitious owner eventually evolved into a publisher. Naturally, the store had a close relationship with local authors.

The Hudson's Bay Company department store had a good book department too. Moreover, it sponsored the annual Beaver award for the best submitted unpublished manuscript. In 1970, my mother returned home late one evening teary-eyed with excitement and clutching the golden trophy – 'My Beaver' – and $500 for *The Moneylenders of Shahpur*. She was very proud of that award and kept it permanently on display.

In the later 1960s, my mother was working on her novel *Liverpool Daisy* when a reporter proved to be an unexpected source of inspiration. As she explained later:

> I had written three novels, the latest one being *The Latchkey Kid*, and had had some success. The local Canadian newspaper, therefore, sent a young reporter to interview me – this city did not have many authors in those days.
>
> I brought out my best [snowdrops] tea set and made tea and cookies for him, and we had quite an amiable hour together. Imagine my horror when, a few days later, there was a page in the paper about 'this sheltered little professor's wife sitting amid her priceless English teacups. What did she know about life, still less about Canada?'
>
> I was terribly, terribly angry. His interviewing had been totally superficial and he never asked details of my life. I was in the middle of writing *Liverpool Daisy*, but I put her on hold and, in total rage, wrote *Twopence to Cross the Mersey*.

Helen consulted her family members back home before embarking on her first memoir. 'I told [my mother] it won't be very nice, but she said "go ahead and be as kind as you can".'

My grandmother visited Canada in 1968 and stayed with us for several weeks. I found her difficult to get along with and I don't think my mother enjoyed the visit much either. None of us was used to the kind of intrusion that house-guests bring. Lavinia died in 1972 before *Twopence* was published. My auntie Avril cared for her in her final weeks and Helen provided support by letter and telephone. After she passed away, Mum tried to book a flight to England to attend the funeral but found it impossible to get there in time and at an affordable cost so she grieved for her mother quietly, in her own way. Her childhood had been difficult and her relationship with Lavinia had often been fraught, but the loss of her second parent severed a link to the past.

Before sending *Twopence* out to publishers Mum changed all the names and used the pseudonym Helen Forrester for the first time to give herself an easy-to-pronounce English name and so that her siblings need not be identifiable. In fact they were proud of the book and told all their friends about it. Ten publishers rejected *Twopence,* with one editor saying he couldn't believe the suffering depicted and another complaining that it wasn't humorous. The editor at Jonathan Cape who accepted the manuscript, Tom Maschler, understood because he had seen and experienced similar hardship in Germany during the Depression.

I can personally attest to the long hours my mother spent checking facts. As far as possible, she confirmed memories with family members and friends to make *Twopence* and its sequels as accurate as possible. She wrote it, only partly consciously, in an innovative style, with a significant amount of direct dialogue. This style was unusual in autobiographies at the time. Helen wrote to a Canadian critic who had commented positively on the use of dialogue in the book: 'Your remark about the conversation in *Twopence* is so right. I still have living five brothers and sisters [Fiona had died of cancer in 1969] and between us we were able, knowing our own speech patterns, to reconstruct fairly accurately some of the conversations. Some are seared on my memory, like the ones with the old man in the park, God bless.'

In contrast to her experience with *The Latchkey Kid*, reviewers in both England and Canada heaped praise on *Twopence to Cross the Mersey* on its publication in 1974. My mother had often talked to me about her childhood so by the time I read it, at age nineteen, I already knew much of the story. All the same, it was compelling reading, and it made me cry.

This was the book with which my mother had truly found her voice as a writer. In subtle ways, she was evolving from a mother and housewife who wrote, into an author who was still a dedicated wife and mother. The big success of *Twopence* didn't come until five years later, when it was reissued, but soon after the original publication, almost imperceptibly at first, her confidence began to grow.

Writing the book had a cathartic effect on Mum, too. It forced her, as a mature adult, to work through in her mind the traumatic events she had experienced. Helen said she never understood her parents but I think writing helped her to put her experience into a longer-term context of her life and theirs.

Many readers were inspired by Helen's resilience and they wrote to share stories of their own suffering during the Depression. While the book resonated most directly with those who had lived in the ravaged cities of the North of England, the stark hardship also struck a chord with Canadians who had suffered mightily on the drought-stricken prairies during the 1930s.

Quite unexpectedly, Helen felt the love and admiration of thousands of strangers. Even today, loyal fans maintain a Facebook page dedicated to her books and her memory.

Chapter Twenty

I was determined that [my son] should be thoroughly prepared for a better life than I had, and at a time – the 1960s – when it was the fashion to lie about and smoke hash – he got propelled through university, my husband being of a like mind to myself.

During the late 1960s there was a lot of talk about the 'generation gap' between parents and children, but in our family it was pretty mild. There may have been bruised feelings occasionally, but I never felt any real alienation. I was always very close to Mum and I grew closer to my father when I was sixteen, after an odd opportunity arose for us to spend time together. Dad had to travel to Vancouver for a colleague's PhD student's final examination. It happened to fall on a Friday and he asked if I would like to come along for the weekend.

The celebratory dinner for the student took place in Vancouver's Chinatown and was the most unusual feast I have ever attended, consisting entirely of dishes that would never be found on English-language menus at the time such as Peking duck and whole baked cod (complete with eyes and fins). We went to see the James Bond movie *Diamonds Are Forever* and attended our first professional hockey game. This little trip marked the first time I saw my father travelling and working on his own, without my mother. Dad's competence and independence surprised me because I had always viewed her as the person who organized everything. Dad and I grew closer that weekend and continued to be close afterwards. Even after I moved away from home, we used to take evening walks together during which we discussed whatever aspect of life needed discussing.

After finishing school, I studied Economics at the University of Alberta, which had the huge advantage of being just two minutes' walk from home. One afternoon in March 1974, I came home from classes to find my father in bed and my mother at his bedside. She had just called an ambulance as it appeared Dad was having a heart attack. That turned out to be the case. It was scary; he was pale and was quietly suppressing the pain as we flitted in and out of the room watching for the ambulance. Years of pipe smoking and being overweight had caught up with him. Fortunately he received very good medical attention, along with strict orders to lose weight and stop smoking forthwith.

When he had recovered sufficiently to return to his lectures in September, this opened up a new cycle for my mother of caring for my still-fragile father. She had to learn how to cook without salt or butter, a skill she soon mastered after an initial panic at the impossibility of such a change. On about the fourth warning from an exasperated cardiologist, Dad's pipes were ceremonially dispatched to the garbage.

Writing was sidetracked for months but not abandoned. Helen completed a formulaic romance novel called *Most Precious Employee*. It was published in 1976 under the pseudonym June Edwards because it was written for a different market from her other books and has the distinction of having been translated into Dutch and Italian. This type of novel could be quite lucrative for writers able to produce them in bulk but Helen dipped her toe in and wisely stepped back.

Liverpool Daisy, the story of a woman who turns to prostitution to support her family and pay for her friend's medical treatment, was completed in 1976. It was promptly turned down by Jonathan Cape, the publishers of *Twopence*. When submitting it to a senior editor at The Bodley Head, Helen wrote in her covering letter:

> The pile of letters of approbation and the phone calls I have received as a result of the publication of *Twopence to Cross the Mersey* confirmed to the hilt the accuracy of that manuscript. And I feel the same acceptance will be extended to *Liverpool Daisy*.
>
> I lived for many years within two blocks of Catherine Street, a well-known red light district of Liverpool, and walked through it most evenings for seven years on my way to night school. It was a very harsh introduction to the idea of sex. As a social worker I often came into contact with women like Daisy.
>
> If I have any expert knowledge of anything, it is of poverty, having lived in it and worked three years to alleviate it amongst others. My wanderings in Liverpool, in India, in Mexico, in New York and even here, in Edmonton, have added to it.
>
> You will have probably heard Rod Stewart singing his smash [1971] hit, 'Maggie May', in praise of the present generation of Liverpool daisies, who specialize in young men. They don't seem to have changed much.

The Bodley Head turned it down. Helen was forever grateful to Robert Hale for publishing *Liverpool Daisy* in 1979.

She had a particular affection for her smelly, maternal prostitute; she always smiled and her eyes lit up when talking about her. I think she felt she had created a uniquely sympathetic character, firmly based in reality, one whose story deserved to be told.

In one memorable scene Daisy, wife of an absent seaman, is confronted and engaged by three drunken seamen on a dark street. While not exactly politically correct by twenty-first-century standards, Helen describes the events with deft humour:

> 'And there, in no time at all, at all, Mog, I found meself with another half dollar [half-crown] in me hand,' she later told her stony-faced cat. 'And another one coming up t' jigger at me.'
>
> As the third youth approached, it seemed to Daisy that her real self stood outside her body watching in scandalized horror a completely alien Daisy, filled with excited anticipation, await the boy coming towards her.
>
> 'Mog, it was as if the divil himself was in me. At first I thought I'd run away up to top of t'entry. But I could hear the rats rustling in the dustbins – and I'm more afraid of rats, as you know, Mog, than I am of any boy. So I waited for him.'

It is a testament to the broad appeal of the story that it resulted in another Beaver trophy (also displayed proudly) just before it was accepted for publication.

*

Helen paid a great deal of attention to the use of Liverpool dialect (Scouse) in her books. She wanted to give just enough to ensure that the characters sounded true to their Liverpool roots but stop short of it becoming obtrusive to readers elsewhere. When a reader wrote to her querying the use of t' instead of the, as in the passage above, Helen replied:

> You raise a very good point about the sounding of the word 'the' in Scouse. Although all the dialects are now getting flattened out, alas, as you may know, there are at least five distinct dialects in Liverpool, not to speak of variations in specific localities. When I was a social worker in Bootle, my senior colleague could, if a person had lived all his life in one street, tell him within a street, where he lived! It always used to surprise them.
>
> The sound I was trying to convey is a kind of swallowing of the word 'the', so that it hardly sounds. And I agree with you that t' is not the best way of showing it.
>
> I think that it is more accurately what is known in German as a Glottal stop, a fractional pause used in German between words. I think it has come down from a very long time ago to us, possibly from an early form of German.
>
> When I was travelling down from Liverpool to London just before Christmas, I sat by an old lady of 88, who had lived all her life in or near Park Road, and her speech was full of these abbreviated the's.
>
> To really translate Merseyside speech onto paper is impossible, if all one's readers are to understand, bearing in mind that many of those readers are Americans, Australians and Canadians.

It was also no coincidence that Daisy confided in her cat. Helen loved cats and owned a series of them through much of her time in Canada. All her life, she recalled the way cats like Mog struggled to survive back in Liverpool in the

1930s. My son recalls seeing a note with feeding instructions from the vet, on which Helen had carefully crossed out, and doubled, the quantities.

*

From 1978 to '79, Avadh spent a sabbatical year at Oxford University, while I stayed behind in Canada. Helen particularly enjoyed it there since they had the company of one of Avadh's close collaborators and his wife, Norman and Joan March, who had became good friends. At Christmas that year, my parents travelled to India and combined lecturing, family visits and holidays. I joined them for five weeks, my first visit to India. As I travelled around, staying some of the time in university guesthouses, I was introduced to hundreds of the tiny vignettes that make life in India so fascinating.

At the Indian Institute of Technology in Bombay, we were invited to the faculty New Year's Eve party, the best New Year's Eve I have ever experienced. It was dominated by children performing impromptu dances and running around with endless blowout noisemakers. Huge quantities of Indian snacks and sweets were on offer together with fresh lemonade. The excitement was unbridled.

During that trip my half-brother, Vijay, travelled across the country from a remote part of eastern India to see us. My father had funded him through university and he was now a highly successful professional engineer of almost thirty years of age. He greeted us warmly and presented me with a length of silk, which a tailor in Varanasi made into a shirt overnight. We got on well and in 2014 I would return, with my wife, Dianne, to stay with him and his family during Diwali, the Hindu Festival of Lights. It was a fabulous experience.

In Old Delhi, a walled city inside Delhi, we visited my

Doctor Uncle, who had been so instrumental in helping Avadh through his marriage crisis. I also saw the fine old family house and compound in Bulandshahr, which had become a home for the family's widows and was decaying sadly. We then spent a few days in Kanpur, a large industrial city. My Kanpur uncle, a charming, funny and self-effacing man, was an expert in ceramics, a significant industry in the city. He and his wife and his children and their families entertained us and showed us a very interesting Indian city where few tourists go.

This, my first trip to India, was my mother's first return to India after almost thirty years and my father's first visit in at least ten years, and we all enjoyed and appreciated it from our own perspectives. To me it was new and exciting; to my father it was familiar and a source of great pride. Not only was he able to show me his country of birth but, as a scientist successful in the west, he was revered and in constant demand in the university communities. My mother enjoyed observing both my reactions and the welcome extended to my father by the family and by fellow physicists. She, no doubt, enjoyed renewing her love affair with the country.

I came back with a strong feeling of connection to India, quite unlike that for any other country I have visited – except, not surprisingly, England.

*

While my parents were in Oxford, my father, never very strong, had begun to feel more tired than usual. Back in Edmonton, the doctor diagnosed a form of anaemia for which there was no cure. The only treatment was to have massive infusions of red blood cells every six or seven weeks.

For my parents, life began to be timed in intervals between

these infusions, which gradually got closer and closer together. My father continued to teach and do research while my mother did everything she could possibly think of to help him and to keep him safe from infection, to which he was highly susceptible.

While Jonathan Cape had sold all its copies of *Twopence* on first publication back in 1974, the print run had been limited. In the late 1970s, The Bodley Head agreed to republish *Twopence* if Helen would like to write another volume of her own life story. In a speech in Edmonton, she described her response to this offer:

> I did. It was called *Minerva's Stepchild* [later changed to *Liverpool Miss*]. Sales climbed. Letters from fans came by shoals. 'What happened next?' they asked. So I wrote *By the Waters of Liverpool*. And that, I thought, is that. I was fed up with writing about myself.
>
> I happily published two novels [*Liverpool Daisy* and *Three Women of Liverpool*], both of them doing very well. Both hit the bestsellers list.
>
> But my fans were not satisfied. They asked for more of my life. So I wrote *Lime Street at Two*, a quiet tale of a war, my war.
>
> In May 1983, I went to Britain to do a tour promoting *By the Waters of Liverpool*. Little did I realize, dear Readers, what I was starting.
>
> The tour lasted ten days. Some thirty thousand copies of the book had been ordered by bookshops and Fontana [the paperback publisher] was delighted. There was also a good demand for the earlier books, so they hastily put in orders for reprints of them.
>
> Well, when I arrived in Liverpool, to do a signing at W.H. Smith & Sons, the shop was so packed that they had had to form a queue, which went right round

> the block. That afternoon I signed 600 books in Smith's and 441 in Pritchard's at Crosby. At Smith's, Birkenhead, the next morning I signed 820 copies and in the afternoon 545 at Bookland, Wallasey. And so it went.
>
> In connection with this promotion tour, the Fontana people gave me a marvellous party on a ferry boat. They asked 150 north-western booksellers to it, and 180 came – typical Merseyside.
>
> En route to the airport, to come home, I went to Russ Hill Hotel nearby, where Fontana Paperbacks was having an annual sales meeting. I received a standing ovation as the computer ticked over 250,000 in sales for the trilogy. Books were selling that day at the rate of two thousand per hour, and the whole Fontana organization was concentrating on my books.
>
> Engulfed in flowers, I was escorted to the airport where the bookshop was simply covered with posters and copies of my book. It was the most exciting day of my life.

Avadh described this day in his diary: 'Fontana gathering of sales representatives. Beautiful surrounding. Stupendous reception of Helen, with introduction as best selling author of Fontana. H's speech very nice. Flower bouquet to H. Very moved by it all and very happy for H.'s success after all these years.'

I did not accompany Mum and Dad on this occasion but when they landed back at the airport in Edmonton, I heard about her momentous trip in detail.

It was unspoken, but we all knew how important it was that my dad was able to be there. His struggle with anaemia was getting harder. There was not much time left.

Chapter Twenty-one

It was a love affair which lasted 34 years, and I cannot imagine life without him.

In 1974, while at the University of Alberta, I had met Dianne, who was studying to be a teacher. We were married in a university chapel, filled to capacity with 150 guests, on a very hot day in July 1981. Very hot, but nothing compared to Ajmer – and there was no fire to walk around. My aunt Avril and her eldest son came from England for the occasion.

By this stage, I had spent a year at Queen's University in Kingston, Ontario (1976–77) then come back to Edmonton, where I was lucky enough to get a good position with the government of the Province of Alberta. My mother wrote to a reader, 'The boy is now an economist, with a great interest in how people manage.' This comment, when I was still in the early stages of my career, was particularly perceptive since leadership and executive coaching have been my focus for the past thirty-five years.

My mother regularly told me about her writing and what her characters were doing or might do in the future. A number of times she entrusted me with early drafts of her books on which I would comment honestly but always with the conclusion that it was going to be wonderful.

During the summer of 1984, the year following the Fontana sales conference in Liverpool, my dad was told he had just months to live. He was compiling a book, to be called *Mechanics of Deformable Media,* with a post-doctoral fellow from India, whom he liked very much. Throughout the summer the young man visited frequently and they worked together, with him sometimes sitting by my father's bedside.

By August, Dad could no longer eat and we all knew the end was getting near. He wanted to be at home but the medical system only provided minimal support. Fortunately a physician who had recently moved in next door realized what was happening and, with great compassion, took over the medical side. The strain on Mum was enormous as she cared for him one way or another, all day, every day, knowing that the only possible outcome was that she would lose him. She had no time to do or think of anything else.

At the end of September, Dianne and I dropped by after going out for dinner for my birthday. I sat with Dad holding his hand while Dianne and Mum talked in the kitchen. After ten minutes or so, the raspy irregular breathing from my stick-thin father stopped.

Our first reaction was for the three of us to embrace and laugh with the extraordinary relief that his long struggle was over, but of course that was very quickly supplanted by grief.

My mother wrote to inform her cousin Marjorie, who had lived with Helen's aunts and grandmother in Hoylake, in simple but moving terms:

> This is just to tell you of the death on 27 September of my darling Avadh, after much suffering.
>
> It was a love affair which lasted 34 years, and I cannot imagine life without him.

Dad was a Hindu. He practised his faith privately and was not connected to a Hindu temple or community, so my mother and I had had to consider the appropriate form of funeral for him. Well in advance, we approached the local Anglican [the Canadian equivalent of Church of England] priest at a church three minutes' walk away from our house. We explained the situation and were received warmly and graciously. He visited my father a few times and, when the time came, we had a simple service at the church attended by several dozen friends, colleagues and family. Dr Stuart Woods, a long-time physics colleague delivered the eulogy. Exhausted and numb with pain, my mother coped with the ritual well but, as people left, she pleaded with them not to forget about her.

In fact, in the early days, she received many offers of help – not all of them useful. To a Canadian acquaintance who worked in publishing, she wrote:

> I have, of course, heard about Betty Jane Wylie's book for widows, and thanks for reminding me about it. I am not sure that for the moment I can stand any more advice upon the subject of being a widow! I seem to have entered a mysterious, secret world of widows, all of whom give advice! It is all very well meant but nothing goes in, really. I am quite capable of managing the business side and I had been doing this steadily – it is practically a full-time job. The rest of me has to sit quiet until the shock has passed, before I can do anything. I exclude my writing, because that is a world

apart from my dear husband, which I am now able to cope with; everybody says I am lucky to have it, so I suppose I am. In a little while, maybe I will be able to face Betty Wylie's book.

Thanks for sharing my grief and for all your help. I'll be better soon.

A month later Venket and Bharati [the friends from India, who eventually moved to Calgary, Alberta] and their son, and a few other friends joined Mum, Dianne and her parents, and me on a cold November day to sprinkle Avadh's ashes near a gravestone of red Indian marble. Mum told her brother, Brian:

> The saddest thing I ever had to do was to sweep the snow off his grave plot, so that we could scatter the ashes on the earth. Somehow, it got me down that the snow came before we could hold the ceremony. A Brahmin read from the *Gita* [a Hindu scripture] and an old friend sang a song much loved by Gandhi, about freedom of the spirit. Then some 20 old friends came home for tea. After they left, I was alone in the house throughout the weekend, and frankly, it felt terrible. Then I was also alone the Remembrance Day weekend, and it was just as bad. At least at Christmas I shall be with Rob and Dianne and her family.

Just a few weeks later, I told Mum that Dianne was expecting our first child. The news of a grandchild, to be born nine months after my father's death, gave her some comfort in her grief.

Chapter Twenty-two

I never know quite what will come out until I begin to write. Then characters crawl out of the woodwork and from them the plot evolves. However, I am always reading, with an eye to a future book.

During 1984, as my dad's illness worsened, Mum's career had continued to flourish. Robert Hale Ltd., which had published *Three Women of Liverpool,* offered, out of the blue, to publish *The Latchkey Kid* in England. Fontana was contemplating republishing *Alien There Is None* as *Thursday's Child* and Helen was snatching whatever time she could to work on *Lime Street at Two.* She was also toying with the idea of a Lebanese heroine, who would form the backbone of *The Lemon Tree.*

My mother was exhausted physically and emotionally from the burden of caring for Dad, never mind the pain of actually losing him, but she did not wait long after his passing to throw herself into the book world again. In December 1984, just two months later, she was off to the south of England to promote her books. One result of this trip was her decision to engage an agent, Richard Scott

Simon, at long last, as her career was burgeoning and its complexity was growing.

In early 1985, after completing *Lime Street at Two*, she wrote to an old friend:

> This is absolutely the last book I write about myself. Everybody is rushing round me, saying, 'You must write the love story of you and Avadh'. But they have had it. As if they have no idea of the pain inside one! It is very well to write of things that happened 45 years ago – 40 years is just about time in which to recover. Anyway, with the success of *Three Women of Liverpool* and *Liverpool Daisy*, they know that I can write novels, so at least the publishers will probably shut up.

On the morning of 6 June 1985, Mum's sixty-sixth birthday, I was scheduled to take an aeroplane tour of irrigation facilities in Southern Alberta but, on a hunch the night before, I cancelled it. It was just as well. As Helen wrote later that month: 'I was blessed on my birthday this year by a special gift. Stephen James Avadh Bhatia made his entry into the world a little early. He is a very small baby, but healthy and Dianne is simply marvellous with him. She is feeding him herself.'

At the same time she was moved beyond measure by some other news:

> The University of Alberta also wrote to tell me that the physics building will in future be called The Avadh Bhatia Physics Laboratory in honour of Avadh. It made me weep because, like most prophets, Avadh was not honoured in his own country, and I think it is only since he died that the University has realised what a great man sat in their midst.

Later in the year Helen moved from the house she had shared with Dad to an apartment with floor-to-ceiling windows looking over the river valley and across to the University. Not only was the apartment less work and easier to leave when she wanted to travel, but it was also a symbol to Helen of her independence and success. She put her stamp on it by surrounding herself with books, the collection of fans she had been accumulating slowly since the 1970s, some treasured mementoes from India and floral-patterned bedspreads, cushions and teacups. More than one visitor commented that it looked like an English cottage. Her grandson, Stephen, enjoyed looking at all the interesting things in her apartment and hearing the personal stories that accompanied them.

While the trauma of Avadh's illness and death faded excruciatingly slowly, this was an intensely creative and productive period in Helen's writing. There was an added boost when she heard Fontana would be publishing yet another book in 1987: *The Moneylenders of Shahpur*, which had been languishing unloved by publishers for a long time. Helen wrote enthusiastically to her editor at Fontana, Andy McKillop, about several future books.

> I think that Richard [her agent] jumped the gun when he said I was about to embark on a novel with Indian settings and Liverpool connections. I obviously did not make myself clear. What I meant was that, if *The Moneylenders of Shahpur* is a reasonable success, I could write another Indian novel, perhaps giving it Liverpool connections.
>
> As you know, I am at present writing a novel about Liverpool [*Yes, Mama*], set in its most prosperous time, 1886 to 1922. It is a picture of a well-to-do family carefully burying a scandal, a bastard child, running

parallel with the horrific life of the slums which form the background of the child's nanny. The child's slow realization of why she is treated differently from other children corresponds with [the] financial decline of the family, and I propose to allow her to escape to Canada – finally.

I still have in mind to write a book with the background of the Liverpool soap trade [what would become *The Lemon Tree*], following the above, provided I can put together all the facts I need. In this, I also want to show the connection between the British and Lebanon in those days – there were many Britons in the fruit and silk trades out there. I thought I might take a girl from Lebanon and drop her into a middle-class soap merchant's home in Liverpool. Remembering some of the astute women I had met in India who were purdah bred, I thought I might make her into a sort of Helena Rubenstein of the Liverpool soap trade. (Helena Rubenstein rose to be one of the greatest producers of cosmetics who ever lived, in case you don't know the name.) This is why I mentioned that I had been reading histories of the Middle East, not to speak of travel guides, et cetera. None of it will actually go into the book, but it gives me the rich background of a potential heroine . . .

I was very interested in your remarks about writing longer books. It is sometimes nice to have more elbow room in which to develop characters.

In April 1987, a fan from Prince Edward Island wrote to Helen 'one of the most marvellous letters that I have ever received'. It began a friendship and planted the seed of a new book. Vincent Elordieta had been a member of Liverpool's Basque minority and wrote to Helen to share his history of Spanish people in Liverpool and his wartime experiences. His story was compelling and had connections to Helen's own experiences. She replied to him:

> It was ironical that you should be in a ship in the Mersey River at the time of the May Blitz. I was working at the petroleum installation during that terrible week and probably saw your ship sail into port from my office window. I thought you might enjoy the enclosed book, *Three Women of Liverpool*, in which I used the raid as the basis of a novel. It has been one of my most successful books.
>
> You mentioned seeing the *Mauretania II* being launched [in 1938]. Presumably, you were actually in Cammell Laird's as it slid down the slipway.
>
> You will be amused to hear that, standing on the Pier Head, was a very hungry young girl spending her lunchless lunch hour watching the same launch. Of course, it looked quite small from where I was, but it is the only ship I have ever seen launched, and I was quite excited.
>
> It is so strange, because we probably passed each other in the street at times.
>
> I can understand how hard it was for you to come home to Canada after being in Liverpool. It is as if it is impossible to tear free from one's roots entirely. Of course, my real childhood was not spent in Liverpool, but I get the same lost feeling after returning to Canada from any part of Britain.

She and Vincent began an active correspondence that took her down a creative path she had never anticipated. Within a few months, she decided to visit him in Prince Edward Island, where she interviewed him for hours, and his story became the inspiration for *The Liverpool Basque* (published in 1993), which followed *Yes, Mama* (1987) and *The Lemon Tree* (1991).

Helen's life was madly busy in the decade after Avadh's death, not least as she became grandmother to another baby. My and Dianne's second child, Lauren, arrived on 6 June 1988, sharing her birthday with her older brother and her increasingly famous granny. Organizing birthday celebrations for the month of June was a complex business in our household since the guest lists and interests of the honorees were rather different.

At the start of 1988, anticipating the new baby and acknowledging her growing fame, Helen wrote to a friend:

> I shall be away from Edmonton quite a lot this year – a Canadian publicity tour during March, a speaking tour on Merseyside in Britain in April, Writers Union Annual Meeting in Ontario in May, Rob's and Dianne's baby requiring my presence (they are due in June), a week lecturing at the University of Western Ontario in August, a tour of Western Canada with my brother [Tony] and his wife throughout September, another publicity tour (probably but not certain) in England in October and a 16-day visit to India in November. And looking at this paragraph, I feel tired and wonder what it's all about! Except for the visit to India, to which I am looking forward.

On top of these other plans for the year, Helen received the thrilling news early in 1988 that the University of Liverpool had decided to bestow upon her an honorary Doctor of Letters. The ceremony was to be on 8 July, perilously close to the baby's due date, but it was agreed that I would accompany my mother to Liverpool.

We flew over and stayed at the Bowler Hat Hotel in Birkenhead. Brian and Avril attended the ceremony and sat alongside me as Helen went up on stage in cap and gown to receive her doctorate. The citation was delivered by an Emeritus Professor to Lord Leverhulme, grandson of the founder of Lever Brothers soap company (now Unilever), and it included many lovely sentiments, including the following: 'We honour a woman of immense character, a woman with the will to emerge with undiminished spirit from the greatest adversity, and the skill to describe that triumph with heart-warming humility.'

It was a proud moment for me to see my mum receive the recognition that I, together with her millions of readers, felt she so richly deserved. It was also particularly fitting for her to be honoured by a university. Her thirst for learning had led her to develop a deep and broad knowledge far beyond what could be expected of someone with so little formal education, and this contributed greatly to the success of her writing. In different circumstances, Helen's intellect would have propelled her into higher education. That the recognition should come from Liverpool was entirely appropriate and very welcome; it was, of course, the same university that had granted Avadh his PhD in physics years before.

Afterwards she wrote to her brother Alan: 'The ceremony went off very well and everyone was very kind, both to me and to the family. I found it rather a joke to receive the doctorate from Lord Leverhulme, because I have made his grandfather something of a villain in my new book [*The Lemon Tree*]. I must now do some fast rewriting!'

To a friend, she confided:

> When the University of Liverpool gave me an honorary doctorate, I would normally have hung the certificate on the bedroom wall and forgotten it.

Lord Leverhulme, however, a very wise old owl, who was the Chancellor of the University and was my host, took my hand and said, 'Be sure to use the doctorate, my dear. It will help you.' He gave me such a knowing grin that I think he understood how white-haired little old ladies get patronized and shoved on one side.

So I've used it – and he is right. It helps me in a whole lot of hard situations. But forgive my flaunting it at the top of my notepaper – it's useful. I could never have earned it – I simply don't have the brains, never mind the opportunity!

*

In 1993, Helen described her approach to research and developing character in a letter to a Canadian acquaintance in the publishing world.

You asked me what my techniques are in historical research. There goes the trained mind! I have a mind almost completely unformed by ordered teaching, so I have always invented my own systems, no matter what I am doing. I occasionally reinvent the wheel, of course!

I lived with Wallace Helena [the heroine of *The Lemon Tree*] for five years, through two previous books, while I sought for a way of using her. She was sparked simply by the newspaper headlines regarding the war in Lebanon. I had, of course, read a fair amount about the Middle East and knew about the horrors of the Christian massacres under the Turks and Druze. So, to confirm this knowledge, I read Hitti's *The Near East in History*, an excellent book. Then, I had to think how to set the book in Liverpool, to please my publishers, and I hit on the soap industry. Soap firms were marvellous in giving me information about their companies and how they began – and there are many hippie books on soap making at home. And all the time, I was picking up bits from other books to strengthen my idea of Wallace.

I knew Chicago had many Lebanese millionaires, who had been refugees of the massacre, but who took their money back to Beirut – and made it, incidentally, the banking centre of the Middle East. But Chicago was too easy to sustain the kind of hardship that would make a really strong woman. Hence, the idea of bringing her to Edmonton, a place which she could not easily leave. I literally learned the history of Edmonton from scratch.

There comes a point when you close all the books you have read and start to write, to see what comes.

I have a Safeway's bag into which I drop cuttings and small books on the subject I have in mind, and a bit of bookshelf to hold the bigger tomes, and when I am ready to seriously start writing, I tip everything out and see what I have.

In amongst the hard work, Helen did make time to travel for pleasure. She particularly enjoyed Swan Hellenic cruises on the *Orpheus*, where she could listen to talks by scholars on a number of subjects. She also travelled to India and France, and made a number of friends on these trips with whom she corresponded regularly. While she took an active interest in my own little family, much of Helen's life was lived in her fictional world and in the very active correspondence she maintained with her readers, agent, publishers and other friends in the book industry.

Helen stayed in very close touch with most of her brothers and sisters and wrote regularly to Alan, Brian and Avril in particular. In her book world, she guarded their privacy carefully but readers often wanted to know what had happened to them. In 1993, she wrote this to a schoolmaster whose class she had visited.

> My four brothers have never, to my knowledge, read any of my books! True brotherly love! They did, however, know what was in *Twopence* because I talked to them about it. Three of them are some of my best salesman, but the fourth one [Edward] is a bit shy of being identified as one of the children in the book, probably because he became a headmaster!
>
> My sister [Avril] reads them avidly, and is at present immersed in my latest one, *The Liverpool Basque*. My second sister, Fiona in the book, died in middle age of breast cancer, much to the grief of all of us. She left five adopted children who were brought up by her husband.
>
> All my brothers and my sister are now retired and on their second careers. Alan and Brian spent their youth fighting in the war, seven years of it. Afterwards Alan became a sales rep and then bought a small hotel. He now designs gardens. Brian left the Navy loving boats but hating the Navy, and joined the Customs Service. His great interest was [coaching] boxing, but he cannot do much now, because he is very frail as a result of his war service.
>
> Tony was called up for the RAF and did two years' service. He went into the Civil Service and eventually became an expert on VAT [Value Added Tax]. Retired, he now advises foreign governments on how to organize this particular tax. Edward is an MA and was the principal of a big college at his retirement. He now does a lot of social work.
>
> Avril went to work at fourteen and then to night school as I did. She eventually was qualified to teach

and she became the Head of a Commerce Department in a high school. Retired now, she has her own business training women to return to the workforce.

*

On one of her Swan Hellenic cruises she met a retired but very active professor of Greek history, Professor Frank Walbank, and he became a good friend. She wrote to one of her other cruise friends about him:

> I . . . have an invitation to stay for a few days in Cambridge, with a darling old professor whom I met on my last cruise last fall. He is 83 years old, so I am afraid that my honour is rather safe! However, he is a delight to be with, a specialist in the history of the Aegean Sea. He knows Liverpool well, having been the Rathbone Professor of Ancient History and Classical Archaeology at the University there. He has also served as visiting professor at Pittsburgh, Berkeley and Princeton – so he is no mean scholar. He is now Professor Emeritus at Cambridge.
>
> I feel quite sad that we are both embedded (of necessity, almost) among our respective families over 6,000 miles distant from each other. I feel that something really good might have come out of our meeting if it had occurred earlier. He lost his wife a good many years ago. He did not do too well alone, so now he has come to live next door to his daughter, a professor of Egyptology. Anyway, I have accepted the invitation – a little is better than nothing.

Is this a hint that there could have been some romance in the friendship had they met a few years earlier? Later she wrote to Alan about him.

> His father owned a corner shop in Bingley and wanted his only child to become a teacher, so he was sent to university. To his father's alarm he stayed and stayed and stayed at University, and finally became a world expert in things Greek. He speaks German, Latin, Greek, Hebrew and Aramaic (Jesus's language). I believe he can speak Arabic and some French too.

Professor Walbank combined relatively humble beginnings with extraordinary academic achievement. Helen corresponded with him regularly and visited him a number of times. In 1996, she wrote to another Swan friend:

> I went to Cambridge and had such a good welcome there. Frank and I went some great walks in the backs by the river and had lunch in a famous room called the Combination Room, which is a sort of club room for the various college profs. It is a classically beautiful room, dating back, I believe, to the 16th century.
>
> One of his daughters invited us to dinner. She has such a pretty home and the conversation and the dinner were both excellent.
>
> There are times that, when I am with Frank, and we meet other professors, I feel like the American lady who married the poet, C. S. Lewis, and came to live with him in Oxford and found herself being patronised. I don't know whether you saw a film called *Shadowlands* about them, in which this point was beautifully brought out and smartly dealt with by the American. I am not so smart. But as long as Frank does not care, I don't care either.

Mum had a variety of male and female friends and acquaintances in both Canada and England and maintained some connection with very old friends including John, the colleague in Liverpool who had lent her money back in 1949 when she was saving to get married to Dad. But few friendships gave her the depth of connection she longed for. A natural reserve, her unique experiences, a distance from Canadian society that she never fully bridged, the physical distance from England, her professional accomplishments without matching academic credentials, and the time and energy demanded by her work, all contributed to varying degrees of loneliness after Avadh's death.

No one could ever replace my father as her soul mate and companion. He was the person with whom she had made a home in three different continents, who had encouraged her to write and understood her like no one else. After losing your great love, she found, life can still be rewarding, it can still be amusing, but it is never the same again.

Chapter Twenty-three

I am not particularly scared of the changes which are taking place. We tend to forget the heart-turning changes which have taken place in previous times.

Helen's primary market was always in England and she often complained about a lack of recognition in Canada, but she was active there as well. She travelled all over Alberta to speak at schools, libraries and a Native reserve in the south, which she enjoyed immensely. She visited various places in Saskatchewan, did book tours in Ontario, and had a good following in Victoria, British Columbia, which had a significant English-born population and very strong bookstores. She acted as writer-in-residence at the Edmonton Public Library and in 1992 delivered the annual lecture in honour of the founder of the University of Alberta.

In addition to her Beaver trophies, she received a number of local and regional awards. In 1993, the University of Alberta conferred on Helen an honorary Doctor of Letters degree 'in recognition of an outstanding citizen for her contributions to Literature and to the cultural life of Alberta'. It was wonderful to be able to celebrate another honour with my mum, and this time Dianne, Stephen, Lauren and the rest of our family were there.

Granny loved her grandchildren dearly, would babysit whenever asked and tried hard to relate to their busy modern lives. They appreciated her kindness and cheerfulness when they were little.

> My grandchildren have suddenly become interested in me. I think that earlier I was just part of the furniture, a granny who could not get down on the floor to play [by this time she suffered from arthritis], for example. Now they really know what I do, I have had some wonderful sessions with them about India, when I showed them photos that I have. We also tried putting on a sari and making a turban.

Lauren recalls going to a reading her granny was giving at a local library and, along with her older brother, being called to the front afterwards to be shown off to an appreciative audience. *Mourning Doves* (1996) is dedicated to Stephen and Lauren.

Back on the other side of the Atlantic, a rock band called Alternative Radio played a song they had written based on *Twopence* at a reception that Helen attended. The group approached Helen with the idea of developing a musical based on *Twopence* and she agreed straight away. Rob Fennah, who wrote the script, worked closely with Helen to ensure that it captured the story accurately. The musical was first performed in Liverpool's Empire Theatre on 5 April 1994. Helen attended and, moved to tears, led the standing ovation as the curtain came down. Over 27,000 people attended the first run of the production and it has been restaged four times. It has now been made into a fine play, without music, which I attended in 2015.

In 1996, in her relentless pursuit to develop compelling characters, Helen called upon a friend who had served in the French Resistance to help her devise a Norman farmer whom she could pair up with a Merseyside widow for *Madame Barbara*. They exchanged letters over several years about numerous aspects of French life and custom, land tenure law, and especially wartime in Occupied France.

Her character Barbara travels to France to visit the grave of her husband, just as Helen had travelled there to see Eddie's resting place soon after the war. She wrote to her editor:

> The book is, indeed, grim. Most of my books are because they deal with the Depression and wars, etc. . . . It was strange, when I was in Normandy, in October, to find a sense of the frightful aftermath of the invasion still there, though most of the present population are too young to remember it, although most of them must have lived amid the ruins for years; and you can buy ice cream and sodas on the cliffs above the Juno and Sword landing places. There are no houses, except the new cafe, within sight. A little way away, tucked into the coast is Arromanches which was, along the seafront, totally ruined when I saw it in 1948.
>
> Brittany and the Loire Valley did not have this weird aura. Britons know very little about the French civilian population caught in the invasion, and I really hope to remind them of it!

While researching this novel, Helen visited Eddie's grave again, her own very personal emblem of Britain's sacrifice in France. Through the process of researching and writing and, in particular, creating the character of Michel, Helen developed a much better understanding of and empathy for the French who died during the war, or who survived to live on in the devastated landscape of northern France. *Madame Barbara* was published in 1999, just after Helen's eightieth birthday.

*

Unlike many of her generation, my mother was quick to embrace new technology. In 1992, as soon as I thought home computers were usable for word processing, I taught her the basics. While there were the inevitable frustrations we have all endured, she soon took to computers and abandoned her typewriter. She never adopted email but as the Internet developed she saw that it was important to have a presence online. Her grandson Stephen developed a website for her just as publishers and other authors were beginning to emerge online. I counselled her not to panic about online theft of her work – something many authors feared in the early days –and just to focus on producing great stories.

In 2000, she wrote a thoughtful letter to her agent, Vivien Green, who had taken over from Richard Scott Simon, putting the new technology in a broader historical context.

> Most of the more recent developments have been along a pretty narrow road: they are not nearly so earth-shaking as Microsoft would have us believe. They are just improvements on existing technology. It will all settle down, like the telephone, the car, the TV and so on. Remember those happy days when you simply telephoned (the latest technology!) to the grocer and said what you wanted that week – and it was delivered. Ah, happy days! What's different doing it on the Internet?
>
> Just imagine how horrifying the advent of trains

must have seemed – the whole countryside being torn up for the ugly monsters. Why could they not have stuck to horses, carts and carriages, my grandmother always wanted to know!

Though my grandfather [Paul Huband's father] was a director of what became the Great Western Railway and had free tickets, not once in her life did my grandmother travel in a train, and she lived until 1939! 'Dirty things where one had to mix with the vulgar, who all want to go to Blackpool – for a holiday! Who would ever believe it could happen?' Yet the train changed life fundamentally for the better.

I often compare the last 50 years to the last 50 years of the 18th century, when basic inventions brought in the Industrial Revolution and the awful uprooting of thousands of country people. They were stuffed into factories and appalling slums and learned to be machines. (They used to bury the dead child labourers from the factories at night, so as to avoid a public outcry.)

And a great number of adults were left helpless, because they could not read or write, just like the yobs of today, who will never be computer literate and will expend their frustration at others getting richer, by rioting in exactly the same way. Remember Peterloo and the Corn Riots? But the grandchildren of our yobs will wonder what all the fuss was about.

Yet, out of the 18th century came wondrous architecture, art, philosophy, literature, music, further inventions which raised the standard of living unbelievably. Today, there is tremendous intellectual ferment in philosophy, ethics, the true origins of life, the falsities of war, etc., running parallel with the Internet.

Though I appreciate that the mechanical changes

> taking place now are going to cause a deal of pain to many people, including us, I don't think they will be quite as soul-destroying as many fear.
>
> Frankly, I don't think the world is changing as fast as people imagine – the media TELL them that it is; and big business keeps bringing out new toys to rouse up sales and does all its ordering through the Internet, because it is quicker than mail; yet, the mail itself was a wonderful invention which changed the lives of both businessmen and laymen.
>
> I can imagine that you have problems in trying to get contracts that protect your authors and their copyrights – and it is a worry to all of us. But as the years go by, the problems and advantages will sort out; in fact, some of the problems are probably already clarifying. It is funny to remember that the idea of written contracts, in its initial day, was thought subversive and that business would fail to thrive under such restriction! And there was no such thing as copyright??

After fifteen years of writing books that required intensive research on unfamiliar topics, Helen decided she would like to return to a setting and characters that she knew well from her life in Liverpool and her work as a social worker. She chose to focus on a segment of Liverpool society that she told me 'were probably the only ones poorer than we were'.

In *A Cuppa Tea and an Aspirin*, she zeroed in on the life of Irish Catholic Liverpudlians in a court, a notorious form of slum housing of the late 1930s. As she finished the book in May 2002, she wrote to a Canadian friend:

> It is a very controversial book. I have probably offended the entire Roman Catholic Church; the entire collection

> of respectable, skilled craftsmen who are descendants of what was once a primitive community of semi-illiterate Irish Women on the Dock Road, who fought and stole to keep their children alive; every owner of a Private Home caring for the elderly poor (very common in Britain) holed up in ancient Victorian mansions, and all my usual readers who won't want to believe a word of it!
>
> The joke about this book is that it is likely to be my last, so even if it is turned down now, my death will cause enough publicity for several publishers to enquire immediately what MSS I have left unpublished; and one of them will snap it up. So Rob will benefit.

The book was quickly accepted for publication but Helen had a lot of discussion with one of her editors about the inner thoughts and beliefs of her impoverished Catholic characters. In January 2003 she lamented to her senior editor:

> As you probably know, Jane and I are at odds as to the reality of the Virgin Mary, who makes her presence felt in this book. In response to her queries, I have fudged matters slightly, though I think I have spoiled the touching belief of my heroine that She really does come to her to comfort the truly penitent and will intercede for them.
>
> I discussed this problem with educated Roman Catholics here, and they were heated in their defence of the Dear Lady's reality. It amazed me. I am an Arya Samaji Hindu and have been for 50 years, so I do not have an opinion of my own on the subject. All I know is the ideas behind elephant-headed Gods – and, of course, a lot about Dockside shawl ladies!

In the end, Helen accepted what she viewed as a watered-down portrayal of their absolute faith. She was just too exhausted to fight. All the same, *A Cuppa Tea and an Aspirin* is in my opinion one of her best books. It is a simple but full-bodied urban survival story.

After that, Helen did not want to write any more. At one point I suggested we work together on a kind of autobiography (similar to this) but the thought of the effort was too much for her.

In 2003, my mother was feeling the loss of numerous friends and acquaintances, most recently her youngest brother, Edward. As she entered her mid-eighties, her energy diminished, her professional life began to fade away and her life narrowed noticeably. She ached from painful arthritis and found it hard to get enough exercise. She attended family events but gradually her interest in the world diminished. By 2006, signs of dementia were beginning to show and in 2010 she had to be moved into a nursing home.

She passed away on 24 November 2011.

In her final years Mum had occasionally attended services at All Saints Anglican Cathedral in Edmonton and we arranged her funeral service there. Perhaps a hundred people attended, people whose lives she had touched more deeply than she was aware. Her ashes were interred at the same gravesite as Dad's and her name inscribed next to his.

Postscript

As I sit and wonder how my mother not only survived but excelled against the odds, I can pick out a number of traits that I think made it possible.

From her childhood in the idyllic English countryside, to the slums of Liverpool, the colour of India, and the rapidly changing society of western Canada, Helen was a keen observer of people and their environment. Whether it was from the perspective of a child, a young teenager in a devastated urban society or as a faculty wife, she observed people closely. Subconsciously or consciously, she asked herself: 'Why do they act that way?' 'What makes them tick?' The breadth of her experience, combined with her careful observation, gave her characters and stories veracity and variety. Moreover, her difficult and complex life spanning three countries and cultures enabled her to write with balance and perspective as well as great empathy.

Helen was a shrewd judge of people, able to understand them and to steal tiny threads of personality to compile with countless others into the rich tapestry of her fictional characters. Her judgment also enabled her to be successful in both social work and business. Not many people were ever able to put one over on her. The downside to this shrewdness showed in the selectivity of her friendships.

She was deeply interested, in many, many subjects. Her knowledge of nature often surprised me but she had retained and built on the lessons of her auntie Phil in Hoylake and her nanny, Edith. She knew a remarkable amount about flowers, trees, birds and animals.

She followed social trends carefully and had a good understanding of business. She was an astute observer of world events. She had read English literature intensively, studied history deeply and explored other societies widely. She retained knowledge for her own pleasure so that, when the time came to write, she had a vast store on which to build with specific research.

Readers of *Twopence to Cross the Mersey* and its sequels can't fail to be impressed by Helen's determination, persistence and hard work in the face of poverty, war and grief. But those characteristics did not disappear when *Lime Street at Two* ended.

My mother was basically very healthy, in part because despite the turmoils of her teenage years she was well-nourished as a young child. She had immense endurance and the will to push herself through fatigue and hardship. At times there was no goal other than survival, but that iron will helped to ensure that she did indeed survive.

In her twenties she applied that appetite for hard work to her career in business and then after her marriage she did everything possible to help my father (and later me) to be successful in our careers. It is not surprising that she had the discipline and stamina to write book after book.

If success comes from a combination of talent and hard work, Helen's was no exception. I can attest to the stacks of books she read – and they were serious books – as both general background and specific research. Her files had extensive notes sketching out descriptions of her characters and timelines. No detail escaped her; she took great care, for example, in matching a character's manner of speaking to their social standing and class. If probed, she could describe any of her characters in detail.

Each book required hard thought and reflection over an extended period of time, and her experimentation sometimes failed. *Twopence* was started in a different form and scrapped after several chapters, for example. Substantial rewriting, a minimum of three complete drafts, and painstaking fact-checking were all completed before she even considered submission to a publisher. The disappointment of rejection often followed but in the end only one of her manuscripts remained unpublished, a well-researched but somewhat incongruous story of the police force in a Canadian town.

All her books, except *Most Precious Employee*, remain in print to this day. This is no mean feat!

Her four volumes of memoir were successful in their own right, but they also had a wider impact in publishing as a whole. According to her obituaries in both the *Guardian* and the *Daily Telegraph*, her honest style of writing, devoid of self-pity, spawned a new type of 'gritty, working-class memoir' which became very popular in the 1970s and 80s and which still sells strongly today.

With her experience and knowledge in business, Helen always made sure she understood her contracts, and she knew the importance of promoting her work, whether at gatherings in tiny libraries in Northern Saskatchewan or large bookstores in London. She was aware of herself as a public figure and, while she did turn down some requests, she graciously accepted most. Her most frequent complaint was being kept so busy at events that everyone else got to eat except her!

In some ways writing is a solitary profession, with long hours spent alone at the typewriter or computer, but Helen knew that her success also depended on her relationships with her agent, publishers, booksellers, librarians, the media, readers and potential readers. While the sparks flew a few times with editors or critics – for example, of *The Latchkey Kid* – Helen respected the role of each of these participants in the book world. She tried to understand their needs as well as her own and was pragmatic in striving to meet both. She was warm and appreciative of the people she dealt with and scrupulous in responding to fan letters.

In return she engendered respect herself. She told a representative of the Writers' Union of Canada who was organizing a regional meeting:

> One thing which interested me on your agenda, was the proposed discussion of the treatment of women writers. I have been writing from the early 1960s and I honestly can say that I have never felt that, as a woman, I was being discriminated against. I have had both men and women as editors and publishers – and as critics – and have no complaints against any of them. It may be that I have received good treatment because I am an experienced businesswoman and, simply, will not tolerate being patronized.

Reflecting the era in which she was raised, she was very sensitive to the way others perceived her relationships with men. Nevertheless, in addition to two fiancés and a husband, and a close relationship with her brothers, she had a lot of interaction with men at work and at various times in her life had male friends. In her later years, she developed several strong friendships with sophisticated men in both

England and Canada. This extensive interaction with men further widened the perspective of her writing.

My mother was far more intelligent than she was ever prepared to admit and this intelligence enabled her to bring all these skills together to be the successful writer that she was. She was rightly proud of her professional accomplishments.

In her personal life too, her judgement, perseverance and dedication paid off. In each other, my mum and dad found their soulmates and together left an enduring legacy of love.

Helen wrote a postscript for *By the Waters of Liverpool*, the last paragraph of which reads as follows.

> Now I live in western Canada with my dear Professor and our son. As I write, it is the beginning of 1981, and I have trunks full of letters, a much, much, happier collection [than those received from her fiancé, Eddie]. Pictures of Fiona's and Avril's beautiful weddings, and those of the boys – what funny hats we wore; snaps of a dozen or more nephews and nieces; letters from my publishers accepting the manuscripts of *Twopence to Cross the Mersey* and *Minerva's Stepchild* [later retitled *Liverpool Miss*], in which I described the sufferings of our family when we first came to Liverpool; lovely letters from my kind Indian in-laws. And my husband's long letters written to me from India before I went there and others from time to time when he has been away from me for a few days. How much I owe him for making my life anew. We came out to this wealthy country so that he could continue his research, and here was born our son.
>
> My cup runneth over.

Chronology of Helen Forrester's Life

1848	Paternal grandmother, Elizabeth, born
1894	Father, Paul Huband, born Mother, Lavinia, born
1914	Paul joins the army, aged 19
1918	Paul marries Lavinia; goes to fight in Russia
1919	Helen born in Hoylake, Cheshire on 6 June
1920s	Hubands live in Ludlow, Bromfield, Ross-on-Wye, and Nottingham
1920	Brother, Alan, born
1921	Future husband, Avadh, born in Barabanki, India (near Lucknow)
1922	Sister, Fiona, born
1924	Brother, Brian, born
1927	Brother, Tony, born
1928	Sister, Avril, born Father has heart attack
1929	Stock markets crash triggering the Great Depression
1930	Edward born Father goes bankrupt and loses job
1931	Father moves family to Liverpool

1933	Helen attends school for six weeks until her 14th birthday
1934–35	Completes First Year Commercial Course at Granby Junior Evening Institute, Liverpool
1936–39	Helen studies shorthand, English and commercial correspondence, arithmetic and accounts, and German at the Oulton Senior Evening Institute, Liverpool
1934–41	Employed at Liverpool Personal Services Society, starting as office girl and ending as assistant district head, Bootle, Liverpool
1939	England and France declare war on Germany
1940	First fiancé, Harry, dies at sea
1941–45	Employed at the Petroleum Board, which managed wartime distribution of petroleum; starting as shorthand typist and ending as secretary to the manager of Texas Oil Company
1944	Second fiancé, Eddie, killed at the Battle of Caen, France
1945	Second World War ends
1945–47	Employed at Broadcast Relay Service as secretary
1947–50	Employed at Metal Box Company. Positions included secretary, female staff supervisor and customer liaison officer
1947	Avadh comes to Bristol, then Liverpool, to complete his PhD in Physics
1949	Meets Avadh in March Avadh leaves for India in December
1950	Travels to India in April/May Adopts Hinduism and an Indian name Helen and Avadh are married 24 May

1950–52	Ahmedabad Avadh works at Physical Research Laboratory
1952–3	Edinburgh. Employed at Scottish Agricultural Industries
1953–55	Ottawa Writes her first novel
1955	Edmonton Avadh works at University of Alberta
1955	Son, Robert, is born, Edmonton
1959	*Alien There Is None* (later called *Thursday's Child)* Summer spent on Merseyside
1963–64	Avadh on sabbatical leave at University of Liverpool. The family live in West Kirby, Cheshire.
1964	Helen's father passes away
1971	*The Latchkey Kid*
1972	Helen's mother passes away
1974	*Twopence to Cross the Mersey*
1976	*Most Precious Employee*
1979	*Minerva's Stepchild* (later *Liverpool Miss*) and *Liverpool Daisy*
1979–80	Avadh on sabbatical leave at Oxford University
1981	Robert marries Dianne *By the Waters of Liverpool*
1983	During a publicity tour in May sales of the three memoirs reach 2,000 books per hour
1984	Avadh passes away *Three Women of Liverpool*
1985	Grandson, Stephen, is born. *Lime Street at Two*
1987	*The Moneylenders of Shahpur* *Yes, Mama*

1988	Granddaughter, Lauren, is born.
	Honorary Doctor of Letters, University of Liverpool
	Seven-city publicity tour across Canada
1990	*The Lemon Tree*
1993	Honorary Doctor of Letters, University of Alberta
	The Liverpool Basque
1994	*Twopence to Cross the Mersey, The Musical* premieres
1995	Becomes a Canadian citizen
1996	*Mourning Doves*
1999	*Madame Barbara*
2003	*A Cuppa Tea and an Aspirin*
2011	Helen passes away 24 November

HAVE YOU READ THEM ALL?

'Should be long and widely read as an extraordinary human story and social document'

Observer

ALL AVAILABLE NOW

TWOPENCE TO CROSS THE MERSEY

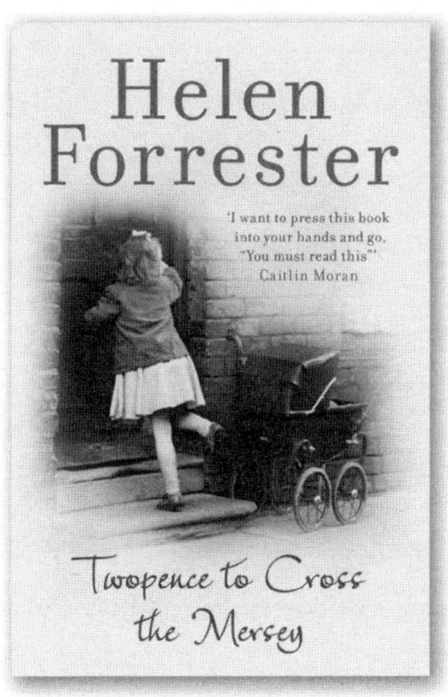

This major best-selling memoir of a poverty-stricken childhood in Liverpool is one of the most harrowing but uplifting books you will ever read.

When Helen Forrester's father went bankrupt in 1930 she and her six siblings were forced into utmost poverty and slum surroundings in Depression-ridden Liverpool. Writing about her experiences later in life, Helen Forrester shed light on an almost forgotten part of life in Britain. Written with good humour and a lack of self-pity, Forrester's memoir of these grim days is as heart-warming as it is shocking.

LIVERPOOL MISS

The second volume of Helen Forrester's powerful, painful and ultimately uplifting four-volume autobiography of her poverty-stricken childhood in Liverpool during the Depression.

Written with an unflinching eye, Helen's account of her continuing struggles against severe malnutrition and, above all, the selfish demands of her parents, is deeply shocking. But Helen's fortitude and her ability to find humour in the most harrowing of situations make this a story of amazing courage and perseverance.

BY THE WATERS OF LIVERPOOL

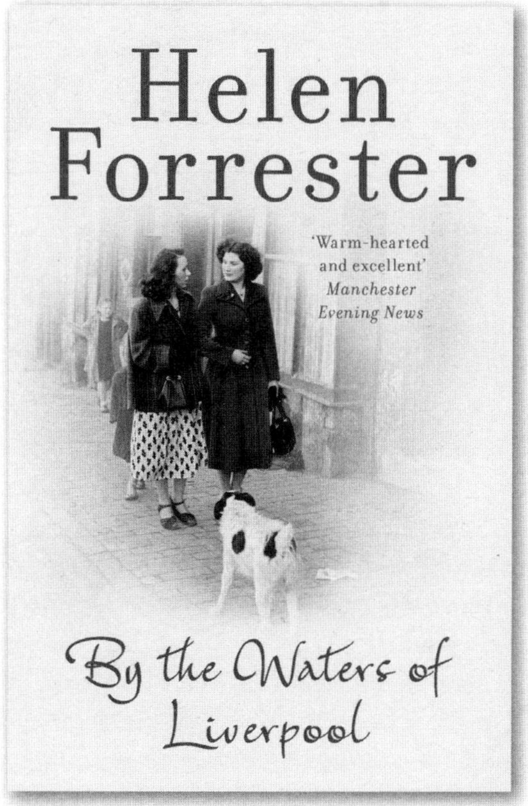

Helen Forrester continues the moving story of her early poverty-stricken life with an account of her teenage years and the devastating effect of the Second World War on her hometown of Liverpool.

Helen will experience at first hand the horror of the Blitz and the terrible toll that the war exacted on ordinary people. As ever, Helen faces the future with courage and determination.

LIME STREET AT TWO

The fourth and final part of Helen Forrester's bestselling autobiography continues the moving story of her early poverty-stricken life with an account of the war years in Blitz-torn Liverpool.

In 1940 Helen, now twenty, is working long hours at a welfare centre in Bootle, five miles from home. Her wages are pitifully low and her mother claims the whole of them for housekeeping but she is still thrilled to be working and gaining some independence. The Second World War is affecting every part of the country and Hitler's Luftwaffe nightly seek to wreak havoc on her home city of Liverpool.

Then, tragedy is brought shockingly close to home and Helen is left reeling when she receives some terrible news. A move brings more trouble for Helen, but she is determined that she will face it, as ever, with courage and determination.